The Economics of
African Development

PRAEGER SERIES
ON
INTERNATIONAL ECONOMICS
AND
DEVELOPMENT

ISAIAH FRANK

CONSULTING EDITOR

The Economics of
African Development

BY

Andrew M. Kamarck

PREFACE BY

PIERRE MOUSSA

FREDERICK A. PRAEGER, *Publishers*
New York · Washington · London

FREDERICK A. PRAEGER, *Publishers*
111 Fourth Avenue, New York, N.Y. 10003, U.S.A.
77–79 Charlotte Street, London W.1, England

Published in the United States of America in 1967
by Frederick A. Praeger, Inc., Publishers

© 1967 by Frederick A. Praeger, Inc.

Library of Congress Catalog Card Number: 66–26553

Printed in the United States of America

Contents

*Four maps of African political divisions and economic development
follow page 66.*

Preface

BY PIERRE MOUSSA

The problem of the economic development of Africa is of great importance in today's world; it is without doubt one of the tests by which our generation shall be judged.

Many books have been written in the past few years on various aspects of African economic development; there are numerous studies illuminating one aspect or another of the economic growth of particular African countries or regions or of particular sectors of the economy, either for a part or the whole of Africa. However, very few syntheses have been written on the economic development of Africa as a whole, covering all sectors; this is because it is difficult to know all fifty countries, independent or dependent, of Africa; very often comparable information is lacking from one country to another and it is therefore very difficult to make meaningful generalizations.

The great merit of Andrew Kamarck, who knows Africa very well— from north to south and from east to west—is that he did not shrink from this considerable task. I think he made a great success of it, and I am honored that he asked me to write the preface to his book. After all, to do so is for me the mark of a permanent friendship that has existed for more than ten years (beginning even before the three years when we worked together in the African Department of the World Bank), since he and I became acquainted at a colloquium on Africa in Princeton, and were happy to find that even though we came from very different backgrounds and had had very different experiences in Africa, we agreed so well on the subject.

Africa must be considered the most underdeveloped continent of the world—at least if the word "underdeveloped" is understood in its literal sense.

In current usage, the adjective "underdeveloped" has come to mean "poor." In this respect, Africa is not the most underdeveloped continent because it is not the poorest one. Although some African nations—Ethiopia, Somalia, and most of the countries situated in the interior, without any contact with the coast—have per-capita incomes comparable to those of India and China, the average African per-capita income is much higher than the Asian. (On the other hand, it is lower than Latin America's.)

But if underdeveloped means—as it should, according to its literal sense—the scant development of the economic potential of a country or region, well, then, I feel sure that Africa is exceedingly underdeveloped. When Mr. Kamarck, in Chapter VIII, treats of electric power, he reminds us first that the African continent possesses two-fifths of the world's total hydro-electric potential—more than Europe and the two Americas put together—and, then, that present production is ridiculously small (all of sub-Saharan Africa, South Africa excepted, produces 12 billion kwh, that is to say, about equivalent to the consumption of a large European or American city). Such examples could be mentioned by the dozen. We can also add that African resources are not only very little exploited, but often very little known. Mineral resources have been relatively little exploited so far; research on tropical soils is at the first stages; knowledge of water resources is minimal (one might mention the case of Lake Tanganyika, the gradual rise of which in recent years engulfed, among other things, a large part of Burundi's port, nobody knowing why and nobody knowing how long the rise was likely to continue). The economist Gabriel Ardant proposed this significant expression to designate the underdeveloped world: "the fallow world." Africa is pre-eminently the fallow continent.

Africa's human resources have lain fallow quite as much as its material resources. In education, Africa lags far behind Asia and

Latin America. In Africa, the percentage of school enrollment of school-age population is 40 per cent in primary school, 3 per cent in secondary, 0.2 per cent in higher education. To reach the same levels as in Latin America, these percentages should be multiplied by two in primary school, by five in secondary school, by fifteen in higher education.

This lack of education is certainly responsible, to a large extent, for the low capacity Africans have shown so far in technical and economic inventiveness. It is quite possible, of course, that the predominant races in Africa are naturally inclined more to excellence in rhetoric than to excellence in technology. In many respects, the African races seem to be "hyper-latin" races. But one must guard against exaggerating ethnic characteristics. More important in this respect was undoubtedly Africa's isolation: for a whole range of reasons, resulting from climate, the winds, the hazards of history, the African continent (above all, Africa south of the Sahara) was cut off from the rest of the world and, in particular, was excluded from the great civilizing adventures of the Occident and Orient. Even during the nineteenth century and at the beginning of the twentieth, Africa's contact with Europe remained astonishingly superficial; the Europeans, in most of Africa, stayed near the coast. Only a few soldiers, a few administrators, and commercial representatives went into the interior (except, of course, in some privileged areas, such as Katanga and the two Rhodesias).

For all these reasons, then, Africa is now, more than any other, *the* underdeveloped continent. (This can be illustrated by output per square kilometer. China produces about $6,200 by the square km., Asia, outside of China, and the Soviet Union produces $5,200, Latin America $2,500, and Africa $930.) The present lag of Africa behind other continents is all the more notable in that, if one considers the history of humanity, the situation was quite different in other epochs. From 7,000 to 2,000 B.C., the great center of civilization was, as everybody knows, the Near East—that is to say, the most western parts of Asia and the northeast corner of Africa. Most of the inventions that are still the basis of our life originated there: i.e., agriculture, livestock-raising, building with bricks, pottery, etc. To go back even further, during the paleolithic era, from 500,000 to 200,000 B.C., one continent was continually ahead of the others, and it was Africa. It was the center of invention, from which radiated all the great technical concepts of the era, especially all advances in stone-cutting.

Today, Africa presents not only an extreme condition of underdevelopment, but also a pure one. Elsewhere, particularly in Asia, underdevelopment is closely bound up with overpopulation (of course, the two phenomena are organically related in Asia). Africa, on the other hand, except in a few regions, is not overpopulated. The problems arising from population growth are less agonizing in Africa than in the rest of the *tiers monde*. This is also why Africa can practically ignore the agrarian problems which for Asia and Latin America are fundamental economic and social issues. Africa poses the question of how to break the vicious circle of underdevelopment in a pure form, while the other continents pose the same question in a form complicated with other essential problems.

To break this vicious circle, assistance from industrialized countries is essential. I, as well as Andrew Kamarck, am among those who believe that international aid to underdeveloped countries must be progressively increased. But I would like to mention here why I think that Africa has a right to very special treatment as regards aid from the West.

The first reason why Western countries cannot forsake Africa is based on the fact that Europe has a serious responsibility for the present situation in the African continent. I do not mean, as some assert in an overly tendentious way, that the colonial period was a disaster for Africa; on the contrary, I think that the colonial period, despite grave defects, brought some incontestable benefits, notably in the fields of peacekeeping and public health. In my view, the West's main fault lay in the slave trade, rather than the colonization. Mr. Kamarck is right to refer several times to the importance of this trade, although, thank God, it belongs almost completely to the past. Nobody can assess the damage that must have been done to Africa, over generations and generations, by the continuous removal of a great number of people (who of course were chosen from among the best and strongest Africans) and their transfer to another continent. Mr. Kamarck estimates that between 12 million and 15 million were transported out of Africa; in addition, as he himself points out, there should be added to these figures the great number of human beings who were killed in the slave raids or who died during the trip. This is not all: to obtain this human merchandise, the Europeans encouraged inter-tribal hostilities, and the seriousness of this error is evident when one considers that excesses of tribal feelings are to this day one of the plagues of Africa.

The second reason that I would like to advance as to why the West has a special obligation toward Africa is that Africa needs Western aid more than any other continent. In *financial* terms, Asia and Latin America need capital from the industrialized countries as much as Africa does. It is in *human* terms that the difference becomes apparent between Africa on the one hand and the rest of the *tiers monde* on the other. Asia and Latin America are better endowed than Africa with educated people and leaders. But for a long time, most African countries will be unable to function or to develop satisfactorily without large-scale technical assistance—as is the case today, since around four-fifths of the total number of technical-assistance personnel on duty all over the world are on the African continent, although in terms of population Africa represents only about one-seventh of the underdeveloped world. In the rest of the developing world, foreigners represent only 1 per cent of the high-level manpower; in Africa, four-fifths.

Not only does Africa badly need the help of the West in personnel; it must also take over from the Western countries their languages and, to a large extent, their philosophy. One can assert, without offending the respectable and humanly attractive deep-lying African traditions, that they cannot constitute for the African civilization of tomorrow a spiritual framework to be compared to what China or India can derive from their own philosophies. In other words, Africa depends much more than Asia on the West's intellectual contribution.

Without a large-scale financial and human contribution from the industrialized countries, the destiny of the African countries is scarcely in doubt: the peril that lies in wait is certainly not so much the adoption of Communist governments (at least within the meaning of the term in Europe and Asia), but rather an immense anarchy, a regression to the darkness of the Middle Ages.

Foreword

Most of this book was written at the African Studies Center of the University of California at Los Angeles during my stay there as Regents Professor in 1964–65. Without the freedom from day-to-day routine I enjoyed there, and without the favorable atmosphere of the Center, this book would never have been written. I owe a special debt of gratitude to Professor James S. Coleman, Director, and the other members and staff of the Center.

The origins of this book lie in the course in African Economic Problems which I have given for a number of years in the African Studies Program at the School of Advanced International Studies of the Johns Hopkins University—a program under the benevolent leadership of Professor Vernon McKay. I have also, of course, drawn on my practical experience of a decade and a half of economic work in Africa for the World Bank Group.

In some of the chapters, I have drawn on material published at various times in the past. These include: "Recent Economic Growth in Africa," *The Annals of the American Academy of Political and Social Science*, CCCLIV, 1964; "The African Economy and International Trade," in *The United States and Africa* (rev. ed.; New York and London: Frederick A. Praeger, for The American Assembly, 1963); "Economic and Social Imperatives," *Symposium on Africa* (Wellesley College, 1960); "Economics and Economic Development," in Robert A. Lystad (ed.), *The African World* (New York and London: Frederick A. Praeger, 1965); "The Development of the Economic Infrastructure," in M. J. Herskovits and Mitchell Harwitz (eds.), *Economic Transition in Africa* (Evanston, Ill.: Northwestern University Press, 1964); "Some Problems of African Development," *The Fund and Bank Review*, I, No. 2 (September, 1964); "The Activities of the World Bank in Africa," in Colin Legum (ed.), *Africa, A Handbook to the Continent* (rev. ed.; London: Anthony Blond; New York: Frederick A. Praeger, 1966); "Notes on Under-Employment," in E. F. Jackson (ed.), *Economic Development in Africa* (Oxford: Basil Blackwell, 1965); "Economic Determinants," in Vernon McKay (ed.), *Determinants of African Diplomacy* (New York: Frederick A. Praeger, 1966); "The Return to Lenders and Investors: The Case of Africa," in J. A. Adler (ed.), International Economic Association *Proceedings*, 1965.

Any opinions expressed in this book are my own and do not necessarily reflect the official views of any institution with which I may be connected.

A. M. K.

Washington, D.C.
September, 1966

The Economics of
African Development

I

African Economic Development in Historical Perspective

> *If we could first know where we are, and whither we are tending, we could better judge what to do, and how to do it.*
>
> ABRAHAM LINCOLN

It is now becoming an accepted theory that the first man to appear on earth was an African, that is, that Africa was the birthplace of man himself. Darwin prophesied that the continent of Africa would prove to be the place of man's origin, and he appears to have been right. Recent discoveries of Dr. L. S. B. Leakey in East Africa indicate that not only did man begin in Africa, but for some 600,000 years afterward, Africa was the spearhead of man's progress. It was in Africa that the first cutting tools from stone were made nearly 2 million years ago—making available to early man a whole new source of food and starting him on the road to the machine-based economy of today.

After man had spread to the rest of the world, much of Africa was cut off from the lands north and east of it by the desert that crept across the Sahara and Arabia. Isolated from the rest of the world from about 5,000 B.C., Africa began to lag behind in *material* development. According to Arnold Toynbee, "Geography kept sub-Saharan Africa out of the history of civilization. . . . The desert in the north, the falls at the mouths of rivers which prevented navigation, isolated Africans and deprived them of the mingling of peoples which produces civilization. The result is that they're 5,000 years behind and paying the price for it. I think Africans are as competent as other people, and . . . 5,000 years is really a short time, but they have a long way to catch up." (Toynbee, p. 1.)

In addition to isolation, sub-Saharan Africa also suffered from the fact that her tropical climate and soils made settled agriculture virtually impossible. (See below, chap. V.) Most Africans, therefore, were unable to get the full benefit from one of the fundamental transformations of man's life on this earth—the domestication and cultivation of plants, which elsewhere in the world made settled existence possible and, consequently, the progress in civilization that comes from urbanization.

The obstacles nature placed in the way of economic development in Africa south of the Sahara were so great that they could be overcome only after the rest of the world had progressed sufficiently to have invented self-propelled machine transport (the railway and then the automobile and airplane) and to have a sufficient surplus of wealth to aid Africans to acquire these necessary means to break out of their isolation.

There was a trickle of trade across the Sahara from the Mediterranean from the times of ancient Egypt and Carthage. The western Sudan (including the medieval empires of "Ghana" and "Mali"), after about the eighth century, is supposed to have been the chief supplier of gold to the Western world until the discovery of America. The East African coast was visited by Indian, Chinese, and Arab traders for many centuries before the modern era. And, in modern times, Christopher Columbus is believed to have visited West Africa ten years before his voyage of discovery to America. The entire African coastline became known soon thereafter, long before the coastlines of the American or Australian continents, indeed, even before the coastlines of Europe and Asia (in the distant north) were fully explored. Yet, with all this, to the rest of the world Africa remained a coastline and not a continent until about a hundred years ago.

The Obstacles of Geography and Climate

The geographical and climatic reasons why neither Africans nor the restless Europeans were able to bring sub-Saharan Africa into the mainstream of world commerce and life were formidable, and they are still important today in holding back African economic development. Most of the African coastline below the Sahara is a forbidding one—where the desert does not come right down to the sea, the visitor sees mostly swamp or lagoon. As Toynbee points out, Africa is by and large a plateau, with rivers falling over the escarpment in a series of falls or rapids near the coast. It is usually impossible in Africa to penetrate the interior by sailing up rivers, as was done, for example, in North America; the fact that beyond the falls one could find navigable stretches of water was unimportant for a long time. (The Niger River is navigable, but, because of the mangrove swamps and the division of the river into many distributaries in the delta, this was not known to non-African explorers until 1830.) Africa also has very few natural harbors where ships can lie safely at anchor. Ships had to remain at sea during the few months when it was safe to lie off shore, and their sailors were forced to depend on small boats to get through the surf for any contact with the land.

The second major set of economically significant obstacles derives from the single fact that Africa is pre-eminently *the* tropical continent. Over 9 million of Africa's 11.7 million square miles are in the tropics. This is still a pervasive continuing influence on Africa's development; in earlier centuries, added to other difficult geographical features, it helped to prevent Africa's economic development from even starting. Among the most effective impediments were the many tropical diseases, such as yellow fever and malaria, that levied a heavy toll of death on all visitors to tropical Africa. The diseases carried by the tsetse fly deserve special mention. While the human sleeping sickness the tsetse fly may carry is bad enough, a critical economic factor is the animal disease it carries—trypanosomiasis, which kills horses and cattle and formerly made it impossible to use animal transport to penetrate the interior from the coast. Commerce had to depend on human porters, the most costly and inef-

ficient of all transport systems, and this meant that the only trade of
consequence that could take place over most of tropical Africa was
in commodities of great value and little bulk—i.e., gold and ivory, or
commodities that were provided with their own legs—e.g., slaves.
And these were inevitably the main African exports, particularly
slaves.

The tropics presented other grave difficulties (these will be considered later), but the transport obstacle alone was quite sufficient
to stop any appreciable economic development for centuries.

THE SLAVE TRADE

As far as one can ascertain, slaves were for several thousand years
and until quite recently a major export of sub-Saharan Africa. The
slave trade was certainly going on in the ancient world, albeit intermittently and in very small volume—the possession of the rare
African slave may have been a prestige symbol compared to ownership of the run-of-the-mill European slave. After the rise and spread
of Islam, the slave trade continued across the Sahara and along
the east coast of Africa to Arabia until the beginning of this century—with some small remnants of it still persisting to this day. (*The
New York Times*, December 18, 1964.) This trade assumed a large
volume in modern times when the Portuguese began to import slaves
into Western Europe around 1442, and when the Spanish brought
slaves to the New World after 1517. The large-scale Atlantic trade
with North America, the Caribbean, and South America continued
for three and a half centuries, with the last trickle not ceasing until
perhaps 1880.

While a considerable number of the slaves sold abroad had been
stolen by non-African slave traders—especially the Arab traders in
East and Central Africa in the nineteenth century—in the main,
the trade was an African economic phenomenon. That is to say,
Africans sold slaves to slave traders because this was the only means
available to raise the money to buy the commodities they wanted
(mostly guns, powder, rum, and textiles). As an anti-slavery leader
expressed it at the time:

> We attempt to put down the slave trade "by the strong hand" alone;
> and this is, I apprehend, the cause of our failure. . . . The African

has acquired a taste for the productions of the civilized world. They have become essential to him. The parent . . . barters his child; the chief his subject; each individual looks with an evil eye on his neighbor, and lays snares to catch him—because the sale of children, subjects, and neighbors is the only means as yet afforded, by European commerce, for the supply of those wants which that commerce has created. . . . When we shall have experimentally convinced the African that it is in his power to obtain his supplies in more than their usual abundance, by honest means, then, and not until then, we may expect that he will be reconciled to the abolition of the slave trade. (Buxton, p. viii.)

Unfortunately, the slave trade, in addition to being an inhuman and, in a real sense, immoral activity, was a particularly destructive type of commerce. It drew off from the continent human beings at their most productive ages. Worse still, it encouraged tribe to fight tribe and encouraged conflict within tribes. Finally, and perhaps most important, any advantages that Africa derived from contact with the rest of the world—the learning of some skills, the introduction of new foods such as maize and manioc—were more than offset by the slave trade's plunging vast stretches of Africa back into anarchy. Whatever else economic development requires, it does need a basic minimum of personal security. The fact that rulers along the West African coast were successful in building up states on the middleman traffic in slaves did not mitigate the disastrous impact of the trade on the peoples further inland. (In addition, in their desire to monopolize the slave trade, the coastal states were careful to allow no penetration of the interior by people from outside.)

There are no good estimates as to the total number of slaves exported from Africa from the beginning of the large-scale trade in modern times to its end in the last century. K. O. Dike (p. 3) believes a figure of 5–6 million West Africans is probably right. To these would have to be added the slaves sold from the Congo and Angola to Brazil, from the Sahara to North Africa, and from the lands along the Indian Ocean to Arabia. Altogether, the figure must be at least 10 million and may be as high as 15 million. Countless millions in addition lost their lives in the slave raids, in the journey to the sea in the slave coffles, in waiting in the barracoons on the coast for a slave ship to appear and, finally, during the trip on the Atlantic or Indian oceans to the slave markets of the Americas or Arabia.

The British, who had been principal participants, withdrew from the slave trade when the British Government prohibited it in 1807, an abolition made possible partly by the beginnings of industrialization, which enabled Liverpool merchants to shift from trading in slaves to trading in cotton for the growing textile factories. The government not only banned the trade for its own subjects, but also took active steps to stamp out the traffic altogether. The Royal Navy began to stop slave ships of British and other nationalities, as treaties were made with other nations allowing such actions against the trade. But slave trading continued across the Atlantic under the protection of the American flag. Senators from slave states prevented any American cooperation with the Royal Navy's police actions. Worse still, the United States' insistence on its sovereign rights as protecting any ship flying the American flag meant that a slave merchant caught in the act by a British warship had only to hoist the Stars and Stripes to go freely about his business. It was only when the southern states had seceded during the Civil War that the U.S. Navy was finally freed to cooperate effectively with the British against the slave ships. The North Atlantic slave trade then stopped.

On the East African coast, the slave trade continued in considerable volume even after the British persuaded the Sultan to close the slave market on Zanzibar in 1873. Not until the whole of the coast came under European domination—a process completed with the Anglo-Egyptian takeover of the Sudan in 1889—did the large-scale slave trade stop. The illegal trade that continued to Arabia for many years after that—certainly until World War II—was not of any great economic significance, although the tragedy for the people involved was no less for that.

The abolition of the slave trade initially had a most unfavorable economic impact on the African middleman communities in West Africa.

> Along the coast of West Africa, particularly in those parts where the slave trade formed the basis of the economy of the communities concerned, opposition to abolition was the rule. In the Gold Coast, where European forts and settlements were situated close to the African states, local native resentment against the Act of 1807 led to

serious riots. When Parliament rebuked the Committee of the Company of Merchants for failing to convince Africans that abolition was for the good of the natives, the Committee reported,

"Can the wildest theorist expect that a mere act of the British legislature should in a moment inspire . . . natives of the vast continent of Africa and persuade them, nay more, make them practically believe and feel that it is for their interest to contribute to and even acquiesce in, the destruction of a trade . . . by which alone they have been hitherto accustomed to acquire wealth and purchase all the foreign luxuries and conveniences of life?" (Dike, p. 12.)

As the slave trade was slowly wiped out, its basic economic role had begun to lose its meaning. A substitute for human power as a means of transport in Africa had been found—the steam engine driving the new railway locomotives and river steamers. An alternative commodity to export from the west coast of Africa was also developed at this time. This was palm oil. One of the consequences of the Industrial Revolution in Europe had been that Europeans began to wash themselves regularly, and, with the spread of the habit, the demand for soap could no longer be satisfied with animal fats alone. There began to be a demand for vegetable fats, especially the oil collected from wild palms in West Africa. Palm oil was also needed in the making of candles and for the lubrication of the new machinery. It consequently became possible for Africans to sell abroad something other than slaves and for some of the African traders to turn to the new trade in oil rather than slaves. Later, of course, other exportable commodities were found or introduced into Africa.

The Key Role of Railways

With the invention in the early nineteenth century of the "iron horse," immune to the bite of the tsetse fly, an effective means had finally been found to penetrate the African continent. Economic development, therefore, now was no longer out of the question for Africa. While Lord Lugard's famous remark, "The material development of Africa may be summed up in one word—transport," is too sweeping, adequate transport *is* a necessary condition for progress, and as long as commerce was confined by the lack of adequate transport, the Africans were bound to remain ignorant and poor, isolated from the world and from each other.

But to acquire railways, they have to be paid for, and, unfortunately, they are a particularly capital-intensive investment. In addition, to get any good out of a railway in many areas of Africa, it was also necessary to construct a port first and usually a costly artificial harbor. The amount of capital needed to carry out the minimum required for this investment was completely beyond African possibilities to procure. (This "lumpiness" of investment so often encountered in Africa seems to have been especially true in these early stages.) Africa was caught in the dilemma that for any appreciable economic development to begin, a minimum transport infrastructure was needed, but without the infrastructure it was impossible for the Africans to earn the necessary foreign exchange to get it. The dilemma could only be resolved by help from abroad. Put in another way, the "threshold" over which Africans had to pass to begin economic growth was so high that it was practically impossible for them to get over it without help from abroad. This help did not become available until Africa passed under the domination of European powers, mostly during the period 1884–95. Railway building in Africa mainly began only then.

In this as in so many other respects, South Africa was an exception. With a temperate climate and one of the few good natural harbors of Africa, the European settlers at the Cape did not encounter most of the virtually insuperable obstacles of tropical Africa. But they had enough problems to keep them struggling and poor for two centuries after the first European colonizers had arrived. Railway building here began in 1859 and, compared to the rest of Africa, moved fairly rapidly after the discovery of diamonds at Kimberley in 1867 and the discovery of gold on the Rand at Johannesburg in 1886. In 1897, there were 5,000 miles of railway in southern Africa and 1,800 in the rest of Africa. Of total exports worth some $140 million from sub-Saharan Africa, southern Africa provided some $100 million alone.

Africa is the only continent in the world where large investments in the construction of new railways are still needed—even though the automobile and airplane are now available as more flexible and less capital-devouring means of transport than railways. Artificial harbors and new ports are also still being built where countries did not possess them before. Since 1960, new railway lines have been constructed in Mauretania, Liberia, Nigeria, Cameroon, Swaziland, Tanzania, Congo (Brazzaville), Uganda, and the Sudan; ports have been built in Mauretania, Liberia (a second port, Buchanan, in addition to Monrovia, constructed during World War II), Ghana (Tema, a second port in eastern Ghana, to supplement Takoradi, the artificial port in western Ghana built during the 1920's), Togo, Dahomey, and Somalia.

EUROPE AND AFRICA

Although by 1899 almost all of Africa had come under the rule of European nations, any contribution these governments made to the economic development of Africa was almost purely by the way. The European powers constructed the railways primarily for their own strategic or administrative reasons—in the Sudan to facilitate the re-conquest of the country; in East Africa, inland from Tanga by the Germans and from Mombasa to Lake Victoria by the British, for strategic reasons and to suppress the slave trade; in West Africa, inland from Dakar, by the French for military and administrative reasons. The record of the United States was even worse vis-à-vis Liberia, which, though not a colony, had been established by Americans and where there was at least some moral commitment by Americans to help. Essentially, the basis on which the metropolitan governments operated was that laid down by Adam Smith in *The Wealth of Nations* in 1776, when he said: "Little else is requisite to carry a state to the highest degree of opulence from the lowest barbarism but peace, easy taxes and a tolerable administration of justice, all the rest being brought about by the natural course of things." So, the European powers restricted themselves in Africa essentially to trying to establish peace and law and order, stop tribal warfare, prevent the slave trade, etc. Of course, such activities were a major contribution to economic development in that they did create the necessary preconditions for it. A railway built for strategic or administrative reasons was no less helpful to traders penetrating the interior.

In addition, the British did provide grants-in-aid, part in loans and part as gifts, to colonies that could not meet their necessary expenditures from their own revenues. Beginning in 1929, gifts or loans of up to £1 million a year were made available under the Colonial Development Act of 1929—designed primarily to relieve unemployment in the U.K. By World War II, a total of around $150 million equivalent had been made available to the African colonies under these two systems. The Imperial German Government contributed about $125 million equivalent to South West Africa and Tanganyika before World War I.

While the records of the colonial administrations themselves are mixed, as far as stimulating economic development is concerned, it is fair to say that in almost every case they did make *some* contribution—small or large. They learned something about local agricultural problems, they assembled data on soils, climate, crops. Before and during the colonial period, Western countries introduced a number of new, basic food crops into Africa, mostly from the American continents—manioc, maize, beans, and peanuts (groundnuts)—and they must have made possible a considerable increase in population in some areas where the lack of adequate food supplies was the limiting factor. The colonial governments also made a start on controlling disease. Missionary efforts to create school systems were encouraged, and the colonial governments themselves began to organize and set up schools. Offices began to collect some of the basic statistics that would be needed for policy-making. In particular cases, men like Sir Gordon Guggisberg, Governor of the Gold Coast after World War I, took an active role in initiating what even today would be regarded as good development programs. Guggisberg built the first protected harbor in the Gold Coast, Takoradi, extended the railway and road system, and organized new schools. Many district commissioners or local officers, by introducing or encouraging new crops (such as coffee to the Chagga on Mount Kilimanjaro), left enduring traces of their work.

But by and large, development was initially turned over to private companies or concessionaires given monopoly powers over large areas, much like the companies and proprietors who were given immense grants of land in the American colonies: the Virginia Company, Lord Baltimore's colony of Maryland, Oglethorpe in Georgia, Carteret in New Jersey, etc. Among these companies were the Imperial British East Africa Company, operating in what is now Kenya and Uganda; the British South Africa Company, founded in 1887 in the Rhodesias; the Royal Niger Company; the Portuguese Mozambique Company; the Compagnie de Congo pour le Commerce et l'Industrie; the Comité Speciale du Katanga (CSK); Compagnie des Chemins de Fer du Congo Supérieur aux Grands Lacs Africains (CFL); Comité Nationale du Kivu (CNKi); Société du Haut-Ogooué; the Deutsche Ostafrikanische Gesellschaft; etc. Amazingly, these companies did raise the money to build railways and ports. Private investors before World War I thought Africa would be a new America, that it was needed only to open it up and new wealth would pour forth. In fact, Africa was not a new America, and most of these chartered companies went bankrupt and out of existence. The few that survived, like the British South Africa Company, or Tanganyika Concessions, generally did not pay any dividends for many years, most of them not until after World War II, when the majority of the original investors had long passed from the scene. It was not until after World War II that the European governments began to make a sustained, deliberate effort to help Africa's economic development.

The immediate effects of the chartered companies' early opening up of Africa were not all positive. In the attempt to make a profit or to get their capital back, some of the companies and concessionaires indulged in activities that resembled plundering of the territory under their control more than it did economic development; the forced labor exacted from the Africans to collect and transport rubber, ivory, and timber or to construct roads and railways prevented the Africans from producing for themselves and killed off large numbers from disease, overwork, and famine.

When the Italians invaded Ethiopia in the 1890's, the draft animals they brought in for their artillery may have carried rinderpest with them. In the next few years, rinderpest swept down the east coast of Africa as far as the Cape of Good Hope, killing millions of cattle. This was bad enough, but in addition, as a result large areas returned to bush and the wild animals and tsetse fly moved in, and regions like Bunyoro in eastern Africa have been impossible to reclaim for cattle-raising since.*

* Stanley, on his pathblazing march across the continent in 1887–88, brought with him human sleeping sickness from west to east. This, transmitted by the

The new network of communications brought by the Europeans spread the African diseases throughout the continent while the European diseases were added to them. Together these had such an impact that, until the early 1930's, the dominant preoccupation of local governments was concern about Africa's depopulation. In the Gabon, this continued into the 1960's, when for the first time one began to see evidence that the population was no longer decreasing but beginning to increase. Only since World War II have the advances in medical science applied in Africa begun to encourage a rapid growth in most African populations. (Now, of course, the problem is becoming one of too rapid population growth!)

With the eventual failure of the chartered companies, the colonial governments of African territories perforce took a more active role in economic development. In part, this was inevitable, given the prevalent theory that colonies should pay their own way. This was notably the case in the English colonies, where the British Treasury was particularly firm that civil servants depend for their salaries on the colonial government. With the colonial treasury dependent on the resources of the territory, colonial officials were forced to find ways to increase the wealth of the population. They had to concern themselves, Adam Smith or no, with finding some way in which Africans could earn money that could then be taxed and used to pay government expenses. The pressure of the British Treasury on the Uganda Government to become self-supporting, for example, explains much of the rapid spread of cotton-growing in that country. During the colonial period, agricultural and mineral products of Africa were introduced successfully into the markets of Europe and North America.

Colonial governments also began to borrow abroad in order to provide the needed transportation systems. In the British territories, such borrowing was possible because the British Government, in spite of its position that it could not and should not take any financial responsibility, did pass a Colonial Stock Act before World War I

---

tsetse fly, killed about 250,000 people around the shores of Lake Victoria in 1900–1905, and, in order to stop the epidemic, the lake shore had to be abandoned. One area, particularly, known because of its fertility as the paradise of Uganda, was abandoned to the tsetse fly and is still deserted; it has not been possible to reclaim it successfully from the fly and repopulate it.

which gave colonial government securities the status of trustee investments—i.e., trustees could invest in colonial government securities. This was more important than a merely permissive ruling: since trustees could not invest in securities that did not have trustee status, funds were funneled, *nolens volens,* into colonial investment whenever there were insufficient supplies of U.K. trustee securities. The Act was in fact criticized by John Maynard Keynes for this reason. While the British Government maintained that the Colonial Stock Act did not imply its guarantee of any securities so issued, the actual practice tended to be that when a colony or protectorate had difficulty in maintaining the service on its securities, it was put under strong pressure to improve its finances while the British Treasury simultaneously would make grants-in-aid in order to make continued service on the debt possible.

The French Government acted more directly in guaranteeing loans raised by the colonies on the Paris market during the 1930's. The United States also almost got into the act. After the end of World War I, the U.S. Treasury proposed to Congress that the United States recognize some responsibility for Liberia and make available a loan of $5 million to help in its economic development. Congress turned down this proposal, however, and the entrance of the United States into Africa's economic development had to wait another thirty years.

By 1936, something in the vicinity of $6 billion had been invested in Africa, according to S. H. Frankel's calculations—all of it provided by private European investors with the exception of about $100 million from Americans. Of this total, colonial governments borrowed about 45 per cent and used the money to build railways, ports, and other public works. The rest was borrowed or invested directly by private investors in Africa and used mostly for the development of mines. (Minerals were the major export from Africa right up until World War II, and for practically the whole of the period from 1900 on usually represented well over half of total African exports.) More than $2.5 billion equivalent was invested in the Union of South Africa, about $2 billion in the other British territories, about $700 million in the Congo, $350 million in the French territories, and about $300 million in the Portuguese territories. The distribution of this capital also provides a rough but good

proportional indication of the relative progress in economic development made by the various territories of Africa at the beginning of
World War II.

By World War II, therefore, a pattern had been established in
Africa according to which heavy reliance was placed on the local
government to start economic development. While theorizing about
"African socialism" is fairly recent, the practice of governmental initiative, it is clear, was essentially pioneered by the colonial governments themselves. Direct private investment in the African countries
was most frequent and most successful in mining—and this pattern,
too, continues to prevail.

NEW ECONOMIC THINKING

World War II represented a turning point in the development of
Africa. During it, a sea change in economic thinking and policy took
place that makes the pace of development in Africa in the postwar
period considerably different from the prewar period. The fundamental new assumption was that government has a responsibility for
running the economic system. In developed countries, this assumption underlay the now accepted policy that government could and
should maintain full employment. In underdeveloped countries, it
became the universal belief, to which all governments paid at least
lip service, that government had a responsibility for promoting
economic development. The final implications of these new attitudes
to economic policy are still not yet fully accepted—that in developed
countries the government has a responsibility for bringing about an
adequate rate of economic growth, and that these countries have a
responsibility to aid the development of underdeveloped countries.

But the impact of this change in economic thinking on African
development has nevertheless been enormous. Since the war, African
countries have been able to profit from the prevalence of full employment in developed countries, which has meant that there has
been a continuous demand for African products. In fact, the shift
from the depressed condition of the world market before the war
to the high demands resulting from full employment in the industrialized world has given the African countries favorable prices for
their products over most of the period since World War II. And the

sense of obligation in industrialized countries to help the underdeveloped countries has resulted in a major inflow of public capital and technical assistance into Africa. Since the need for foreign capital to finance most of the investment in Africa has continued, the inflow of capital has been crucial.

POSTWAR AFRICAN GROWTH

The years since World War II can be divided into two phases—1945–60 and the years since. Until 1960, Africa in general did very well economically. The indications are that economic growth in Africa during this period was at least as fast as in any other major underdeveloped region of the world: production and exports grew rapidly; gross national product grew in the vicinity of 4–6 per cent per year in real terms. Only the Middle Eastern oil-producing countries showed a more rapid growth of exports.

It is true that this growth did not take place uniformly throughout the continent. Some areas—like the Rhodesias, the Belgian Congo, Morocco, Gabon, Kenya—grew at rates of 6–11 per cent per year, rates among the highest in the world. These were the countries that enjoyed a large inflow not only of capital but also of key managerial, technical, and entrepreneurial personnel from Europe. In addition, they were (aside from Kenya) mainly mineral-producing countries where a rapid increase in production is more easily secured. Other African lands—Tunisia, Algeria, Ghana, Nigeria, French West Africa, Liberia, Uganda, Tanganyika, South Africa—grew at rates of 4–6 per cent per year, not spectacular but more than satisfactory. And, finally, there were countries where the increase in gross national product barely kept up with the population growth and may even have fallen behind. These were the lands of equatorial Africa (except Gabon)—Ruanda Urundi, Ethiopia, the Portuguese territories, Somalia.

Between 1945 and 1960, another $5 billion or $6 billion of private capital had flowed into Africa. A new feature was that, in addition to this, around $9 billion of capital was provided by governments outside of Africa. In all, something like $15 billion of capital from abroad came into Africa. This large inflow of capital naturally accelerated the transformation of Africa, making possible the minimum of economic infrastructure (ports, roads, schools, hospitals, administrative buildings) without which economic growth cannot begin.

AFRICAN DEVELOPMENT IN THE 1960's

In 1960, a new period began, a new period that roughly coincides with the coming to independence of most of Africa's former colonial territories. It also roughly coincides with the point at which capacity for production of primary products finally caught up with the needs of the fully employed industrialized world. Since 1960, the national rates of growth have consequently changed. The countries that were the most rapid growers in the previous period experienced a stoppage of the inflow of private capital, and, in fact, there has been a sizable over-all outflow. Trained personnel from abroad have also departed in some cases. In such countries (and Tunisia and Algeria also), a main problem has been to achieve a successful transition from an economy where most of the exports and the dynamic elements were concentrated in the sector owned, dominated, and run by foreigners to an economy run by the local people. Of all the African countries, Tunisia has been the first to accomplish the transition by and large successfully, and she has now been able to embark again on a substantially rapid rate of growth. The formerly rapid growers in Africa south of the Sahara are still struggling with this problem.

In other African nations too, there has been some slowdown in the inflow of foreign private capital, and this has naturally affected the growth rate. South Africa, which was greatly dependent on the inflow of foreign capital at the end of the war, has since developed its economy to the point where it alone of the African countries is capable of self-sustained growth and, consequently, no longer has to rely on inflow of foreign capital.

Nearly all African countries have suffered from a deterioration in their terms of trade, but this affects the various countries unevenly and differently from year to year. In the main, Africa must pay prices that are perhaps 10–15 per cent higher today on the average than they were in 1955–57; the prices of the commodities they sell decreased year by year to 1962 and since then have recovered somewhat; but African terms of trade are still 10–20 per cent below 1955–57. This change in the terms of trade has made it much more difficult to meet current needs. In particular, in countries that had been able to finance most of their public capital investment from current revenue (Ghana, Nigeria, Sudan, Uganda), this has helped to make them dependent on foreign assistance to finance their public capital investment. Consequently, Africa's need for foreign capital finance continues and has been reinforced by these price movements.

Political independence has not removed the African nations' great need for help from abroad in the form of trained personnel. There are still some 35,000 Europeans and Americans working for the governments of sub-Saharan Africa. Independent African countries are, of course, pushing as rapidly as possible to replace these "expatriates" with trained people of their own nationality, but inevitably, the "expatriates" have left more rapidly than trained people were available to replace them. Also, even though an "expatriate" may be replaced by a man of the same ability and same standard of training, his replacement will be less experienced. The result has been that the standard of administration throughout the continent has somewhat deteriorated. On the other hand, it should not be overlooked that the governments of the independent countries have often found it easier to mobilize the population and get more voluntary cooperation in achieving economic tasks than the colonial administrators did.

The recent years have seen, therefore, some slowdown in economic growth in most of Africa. In evaluating the great obstacles and problems faced by the independent African governments, an objective observer must, however, be pleasantly surprised that the results have not been more unfavorable. Africa's relative success has been due both to a step-up in the amount of external public aid (net of amortization repayments), which is now running at $1.5 billion a year for all of Africa (more than $1 billion for Africa south of the Sahara), and to the great efforts Africans themselves are making to master their problems. In this latter respect, even with all of her inexperience, Africa's efforts to achieve economic development compare more than favorably with those of other major developing regions of the world.

20 The Economics of African Development

Selected Bibliography

Buxton, T. F. *The African Slave Trade.* London: John Murray, 1839; New York: American Anti-Slavery Society, 1840.
Dike, K. O. *Trade and Politics in the Niger Delta, 1830–1885.* Oxford: The Clarendon Press, 1959.
Ducasse, A. *Les négriers, ou le trafic des esclaves.* Paris: Hachette, 1848.
Frankel, S. H. *Capital Investment in Africa.* London and New York: Oxford University Press, 1938.
Hailey, Lord. *An African Survey, Revised 1956.* London and New York: Oxford University Press, 1957.
Hance, W. A. *The Geography of Modern Africa.* New York and London: Columbia University Press, 1964.
Keynes, J. M. "Foreign Investment and National Advantage," in *The Nation and the Athenaeum,* August 9, 1924, pp. 985–86. Cited by S. H. Frankel, "Some Conceptual Aspects of International Economic Development of Underdeveloped Territories." ("Essays in International Finance," No. 14.) Princeton, N.J.: International Finance Section, Princeton University, May, 1952.
Leakey, L. S. B. *The Progress and Evolution of Man in Africa.* London and New York: Oxford University Press, 1961.
Neumark, S. D. *Foreign Trade and Economic Development in Africa: A Historical Perspective.* Stanford, Calif.: Food Research Institute (Stanford University), 1964.
Pedler, F. J. *Economic Geography of West Africa.* London and New York: Longmans, Green, 1955.
"Slaves Are Still Bought in Africa" (AP dispatch from Lagos), *The New York Times,* December 18, 1964, p. 45.
Stamp, L. D. *Africa: A Study in Tropical Development.* London: Chapman and Hall, 1953; 2d ed.; New York: John Wiley, 1964.
Thomas, B. E. *Transportation and Physical Geography in West Africa.* Los Angeles: University of California, 1960.
Toynbee, A. "Interview," *The Washington Post,* February 16, 1964, Section E, p. 1.

II

The Structure
of the African Economies

> *"Is there any point to which you
> would wish to draw my attention?"*
> *"To the curious incident of the dog
> in the night-time."*
> *"The dog did nothing in the night-
> time."*
> *"That was the curious incident,"
> remarked Sherlock Holmes.*
>
> SIR ARTHUR CONAN DOYLE

While it is possible to speak of an American economy or even of a West European economy, there is as yet no such thing as the "African economy": African countries do little commerce with one another; productive units do not heavily depend on markets or on sources of raw materials or components from areas in Africa outside their own country; there is, in brief, little division of labor among African countries. Economically and financially, African nations are more like a series of islands lying off the coast of Western Europe than like parts of a single continent. Africa today does not, in fact, make up a meaningful economically integrated whole.

Normally, only around 8 per cent of the trade of African countries is with other African countries. And even this figure actually overstates the case, since it is inflated by the substantial trade of goods

21

between South Africa and Rhodesia and among East African countries.* And, to some extent, all statistics on inter-African trade are misleading. They usually include some re-exports of goods originally imported from outside Africa. But on the other hand, they often do not cover a considerable volume of traditional trade across frontiers—the movement of cattle, for example, south from the savannah area in Upper Volta, Niger, and Chad in West Africa toward the coast.

Yet, despite all this, it still makes sense to discuss the African economies together. This is because the various national economies, while having few ties with one another, are still so similar that the total is representative of the separate parts. While broad generalizations about Africa are often dangerous, some generalizations on the economy of the whole area of Africa south of the Sahara are quite meaningful in many ways. There is also probably a greater sense among Africans of belonging to a single entity than there is among people in most of the other major underdeveloped regions; millions of Africans cheerfully disregard national boundaries in gaining their livelihood. This is true of the nomads—the Toureg, who move as freely in the Sahara, across half a dozen national territories, as sailors on the sea; the Fulani, who herd their cattle in the savannah areas of West Africa from Guinea to Nigeria; the different groups of Somali who use the grazing grounds of southeastern Ethiopia; the Masai herdsmen of Tanzania and Kenya, etc. It is also true of the African migrant wage workers: one-quarter of the men of Upper Volta are usually away, working in Ghana or the Ivory Coast, and, inversely, one-quarter of the Ivory Coast's total population of almost

---

* Almost 10 per cent of South Africa's exports in 1965 were to Rhodesia, where they represented about one-third of Rhodesia's total imports. Rhodesian exports to South Africa amounted to about 28 per cent of its total exports and 2 or 3 per cent of South Africa's imports. The breakup of the Federation of Rhodesia and Nyasaland in 1964 resulted in a drop in trade between its successor states, Zambia and Malawi, and South Africa, but trade between Rhodesia and Zambia and Malawi was quite high (Zambia bought 40 per cent of its total imports from Rhodesia) until Rhodesia's unilateral declaration of independence in November, 1965. Rhodesian trade with South Africa, on the other hand, increased in 1965, facilitated by the broadening of the trade preferences that each country gave to the other. A special trade relationship between Rhodesia and South Africa dates back many years, in fact, to the free-trade area that existed in practice between them until Rhodesia began her industrialization in the 1950's.

4 million has come from other African countries, mainly Upper Volta, Mali, and Guinea; the men of Malawi and Lesotho (formerly Basutoland) get the bulk of their paid employment in Rhodesia and South Africa, respectively; a hundred thousand "Westerners" from northern Nigeria and Chad are the backbone of the labor force on the cotton farms of the Gezira Scheme in the Sudan; men and women from Rwanda and Burundi work on the coffee farms of Uganda and make up a large proportion of the miners in Katanga.

Population and Area

Excluding the Mediterranean African countries, Africa has an area of 9.5 million square miles, or more than three times the size of the United States. The population is probably somewhat greater than that of the United States, between 200 million and 250 million in 1966; of these, about 4.5 million are of European origin and 1 million of Asian origin.

Not enough is known about the population size now, and very little about what it was, to make any very confident assertion about what the rate of population increase has been or is. In those areas where somewhat better data are available, that is, in East and Central Africa, rates of population growth range from 1.75 per cent yearly in Tanganyika to 3 per cent and over in Kenya, Rhodesia, and Mauritius. But "figures of 3 per cent and over must be considered with suspicion. . . . In order to get greater representation in the legislature or even for greater prestige, there is a strong temptation to overstate population numbers where before there may have been an understatement because people were taxed per head, or because they were superstitious or distrusted the administration, etc." (Martin, p. 9.)

In any case, it is safe to assume that the rate of population growth in Africa has accelerated since World War II, though probably not as much as the available figures indicate. It will almost certainly accelerate more within the next decade, since the present (still high) death rates are likely to be reduced more rapidly than the birth rate. A rate of population growth of 2–3 per cent yearly is a datum that African governments will have to accept as a planning parameter for some years to come.

In relating the present size of population to the area of Africa—which results in a density figure of 20–25 persons per square mile (9–10 persons per square kilometer), or about one-third that of the United States—the temptation is great to conclude that Africa is underpopulated. But "underpopulation" or "overpopulation" depends not only on the relationship of population to physical resources but on the level of technical and economic development that the people have attained, since this is what determines the numbers the economy can support at any particular point in time. For instance, in Zambia and Rhodesia, with a population living in the traditional way on the basis of shifting cultivation, ash planting, and cultivation with hoes, the land could carry in perpetuity from about 6 to 10 or 12 people per square mile, depending upon how much wood was available to burn for ash. (Gluckman, p. 647.) With the growth of industry—the opening up of the copper mines—the numbers that can be carried have risen considerably. In other words, with traditional methods of culture, Rhodesia could have supported perhaps 1.5 million people, but today she is not overpopulated with 3 million. In the case of Zambia, the size of the population today is still quite close to the number that could live on the land on the basis of subsistence agriculture.

Aside from parts of eastern and northern Nigeria, Rwanda, Burundi, Kigezi in Uganda, southern Malawi, Lesotho, and the "reserves" in South Africa, there does not in general appear to be that pressure of population on *present methods* of exploitation of resources which would lead one to say Africa is overpopulated. On the other hand, there is certainly no evidence that an absolute lack of adequate manpower is holding up development.* Yet, while there is little population pressure in Africa as a whole, the present distribu-

---

* From time to time, complaint is made of the scarcity of labor for a particular activity—e.g., in Liberia in the early 1960's in the rubber plantations. But the difficulty is likely to be due not so much to an absolute scarcity of labor as a scarcity of labor at the low wage being offered. When a low wage ceiling is imposed, as was true in Liberia, it is to be expected that some enterprises will have difficulty in recruiting labor. The very fact that it was felt necessary to establish a maximum wage indicates that demand was raising wages: at a higher wage, more labor might be available, on the one hand, and, on the other, some of the demand for it would disappear; if wages were to be prevented from going up, some enterprises would have to be short of labor at the legal wage.

tion—decided by historical events (the slave trade, tribal wars, etc.) as well as by the agricultural technology of 60–100 years ago—is not ideal. Crowded areas often lie next door to underutilized land, with movement between them restricted by tribal considerations. Still, the absence of severe population pressure at a time when economic development has hardly begun can be seen as an important economic asset. It gives Africa a better starting point than India or Pakistan, for example, where, with about the same level of per-capita income, there are already severe pressures on the available resources.

But a good starting point is not enough. What will count now is the rate of population growth, the rate of growth of gross national products, and the interrelations between these. In this regard, the acceleration in the rate of population growth that is now unquestionably occurring over most of Africa is a strong negative factor.

Generally, what is happening is that fertility remains high—with birth rates of 40 or 45 per 1,000 or higher—while infant mortality rates drop. The number of children rapidly increases, and the proportion of the population who are adults and economically productive drops. Typically, in a country in this stage of development and population growth, 40–45 per cent of its population is under the age of 15; most developed countries have a maximum of 25–35 per cent in this age-group. This means that a larger proportion of the national income in an African country has to be devoted to the feeding, clothing, and housing of nonproducers than in a developed country. As between two countries, then, with the same size labor force and same national income, the one with the lower rate of population growth will have a higher per-capita income. And the difficulty the country with the higher rate of growth faces in saving a portion of its income for investment (to make possible higher incomes in the future) becomes greater just because of the high rate of population increase.

All of these difficulties occur when a country has had a high rate of population growth for many years. But they are aggravated when the rate of population growth is *rapidly* accelerating; during this period, the number of children may double or triple while the number of adults still does not increase (or only slightly, due to improvements in adult medicine). The proportion of children in the population in this way may shoot up beyond the 40–45 per cent mentioned above.

A second factor that comes into play as a result of the higher rate of population growth is this: a much higher proportion of the investment an African country is able to make must go to schools, housing, and other not *directly* productive sectors than is true in developed countries. As between two countries where all else is equal, the country with the lower rate of population growth can not only invest more in total amount but can invest a higher proportion in factories, farms, and other immediately productive enterprises than can the one where the population growth rate is accelerating. Of course, this becomes cumulative: a greater productive investment this year results in a higher output next year, which makes possible still greater investment.*

* A simple population model that may fairly be applied to African countries is as follows:

Total savings and investment, 12 per cent of GNP; investment in the social sector—defined simply as the investment necessary to take care of the growth in population, i.e., schools, housing, hospitals, etc.—3 per cent of GNP for every 1 per cent in the rate of population growth; an average and incremental capital/output ratio of 3 in the non-social sector alone, assuming that the social-sector investment does not have any immediate effects on output. Then, comparing two countries, both with a per-capita GNP of $100, and assuming that Country A has and maintains an annual rate of population increase of 1 per cent while Country B's rate inceases from 1 per cent to 3 per cent within ten years, the following table shows the results in economic growth:

At the end of	Per-capita GNP (in dollars)	
	Country A	Country B
5 years	116	113
10	134	123
15	156	129
20	181	136
30	243	150
40	326	165

At the end of five years, the two countries are still quite close together. But, after twenty years, not only has Country A pulled well ahead but its GNP rate of growth is *accelerating*. On the other hand, Country B's economic progress is slowing down to a crawl. At the end of forty years, Country A has about double the per-capita income of Country B and is well on its way to rapid economic growth. (A more complex model, closer to reality, would show that Country A can do even better than these figures indicate, since, with the higher per-capita income, it could increase its rate of investment quite early on and its rate of economic growth still more.)

In brief, it is not an exaggeration to say that the policy on population adopted by an African nation may well prove to be the most decisive factor in deciding what kind of an economic future lies ahead for it during the next forty years.

The Internal Economic Structure

Africa is a poor continent. The total gross national product (GNP) of Africa, excluding the Mediterranean countries, is estimated at about $30 billion equivalent (at current exchange rates) for 1966. This is nominally less than 5 per cent of the American GNP in money terms. It is roughly equivalent to the total income of the present American Negro population, which numbers less than one-tenth the population of Africa. It is, in fact, well below the annual *increase* in the American GNP in 1964 or 1965. About one-third of the total African GNP is produced in South Africa, which, with 17 million people, has less than 10 per cent of Africa's total population. The proportion of South Africa in the African total has, however, been dropping during the last sixty years. Few estimates have been made of national accounts of African countries before World War II, but a fair indication can be secured from export figures: in 1900, South Africa provided more than two-thirds of the total exports of sub-Saharan Africa; just before World War II, they had dropped to just over half; in 1965, they were around one-third.

Data on African economies are not sufficiently reliable or abundant to make meaningful the application of any very sophisticated analytical refinements. It is possible, however, to make some fairly rough analysis that illuminates how the African economies work.

The propulsive and dominant sectors in the African money economies are external: exports, foreign investment, and other expenditures financed from abroad.* These essentially still determine the size and growth pace of African economies.

An increase in money incomes results almost immediately in an increase in demand for imports—and in upward pressure on prices to the extent that imports are not immediately available. In other words, the marginal propensity to import is very high. This is for a

* See below, chaps. IV and XII.

number of important reasons: the "modern" sector of an African economy is relatively small and inflexible, particularly that part of it producing goods for the home market. The propensity in the private sector to save is also very small. Consequently, an increase in money incomes (whether from an increase in export earnings, from an inflow of foreign investments or foreign expenditures, or from central bank creation of money to finance a government deficit or private activity) is offset in only small part by an increase in private savings. It results instead in increased imports. Because of the inflexibility of local production, the increase in national output is relatively small (the national income multiplier is fairly weak, probably under 2) and the rise in the demand for imports is quite rapid.

What this means for the African nation is that an increase in the price of exports, resulting in greater export earnings, will soon be reflected in greater imports (of consumer goods, if action is not taken to divert or induce the extra funds into investment). An attempt to finance investment or increased government spending by central-bank creation of money soon results in a foreign-exchange crisis.

Per-Capita Income

The average African per-capita GNP (excluding South Africa) is estimated to be somewhere around $100 equivalent. South Africa's average GNP per capita is around $450 equivalent; Rhodesia and Gabon are $200 or more. However, if the non-African elements in the population in Rhodesia and Gabon are excluded, probably Ghana's over-$200 per-capita GNP and Senegal's and the Ivory Coast's per-capita GNPs of about $175 would be the highest in the continent.

Compared to other underdeveloped areas of the world, insofar as the figures can be taken as indicative, Africa's per-capita GNP, even excluding South Africa, is on the average a little higher than that of the South Asian countries and about the same as that of the Far Eastern countries excluding Japan. (No Latin American nation, except Haiti or Bolivia, is in the same per-capita GNP bracket as the African countries; the Latin American countries usually show a figure several times higher.) While the figure for African per-capita

GNP is comparable to those of these other regions, it should be noted that Africa does not suffer from the wide-spread misery that is characteristic in some countries in these other areas. Also, although Africa is still very underdeveloped, the fact that it is no longer behind the Far East or South Asia economically is already a remarkable fact, in the light of Africa's very late start.

Of course, all of the national-accounts figures for Africa must be taken with considerable reserve and should not be regarded as more than generally indicative. Their general significance is, however, corroborated by other indices: for example, literacy is, on the average, below 20 per cent; electric power consumed per capita (excluding South Africa) is about 60 kilowatt-hours a year (compared to 5,000 kwh in the United States); and the number of people per physician is 21,000 (740 in the United States).

National Accounts

Most of the industrialized countries began calculating their national accounts regularly only after World War II. In Africa too, the preparation of national accounts began after World War II, but here they are still rudimentary and irregular. In the English-speaking African countries, the approach used by the United Kingdom, which is consistent with that recommended by the United Nations, was adopted with some local variations. In French-speaking countries, the French system was adopted, which differs in important respects: estimates are presented in the form of tables of uses and resources by commodity groups and a *tableau économique* for the economy as a whole. Most of the information given in a U.N.-style national account can be derived from these tables, but the appearance is quite different.

For most African countries, dependable bench-mark yearly estimates of agricultural and industrial production are not yet available. In addition, most types of economic statistics are still rudimentary, and the number of personnel that can handle them is limited. Consequently, even though formally comprehensive and detailed national accounts have been prepared for many African countries and partial accounts for the rest, their accuracy is not great.

Aside from their incompleteness and lack of accuracy, many of the

national accounts now prepared in Africa differ from those of industrialized countries also in significance. National accounts describe
best a monetary economy (although pitfalls are also present even
there). In a country with a large subsistence sector, as is true everywhere in Africa, the validity of the accounts is considerably at-
tenuated. The problem is that it is impossible to ignore the subsistence activities but almost equally impossible to bring them into
the accounts in a meaningful way. In fact, the process of putting a
price tag on subsistence output is difficult to justify logically: how
do you value something in money terms when its essence is that it is
nonmonetary? As Phyllis Deane, pioneer in this work, has said:
"Where the bulk of goods in a given category are traded, it does not
greatly strain the conceptual framework to impute a value to the
remainder. Where the bulk are *not* traded, it is obviously a highly
artificial process which bears no direct relation to the physical facts
of the case. The figure for subsistence output can never be more than
a token figure." (Deane, p. 226.)

Besides the valuation, one must decide what part of subsistence
activity can be considered economic at all. At present, economists are
not agreed on which aspects of subsistence activity should be regarded as economic and, therefore, valued and included in the
national accounts. For example, the first estimates made of the Nigerian national income for 1950–51 included £4 million as the value
of services rendered by women in the household, this figure being
based on the bride-payment made by husbands to secure their wives.
(Prest and Stewart, pp. 10, 47.) The national-income estimates made
since then have excluded this item, and the figure for Nigeria's income is thereby considerably reduced. A meeting of a working party
of the Economic Commission for Africa in 1960 agreed that all countries should include in their national income estimated figures for
subsistence activities in agriculture, forestry, fishing, building, construction, and land works by households. But it was left up to the
individual countries to decide whether they wished to include processing, storage, transport, and distribution of a household's own
primary output; home processing of goods purchased; and other
services such as collecting firewood and fetching water.

The general practice today is to include a figure for subsistence in
the national accounts, but it is quite clearly not of the same validity

as the rest of the figures. With time, of course, the increased mone-
tization of activities in Africa will give more meaning to the prices
used to evaluate subsistence output. In the meantime, we have to
use more than usual caution in dealing with aggregate figures in
Africa.

Another problem in the meaning of the national accounts prepared for African countries arises from the economic importance in
all these countries of foreigners ("expatriates") and foreign investment. There are two usual ways of presenting material affected by
this consideration in the national accounts. One is to compute them
on a territorial basis, including whatever happens within the territorial boundaries of a country and paying no attention to national
ownership of assets or nationality of the income-receiver. In this way,
one secures what is called Gross Geographical Product (or Gross
Domestic Product, which is practically the same thing with some
minor differences). The second is to attempt to identify the product
resulting from factors of production supplied by *normal* residents of
the country (Gross National Product). But even Gross National
Product, in countries that have a large enclave of foreigners who are
normally resident in the country, exaggerates the real income and
well-being of the permanent indigenous residents. Yet if the foreign
enclaves were completely excluded, the economic position of the
country would be understated, since, after all, the country does
derive some permanent benefit from the expatriates who are present
and from the enclave investments. If in Kenya, for example, where
Africans are taking over most of the farms and remaining Europeans
are likely to become permanent Kenya citizens, the accounts had in
the past excluded this important European farming community, the
"enclave" would now be introduced into the accounts for the first
time and the Kenya national income would show a misleading big
jump.

It has been suggested that a compromise should be effected under
which the account would "show clearly and in detail what part of
the expenditure by expatriate individuals and which of the investments by foreign-owned firms have an effect on the income of the
indigenous inhabitants." (Saxe, p. 5.) This important refinement
will probably have to wait until more progress has been made in
compiling even the usual conventional accounts. In the meantime,

we shall have to make do with what can be produced in the way of figures.

One important implication of the foregoing remarks is that the usual simple index of economic development—increase in real income per capita—has to be applied with even more than the usual caution in Africa. In some parts of Africa, such an increase could come about by an increase in the number of Europeans employed in the country; but one must also have some idea as to whether the real income per capita of the indigenous population has also improved.

All these difficulties in preparing and interpreting national accounts in Africa have suggested to some economists that an alternative approach be adopted. About ten years ago, Dudley Seers recommended that priority should be given to statistics on specific important aspects of the economy, instead of to national accounts. William O. Jones and Christian Merat made attempts along the same lines at providing an indicator of economic well-being and progress by using the data on physical imports consumed directly by the indigenous inhabitants of ten African countries. The data they presented give a good indication of how well Africans were doing. Ghana in 1955–57, for example, clearly came out with much higher per-capita economic well-being than the Ivory Coast or any other African country represented in the data.

As a means of reconstructing the past development of African countries when essentially only trade statistics are available, the Seers-Jones-Merat approach undoubtedly is worth following. But it does not contribute as much useful information as a national account, when one can be calculated, since it is less comprehensive and less flexible in the coverage of rapidly changing economies. It also does not give as much information about economic structure and is not as useful, therefore, for analysis or planning purposes.

SECTOR DISTRIBUTION OF ACTIVITIES

The average, typical African lives from farming or from herding cattle (or sheep or camels). Agriculture produces from 50 per cent to as high as 70 per cent (as in Ethiopia) of total GNP. In countries that were formerly French colonies, this figure is roughly 65 (Bérard,

p. 10, XIII). The subsistence element in the GNP in some cases (Niger, Chad, Upper Volta) may run as high as two-thirds of the total agricultural contribution but has already dipped below one-half in countries such as Ghana and Uganda. In the typical French-speaking country, the subsistence sector is around 40 per cent of GNP. (Bérard, p. 7, XIII.)

In a few countries (South Africa, Zambia, Congo [Léopoldville*], and probably now Mauretania), the contribution of mining and manufacturing to GNP surpasses that of agriculture. Aside from South Africa (where manufacturing contributes 25 per cent of total GNP), only in Rhodesia, Kenya, and Congo (Léopoldville) does manufacturing contribute as much as 10 per cent of GNP.

THE SUBSISTENCE ECONOMY AND THE MONEY ECONOMY

In terms of the activity of the average African man or woman, the subsistence element in most African economies is probably still dominant. That is to say, the amount of time an average African spends on activities that merely keep him alive and functioning is greater than the amount of time he spends working for or spending money; the average African is more in than out of the subsistence tribal economy. For the average African, the goods and services produced within his household or by the families of his kin are still more important and include more of the necessities of life than the goods he buys or sells. Further, "it would not be unreasonable to hazard the guess that in sub-Saharan Africa the greater part of the exchanges of goods and services which take place outside domestic units occur as incidents to the exercise or acknowledgement of authority. Wherever there are kings or chiefs, or even petty headmen, goods and services pass upward in the form of taxes or tribute and back down again in the form of hospitality or gifts." (Fallers, pp. 119–20.)

It is also probably true, however, though here again there are few data to substantiate it, that few Africans now are completely outside the influence of the money economy. Further, the money economy

* This book was prepared for press shortly before the name of the Congo's capital was changed to Kinshasa. References to Congo (Léopoldville) should be read as Congo (Kinshasa).

is becoming a dominant influence for Africans. Certainly in countries like Senegal, Sierra Leone, Ivory Coast, Ghana, Togo, Kenya, Malawi, Zambia, Rhodesia, South Africa, and the southern regions of Nigeria and Uganda, this is already true for the majority of the population. Whereas twenty years ago, say, the importance of subsistence activities was greater in Africa than in any other region of the world, it is now probably not any more important than in the Far East or South Asia.

The permeation of the money economy throughout Africa not only has considerable importance as such but will influence the whole pace of economic development in the future. It is almost impossible for anyone who has not lived in a subsistence economy to appreciate how profoundly it affects one's activities and outlook. To live in a subsistence economy means to live a hand-to-mouth existence in a world of great risk and uncertainty. Without the techniques or facilities for storage of food over any appreciable period, the African depended on the yearly crop or his luck in hunting or fishing. It was impossible to provide a margin of security. He might be able to gorge himself one week and have to go hungry the next. Nearly every people had a "hungry season" when the last season's crop had been eaten and the new crops had not yet come in. And the risk and uncertainty affecting a whole village, bad as it was, was accentuated for any one individual if he tried to stand alone, since any one farmer's crops could be wiped out by a herd of elephants, a flood, a swarm of insects or birds, and he could then survive only if the rest of the community helped him through to the next harvest.

> Many writers have pointed out the profound psychological effects of this situation. In the first place, it inclines to a fatalist philosophy, interpreted often by Europeans as fecklessness or laziness. If the future is both uncertain and uncontrollable, it is better not to think about it—it might be intolerably painful and daunting to do so. It is well enough known in Western societies that there is a certain threshold of security above which forethought and effort is possible and below which resignation and fecklessness set in. (Hunter, p. 14.)

With the spread of the money economy, it is possible for individuals both to create a margin of security for themselves by setting aside a permanent store of value in the form of money and to survive apart from the community. It becomes possible for them to pass above the threshold of security; to plan ahead and to work for goals beyond bare survival from day to day. This now is happening all over Africa. The widespread thirst for education, and the willingness of parents to make great financial sacrifices to procure schooling for their children, is another indication that Africans are passing over this threshold and are losing the passive fatalism of the past.

THE PUBLIC SECTOR

From a comparatively early point in the development of Africa, the governmental role in the economy was a major one. (See above, chap. I.) Except in the Rhodesias, the Belgian Congo, and the Portuguese territories, in all of which private investment in mines and railways was more important, it was the government that became the constructor of railways and the encourager and stimulator of production. The corollary of this is the continuing importance of the government as employer and of the publicly owned sector generally in the national accounts.

In most African nations, current government expenditures usually run to around 15–20 per cent of gross national expenditures. (In the ex-French colonies, this proportion has been calculated at 14 per cent, but the range is from 9 per cent in Togo to 30 per cent in Mauretania. [Bérard, p. 22.]) If one adds the operations of the (usually publicly owned) railways, electricity authorities, ports, etc., and the investment in the whole public sector, the total approaches one-third of gross national expenditure. The public sector and the export sector, which typically produces around one-quarter of the gross national product, together are therefore the dominant economic influence in the money economy of Africa.

The government and public sector is generally also the largest single, if not the major, employer of wage earners. It remains true that in most African countries the proportion of the labor force in paid employment is still small, usually from 5 to 10 per cent. But, of this group, one is quite likely to find a third to a half or more working for the government or government-owned entities. In the typical French-speaking African country, total wages and salaries paid by the public administrations surpass the total paid in the private sector by around 10 per cent. (Bérard, p. 7.) Many African workers or employees therefore, naturally expect the state or a public agency to be their employers. Among other consequences, this has the effect of reinforcing one of the worst heritages of colonialism— the Africans' acceptance of the idea that the best job to have is a government post.* The ablest people, as a result, think in terms of preparing themselves to fit into the public service rather than of looking for opportunities in the economy outside of government. Another, perhaps in the long run even more significant, result is that worker and employee organizations concentrate on improving their lot through pressure on the state. African trade unions, even aside from their alliance with nationalist movements in the pre-independence period, are thus almost inevitably drawn to the political arena to gain their economic objectives.

THE NON-AFRICAN ELEMENT

A non-indigenous or non-African element is significant in the economies of all African countries, but its importance varies from South Africa (where the economy created by European settlers during the last century is *the* economy, and only comparatively unimportant African subsistence activities are not dominated by it) through nations like Rhodesia, Zambia, Congo (Léopoldville), Ivory Coast, Gabon, and Senegal (where the position can best be analyzed in terms of a dual economy—part European-dominated and part African), to the remaining lands where the bulk of the economy is African but non-Africans still play a significant role as owners and managers of large manufacturing, finance, and import-export business enterprises.

Indeed, the relative economic importance of non-Africans in any African country is generally indicated by how many there are in the country. The largest number of people of non-African origin are in South Africa, where there are 3.5 million of European origin. Elsewhere, there are 250,000 Europeans in Angola, 200,000 in Rhodesia, 100,000 each in East Africa (mostly in Kenya), Mozambique, and West Africa (mostly in Dakar), 80,000 in Zambia, 50,000 in the

* See below, chap. III, p. 60.

Malagasy Republic, and perhaps another 100,000 scattered over the rest of sub-Saharan Africa. Of the continent's more than 1 million Asians, the majority, or 600,000, are again in South Africa; another 500,000 are found in the eastern African countries.

De Kiewiet has made the point that: "The development of Africa in modern times can be more easily understood if it is seen as the result of two movements of migration. The first is the migration of European traders, officials and settlers into Africa together with their skills, investments, equipment and governmental organization. The second is the migration of the African tribesmen into the new world created by European enterprise." (De Kiewiet, p. 35.) Now, with independence, a substantial outflow of Europeans has occurred, their places in the public sector taken over by Africans. But even in governmental positions, European officials will still be needed in most African countries for most of the next decade. And, in the private sector, if the economy is growing vigorously, there is often a continued net inflow of Europeans as businessmen, managers, and technicians, even though the African-owned part of the economy may be growing most rapidly. In Kenya, however, Africans are taking over around half, or more than 3 million acres, of the European farms, and most of the European farmers have left; in Ghana, the government has nationalized several gold mines and a major trading firm.

The Financial System*

Public finance in most of the African countries has been handled well—remarkably well, in fact, even in comparison with countries with much higher income levels. The systems of fiscal administration and taxes introduced by the British and French have deteriorated only moderately during their quite rapid Africanization in some of the newly independent nations. Tax rates and total revenue receipts have generally risen considerably after independence, and fiscal systems have successfully coped with these problems.

In terms of tax and revenue structures, African countries are fairly

---

* Africa's money and banking systems, because they are so closely linked to external financial arrangements, are covered in Chapter IV.

typical of developing nations in general: two-thirds to three-fourths of the revenue comes from indirect taxes, mostly customs, export and excise, or turnover taxes. Kenya, Rhodesia, and South Africa are exceptions, the latter two with a tax structure more typical of developed countries—i.e., with a much greater reliance on direct taxes.

Since exports are a major constituent of African GNPs and the principal means by which most Africans come into the money economy, export taxation is a logical type to apply. It does, of course, penalize a type of production that deserves, rather, encouragement; and, by taxing people engaged in export production and exempting people engaged in production for the home economy, it can be somewhat inequitable. But in the African context, where there is little specialization in production, what actually happens is not so much that "A," who is an exporter, is taxed, leaving "B," who is a producer for the home market, free, but rather that both "A" and "B" are taxed in their activity as producers of exports and exempted as producers for the home market.

In addition to export taxes, Ghana, Nigeria, and Uganda have also secured revenues through marketing boards that buy produce from farmers at one price and sell it abroad at a higher price. At least part of the difference is made available to the government, usually to finance development.

Some of the English-speaking nations, notably Nigeria and Uganda, have pioneered in a form of personal direct tax which is well suited to countries where incomes are too low for the usual type of income tax. This locally assessed tax evolved out of the poll tax, and it is graduated in accordance with a few simple indicators of income or income-producing assets—number of coffee trees owned, number of cattle, wages received, etc.

African governments are rather more successful than governments in other developing countries, even at higher levels of income, in raising tax revenues. Total tax revenue (including marketing-board off-take) in relation to GNP in the last few years was, at the median, 15 per cent, the range from 7 per cent (Rwanda) to 24 per cent (Congo [Brazzaville]). Some years ago, the French-speaking countries did less well, with some figures as low as 5 per cent, but in the last few years, most of them, in order to eliminate the need for budgetary support from France, have carried out intensive drives to raise taxes and increase revenues, and their record now is as good as the English-speaking countries.

Success in raising government tax revenues, as evidenced by a high proportion of revenues to GNP, is not a desirable goal in and of itself. It is desirable only if the use to which these revenues are put are socially and economically more desirable than the use to which the taxpayers themselves would have put the money. On the whole, the uses African governments make of their revenues are satisfactory, since the expenditures, in the main, are for apparently quite reasonable activities directed toward the welfare of the people and growth of the economy. (In some African countries, one can come to the same conclusion on the ground that a decision by the legislature, which imposed the taxes, represents at least roughly the collective will of the people. But this is not the case in all African countries.) There are, however, at least two, rather general, exceptions. First, in quite a number of African countries, the governments have included housing schemes at noneconomic rents, subsidized airlines, subsidized luxury hotels, etc., in their budgets and development programs. Now, since the bulk of government revenue comes from indirect taxes, whose burden falls mainly on the poor, these schemes are in essence a scarcely justifiable subsidization of higher-income groups by the poor.

The second exception concerns government salary levels, which are, relatively, exceptionally high practically all over Africa. Originally, these were set on the basis of European salary levels plus an "inducement element," to get the French or British to come to Africa. When the Africans took over the jobs, they took over these salary levels and prerequisites. The typical governmental wage and salary structure, even for unskilled workers, shows a large disparity between the wages offered and the average income outside, especially startling for positions that were usually filled by "expatriates" in the past. So far, with only some minor adjustments here and there, this gap between the average income level and income levels of the government elite has remained, and the drain on government finances with it.

Intra-African Relations

Economically and financially, there are few ties among the African countries either in the form of trade and financial flows or in the form of economic and financial organization. But the U.N.'s Economic Commission for Africa (ECA) and the Organization of African Unity (OAU), both composed of all the independent states except South Africa, are forums for the discussion of economic and financial problems common to all Africa. The exact division of labor between the two has not yet been worked out, but the setting up in 1964 of the headquarters of the OAU in Addis Ababa close to the headquarters of the ECA should help in this process. The ECA has already shown itself to be a useful center for initiating and coordinating economic and financial policy, as well as for improving economic data and policy.

The ECA took the lead in working out the charter and organization of the African Development Bank (ADB), which came into legal existence in August, 1964, and opened its doors for business in Abidjan on July 1, 1966. With an authorized capital of $250 million (but an initial paid-in capital of only a fraction of this) and membership open to all independent African states except South Africa, the ADB has the potential of being a useful catalyst for and organizer of investment projects involving several states. It also should help to attract capital from outside of Africa; the World Bank Group, in fact, has located its West African regional office in Abidjan to facilitate cooperation with the ADB.

The former French colonies and mandates have made various experiments in creating economic and financial links among themselves. The most important ones still in existence are the Conseil d'Entente, the UDEAC (an economic and customs union, discussed below), and two multinational central banks (see below, chap. IV). The Conseil d'Entente, consisting of the Ivory Coast, Upper Volta, Niger, and Dahomey (Togo became a member in June, 1966), is also essentially a political grouping but has some economic significance in that it created a mutual aid and loan guarantee fund in 1966 to finance and guarantee foreign loans for investment projects. The total fund amounts to around $2.5 million a year, to which the

Ivory Coast contributes $2 million; the remaining $500,000 is contributed by the others. The Conseil members also agreed to pool their credit and jointly guarantee international loans raised by any of its members. The Ministers of Finance of the former French territories are also adopting the habit of meeting regularly with the French Minister of Finance to discuss common problems and to prepare for international financial meetings.

In general, however, the independence movement in Africa destroyed more intra-African links than it created new ones. The West African currency shared by Nigeria, Ghana, Sierra Leone, and Gambia has been replaced by individual currencies. The West African airways and the palm oil, cocoa, and rice agricultural research institutes these countries shared have also been divided up, in large part under Ghanaian initiative. Various attempts made by Ghana to create governmental, economic, or customs ties with Guinea, Mali, and Upper Volta, on the other hand, have come to naught, as did the federation of Senegal and Mali. The former economic and financial ties among Rwanda, Burundi, and the Congo (Léopoldville), in the form of a common currency and customs union, have gone.

The economic union of Rhodesia and Nyasaland disappeared, of course, with the breakup of the Federation on December 31, 1963. An agreement between Rhodesia and Malawi to continue the free entry of Rhodesian products into Malawi against payment of monetary compensation for the customs duties foregone by Malawi preserved part of the earlier economic entity, however. Rhodesia and Zambia also have continued to maintain a common railway and a common power organization to control the Kariba power project.

The economic unity resulting from several political unions persists, however: Eritrea with Ethiopia, British and Italian Somaliland into Somalia, British Togoland with Ghana, and British Cameroons in a federation with Cameroon. The union of Tanganyika and Zanzibar into what is now called the United Republic of Tanzania was added to this list in 1964.

In the French-speaking areas, the previously existing federations of French West Africa and French Equatorial Africa were dissolved when these territories became independent. The West African states, excepting Guinea, formed a new customs union after independence. The monetary union consisting of a common central bank and currency which existed under the French still exists except for Mali and Guinea; the customs union has largely broken down. In 1966, the seven states of the customs union UDEAO (Union Douanière des Etats de l'Afrique de l'Ouest), consisting of Dahomey, Ivory Coast, Mali, Mauretania, Niger, Senegal, and Upper Volta, began an attempt to revive it. The finance ministers initialed an agreement to establish permanent institutions consisting of a council of ministers, a secretariat, and an advisory committee of experts. They also agreed to set up a common external tariff and a duty-free internal market (subject to quantitative restrictions) for products originating in member states. The UDEAO was to become operative upon ratification by five of the seven states. This initiative, if it goes through, together with UDEAC, which is discussed below, would mean that the former French territories are beginning to contrast quite strongly with the continuing trend of disruption of market unity in the English-speaking territories.

THE EQUATORIAL CUSTOMS AND ECONOMIC UNION

The equatorial African states—Gabon, Central African Republic, Congo (Brazzaville), and Chad—and Cameroon are united in a customs and economic union, the Union Douanière Économique d'Afrique Équatoriale–Cameroun (UDEAC). The objectives are not only to establish a common external tariff but to work out common internal economic policies in a number of important fields. The customs union came into effect among the equatorial states in 1959 and was extended to Cameroon in 1962; in December, 1964, the Treaty of Brazzaville set up an economic union to come into existence on January 1, 1966. Three organs were established: a council of chiefs of state to make policy, a *comité de direction* to work out the details of policy, and a secretariat to implement it.

On the customs side, the UDEAC system, when it is completed, will have as its main elements:

1. a common external tariff levied on all goods entering member states of the UDEAC except those from other members, from the European Economic Community, and from the African Associated states of the EEC. (See below, chap. IV.) This will be fully in effect by 1968.

2. "fiscal duties" (*droits d'entrée*) and turnover taxes levied on all goods coming into UDEAC nations except those from member states. 3. a "complementary tax" levied on all goods coming into UDEAC except those from member states, the proceeds of which will be given as compensation to those UDEAC members that in accepting its common external tariff had to lower existing national tariffs.

UDEAC will harmonize other tax, wage, and social policies, and investment codes. The member states also agree to coordinate development programs and to secure an equitable distribution of industrial projects within the union. In this connection, there is to be an ingenious tax, paid by producing factories, with the proceeds to go to the countries where their goods are consumed. This will, among other things, compensate member states for any revenue loss they may suffer from consuming goods originating within UDEAC rather than imports.

The UDEAC has already agreed on the location at Port Gentil, in Gabon, of an oil refinery to serve the area (its first), thus sensibly avoiding "oil-refinery inflation," which has strewn a score of oil refineries around the coasts of Africa during the last five years, a good number of them of uneconomic size. And the UDEAC enjoys several other common services, but these largely date from pre-independence: post and telecommunications, a savings-bank system, the Agence Transéquatoriale des Communications (ATEC), responsible for roads, the customs service, export quality control services, etc. UDEAC members are also served by a common central bank and use a common currency.

Altogether, the UDEAC is one of the few bright spots in the picture of African economic cooperation at present; there has been not only no retrogression but substantial progress among its member states. The next organization to be discussed, the East African common market, is not so promising, except to the extent that its continuing existence is a considerable achievement in itself.

THE EAST AFRICAN COMMON MARKET

The three countries of East Africa, like their French counterparts in equatorial Africa, maintained the substantial economic cooperation they had enjoyed as colonies when they became independent.

Uganda, Kenya, and Tanzania (with partial participation by Zanzibar before its union with Tanganyika in 1964) shared a common market, monetary union, and other services and utilities: the railways, post and telecommunications, and the East African Airways. Fiscal and tax policies were closely coordinated, and taxes and duties were collected by a single income-tax department and customs service. In May, 1964, agreement in principle was also reached on the basis on which new industries in East Africa would be located, as well as on the extent to which departure from the common-market principle would be permitted to enable Tanzania and Uganda to encourage more industrialization.

But in 1965, the East African common market began to come apart, although the disintegration is far from irreversible. In June, Tanzania announced its decision to set up an independent central bank and currency of its own; Kenya and Uganda followed suit and announced the imposition of exchange controls on capital movements to the other countries. There has also been an erosion in the freedom of trade in the area. Kenya has from the start maintained controls on the import of certain agri ..ırural products from the other two countries through an agricultural board system; in 1964 and 1965, Tanzania started putting controls on imports of industrial products.

Much of the common-market and economic cooperation still exists, however; in July, 1965, the three countries cooperated to guarantee a World Bank loan to the East African railways and in January, 1966, for East African telecommunications. A common market among sovereign nations is difficult to achieve and maintain anywhere in the world, because the play of economic interests within each country makes it difficult to work out international agreements; someone is bound to get hurt, and the hurt is direct and identifiable, while the benefits are often diffused and less easy to point to. In addition, the political power of different interests within one nation do not necessarily jibe with the economic structure that would result from an international common market. Finally, if there is not an overwhelming *political* desire for unity, any attempt to work out an agreement item by item to take care of every important interest breaks down from the sheer lack of time and manpower to devote to the task. This may in fact turn out to be one of the greatest obstacles to successful economic cooperation.

Selected Bibliography

ABDEL-RAHMAN, A. "The Revenue Structure of the CFA Countries," *IMF Staff Papers* (International Monetary Fund), XII, No. 1 (March, 1965), 73–118.

BARBER, W. J. *The Economy of British Central Africa.* London and New York: Oxford University Press, 1963.

BÉRARD, J-P. "Une république africaine moyenne." (Chapter xiii of Vol. I, *Planification en Afrique.*) Paris: Ministère de la Coopération, October, 1962.

COALE, A. J. "Population and Economic Development," in P. M. HAUSER (ed.), *The Population Dilemma.* Englewood Cliffs, N.J.: Prentice-Hall, for The American Assembly, 1963. Pp. 46–69.

DEANE, P. M. *Colonial Social Accounting.* Cambridge and New York: Cambridge University Press, 1953.

DUE, J. F. *Taxation and Economic Development in Tropical Africa.* Cambridge, Mass.: M.I.T. Press, 1963.

FALLERS, L. A. "Social Stratification and Economic Processes," in M. J. HERSKOVITS and M. HARWITZ (eds.), *Economic Transition in Africa.* Evanston, Ill.: Northwestern University Press, 1964.

GLUCKMAN, M. "Social Anthropology in Central Africa," *Journal of the Royal Society of Arts* (London), CIII (August 5, 1955), 645–65.

HUNTER, G. *The New Societies of Tropical Africa.* London and New York: Oxford University Press, 1962.

JONES, W. O., and MERAT, C. "Consumption of Exotic Consumer Goods as an Indicator of Economic Achievement in Ten Countries of Tropical Africa," *Food Research Institute Studies* (Stanford University), III, No. 1 (February, 1962), 35–60.

KIEWIET, C. W. de. *The Anatomy of African Misery.* London: Oxford University Press, 1956.

MARTIN, C. J. "The Demography of Tropical Africa." Paper presented to Seminar on Contemporary Africa, Northwestern University, February 4, 1963. Mimeo.

PLASSCHAERT, S. "Institutional Framework of Public Expenditure and Revenues in the Newly Independent Countries of French Africa South of the Sahara." Unpublished paper, International Bank for Reconstruction and Development, February, 1962.

PREST, A. R. *Public Finance in Underdeveloped Countries.* London: Weidenfeld & Nicolson, 1962; New York: Frederick A. Praeger, 1963.

PREST, A. R., and STEWART, I. G. *The National Income of Nigeria, 1950–51.* ("Colonial Research Studies, No. 11.") London: H. M. Stationery Office, 1953.

SAMUELS, L. H. (ed.). *African Studies in Income and Wealth.* Chicago: Quadrangle Books, for the International Association for Research in Income and Wealth, 1963.

SAXE, J. "Capital and Trade Flows in Newly Independent Countries: West Africa." Unpublished paper presented at Northwestern University Conference on Indigenous and Induced Elements in the Economics of Sub-Saharan Africa, Evanston, Ill., November 16–18, 1961.

SEERS, D. "The Role of National Income Estimates in the Statistical Policy of an Underdeveloped Area," *Review of Economic Studies,* XX, No. 53 (1952–53), 159–68.

U.N. ECONOMIC COMMISSION FOR AFRICA. "National Accounting in Africa," *Statistical Newsletter* (Addis Ababa), No. 18 (August, 1965), pp. 8–12.

———. "Public Finance in African Countries," *Economic Bulletin for Africa* (Addis Ababa), Vol. VII, No. 2 (June, 1961), chap. I.

U.S. AGENCY FOR INTERNATIONAL DEVELOPMENT, STATISTICS AND REPORTS DIVISION. "Selected Economic Data for Less Developed Countries." Washington, D.C., May, 1964. Multilith.

III

The African Heritage
and Economic Growth

*The Age of Chivalry is gone. That of
sophisters, economists and calculators
has succeeded, and the glory of Europe
is extinguished forever.*

EDMUND BURKE

There are many universal problems faced by all nonindustrial economies, whether in Africa, Asia, or Latin America. Most of the following description of sixteenth- and seventeenth-century England could
easily apply to the African economies of today!

[The] . . . economy . . . was one in which the methods of production were simple and the units of production were small; in
which middlemen . . . were both hated and indispensable; in which
agricultural progress was seriously impeded by the perpetuation of
communal rights over land. The chronic underemployment of labour
was one of its basic problems and, despite moral exhortations, among
the mass of people the propensity to save was low. . . . It was an
economy heavily dependent on foreign sources for improved industrial
and agricultural methods, and to some extent for capital, but in which
foreign labour and businessmen were met with bitter hostility. In it
ambitious young men often preferred careers in the professions and
government service. . . . Men increasingly pinned their hopes on industrialization and economic nationalism to absorb its growing popula-

47

tion; but industrialization was slow to come, and the blessings of economic nationalism proved to be mixed. (Fisher, pp. 17–18.)

But economic development cannot be separated from social and political transformation. The speed and the ease of economic development depends greatly on the character of the societies concerned. And although the problems of economic underdevelopment are much the same from nation to nation, the way these countries cope with them depends to a large degree on their social (and political) structure. There are elements in African society that make development easier and some that make it harder. It is certainly worth while to try to identify those elements in the African cultural heritage and social structure that can positively help to shape Africa's economic future.

This does not mean that Africans should necessarily take another economic system or society—Western (or Communist)—as a model and assume that it is the ideal toward which Africa should move. It is far from sure that existing Western economic institutions or cultures secure the most rapid rate of economic growth or well-being. But, as they have so far been most successful in providing a reasonably rapid economic growth and a reasonably wide-spread diffusion of economic benefits, they do merit weighty consideration.

The African Heritage

OPENNESS TO INNOVATION

In most areas, Africans show exceptional willingness to adapt or change their institutions to the requirements of economic development. Indeed, the African openness to innovation is comparable to, or even perhaps greater than, that of the Japanese and American in the past:

> Africans in general are the most present-minded people on earth. . . . Without significant exceptions, all African leaders . . . share the passionate desire to acquire all the good things which western civilization has produced in the two millenia of its history. They want especially to get the technological blessings of American civilization, and to do so as quickly as possible. The lack of historical consciousness of their people gives the African leaders a great advantage in moving

rapidly toward this goal of modernization. They are not encumbered by written traditions, or by the visible and tangible physical presence of the ruins of their own "civilized" past—as most Asians have been. Therefore, they do not have to reconcile every innovation with the different practices of their past. (Spiro, pp. 5–6.)

Unlike some other developing areas which depended or depend on a socially or ethnically marginal group for innovation, the African "elite" itself, like the American and Japanese, is open to innovation. In those countries where a marginal non-African group exists, of Europeans or Asians, let us say, those groups can function as a transmission belt bringing in new ideas and techniques from abroad, rather than as the sole and alien embodiment of innovation. The very fact that the African countries are conscious of being "new nations" is in itself of great value, as it emphasizes to the African people the value of "newness"—in ideas as well as things. Similarly, the openness of Americans to technical innovation was and is probably related to the American feeling that the United States, although possessing the oldest government on earth, is still a young country.

African willingness to learn has shown itself from the continent's very first contacts with the rest of the world. For example, cassava and maize spread rapidly through much of Africa as basic food crops after they were introduced by early slave traders to some of the coastal tribes, and this at a time when contact was limited and travel difficult. Many other basic African foods (yams, bananas, plantains, domestic forest goats and fowl) are also not indigenous but were acquired in the course of limited contacts with South Asia.

Emphasis on the importance of economic development not only is not in conflict with the traditional African view of the world, but coincides with the African *Weltanschauung*. There has never developed in Africa, apparently, any religious scorn for the world's goods or any feeling that the body is an impediment to reaching perfection of the soul. Quite the contrary, "there is a certain tendency for traditional African religions to make the health, fertility, and prosperity of the living individual and living community matters of central importance. A great deal of the ritual communication which takes place between living persons and spirit world has as its object the maintenance or re-establishment of individual or group well being in a quite material, biological sense." (Fallers, p. 115.)

Traditionally, therefore, the African, like the modern American, is very much a hedonist, putting a high value on what he regards as the material comforts of this world. This does not mean that the traditional African has the same almost unlimited desire for material goods that the modern American has: his desires may be quite limited. But the important point is that there is nothing in the traditional African outlook that in and of itself tries to place a permanent ceiling on the dimensions of an African's wants or to discourage him from having any material wants at all.

THE EXTENDED FAMILY

Perhaps even more important than religious outlook—both positively and negatively—is the influence of the continuing strength of the tribal ties to which nearly all Africans are subject. To begin with, one must consider the "lineage system," or "extended family"— under which an individual has deep ties with and feels obligation to a large number of people beyond the nuclear family of father, mother, and children. Good fortune is shared with many others, and in a crisis, one individual can call on help from many others. For survival value in a difficult environment, it would be hard to conceive of a better arrangement.

Unfortunately, in terms of potential economic development, the extended-family system has many drawbacks: it tends to discourage individual enterprise and initiative, as the burden of family obligations rises with the degree of an individual's success. A big man in the family is expected to be generous in helping others with school fees, doctors' bills, "bride-price," financing weddings and funerals, and hospitality to all relatives. Consciously or unconsciously, the knowledge that a greater income will mean correspondingly greater burdens must inhibit the efforts an individual puts forth.

There are other drawbacks: family crises tend to prevent accumulation of, or to drain away, any capital that may have been accumulated. Not only are savings in general held down, but the proliferation of small entrepreneurs is prevented. Because people with small incomes find it hard to comprehend the greater costs of living of individuals with higher incomes, a successful civil servant or company employee may be unable to withstand the pressure on him to contribute to other members of the family and still live in the style that he and his family believe is socially necessary. Hence, the temptation to accept bribes or to "borrow" from public or company funds may become great. As the manager of an "expatriate" bank operating in West Africa remarked to me—unconsciously revealing his own cultural biases as well as illuminating African ones—"It is very difficult for the African to learn to put his duty to his employer above his duty to his family."

One of the problems of small business everywhere is the difficulty the small businessman has in comprehending the difference between "income" on the one hand, and amortization and replenishment of capital on the other. If he is under pressure to give help to meet some family crisis, convincing other members of the family that the cash he has in the till is not "income" may be almost impossible. This is, in fact, one of the main causes of the failure of some of the programs to provide loans to small businesses in Africa.

A recent book by Romain Gary takes as its theme a remark by a Russian poet, Sacha Tsipotchkine: "Man—certainly. We are in perfect agreement—one day Man will appear. A little patience is still needed, a little perseverance; he cannot be more than 10,000 years away in the future. At the moment, there are only a few traces, a few presentiments, a few dreams. At this instant, the being who exists is only a pioneer of Man himself." In Africa, human beings may have evolved somewhat farther along the road to becoming "man" in relation to their extended family ties than is economically desirable at this time.

Emphasis on accumulating money as against meeting social obligations worried many people in the United States and Europe in the early years of industrialization. John D. Rockefeller was highly unpopular most of his life; English literature is filled with hostile references to the "New Men," such as in Dickens' *Hard Times*. But it can be argued that this is an instance where it was necessary to fall one step back in order to move farther forward.

When the first John D. Rockefeller was asked the secret of business success, he replied, "Never let your wife know how much money you are making." And, as a matter of fact, his wife was still doing her own laundry when he was already a millionaire many times over. In Africa, the secret of individual business success and of national

economic development may turn out to be, "Never let your relatives
know that you are making any money." This is not just a theoretical
possibility but occurs in fact: "A small but apparently growing
number of Digo and Duruma entrepreneurs are learning how to
manipulate this system of sharing so that they obtain more aid and
support than they give and are able to become successful businessmen in the developing market-exchange economy of the Kenya and
Tanganyika coast. Certainly, one thing a coastal African should do
to protect his assets and his reputation is to appear poor, hungry
and needy." (Gerlach, p. 421.)

There are, of course, offsetting economic advantages of the extended-family system. The sixpences and shillings of many individuals can be pooled to finance the education of a bright child. In
Nigeria, Ibo wage and salaried workers away from home band together for mutual aid and become channels for communicating
ideas for development of the rural areas from which they come—
and tax themselves to provide the necessary funds. (Katzin, p. 186.)
In Nairobi, some of the workers from rural areas club together to
finance small development projects; in Cameroon, the family is used
as a surety for small loans to farmers; in Tanganyika, the family,
using the cooperative system in some instances, pools funds to build
maize mills and set up shops, and pools its credit to borrow from
government agencies to help individual farmers.

In some cases, "the very desire to withhold extra earnings
from one's family may deflect the more enterprising members of
the family from a bureaucratic career (where earnings are fixed
and a matter of public knowledge) into a business career (where
earnings are uncertain and can be concealed). . . . Hence, even if
the sharing implicit in the extended family system is resented, the
obligation to share may act like those taxes that stimulate individuals to greater effort at securing non-taxable gains (and at tax
evasion)." (Hirschman, p. 387.) In other words, the Rockefeller
secret of success may not only be something that permits development but may actually stimulate it.

On balance, the extended-family system in Africa so far has probably inhibited economic development more than it has helped, but
there is a considerable potential for the good—for example, if the
extended family were guided more in the direction of acting as a

kind of mutual-investment fund or trust, as in the Tanganyikan and other examples just cited, rather than of being a kind of social-service or welfare pool. If the family system became an effective way to collect small savings and use them to finance the enterprises of its most capable business members, it could become one of the most potent engines of economic development in Africa.

EGALITARIAN AFRICAN SOCIETY

An aspect of traditional Africa that is unqualifiedly favorable to development is the egalitarian nature of her society. There is no such degree of cultural or social differentiation between strata as developed in the course of the last millennium in Europe. In Africa, if a man attains wealth or prestige, he is accepted as such; there is no "color bar" of "bluebloodedness" such as has plagued and to some extent still plagues Europe and, to a much lesser degree, the United States. The rewards of material success in Africa are, therefore, more satisfying, unspoiled by snubs from an earlier privileged class.

An even greater advantage of this egalitarianism is that talent can be recruited from the entire population. There are no class or caste barriers that an able African youngster must surmount like those that discourage members of certain castes in India or the sons of workers or peasants in Italy, Spain, or France. Most of Africa begins, therefore, at a stage that other societies reach only after long struggle—in which economic relations are regulated on the basis of achievement rather than by reason of traditional social rank or status. (Hoselitz, p. 35.) (Ethiopia, the Sudan, Sierra Leone, and Liberia are partial exceptions to this generalization.) African society, while still underdeveloped, already possesses the mobility among both classes and different localities that Hoselitz regards as one of the necessary characteristics of an economically highly developed society. (Hoselitz, pp. 59–60.)

Again, because in Africa there were not the great differences in the distribution of material wealth that one finds in other underdeveloped regions, there is not a tradition of maintaining the status requirements of an upper class demanding large numbers of servants. This kind of waste is largely absent in Africa.

In a few areas of Africa, however, there has been a prejudice against certain kinds of work, and this prejudice may hinder the economy.* In the Sudan and Ethiopia, there is a bias against manual labor, on the grounds that it is fit only for slaves or serfs to do. In Ethiopia, there has been a prejudice against engaging in commerce. In Liberia and Sierra Leone, descendants of the settlers tend to regard only the government and the professions as proper occupations.

In no area of Africa, apparently, can one find a traditional attitude that there is a *positive* value in work as such, without regard to the material results. In the subsistence economy of tribal Africa, one did not find "inner-directed" individuals—driven to work hard, powered by inner guilt feelings. Nor is there evidence of the kind of personality found in and shaped by modern technological societies to whom work is more than an economic imperative—to whom work is a deeply felt habit or inner need. In traditional African society, the individual was "tradition-directed"; as in all traditional societies, time was regarded as the servant rather than as master. "Rationalism" or "efficiency" in effort or work had little priority; the important thing was the social enjoyment derived from performing a task rather than the rapidity or economy of effort. The acquisition of new attitudes toward work represents an important part of the effort to economic development still in the future.

> The cultural situation of the educated African today may well favour a type of personality more suited not to the enterprising Europe of the nineteenth century, but to the organized Europe of planning and giant companies and social conformity in the twentieth. Such a personality may lack the compulsive initiative and perseverance which still persists in the West as a relict of the first industrial revolution.
>
> It is remarkable how well such a view chimes with the present philosophy of African socialism. Perhaps instinctively African leaders incline toward the state-run economy as against competitive free enterprise, knowing that their peoples have neither the taste nor the

---

* The bias toward the political sphere, reinforced under colonialism but stemming from good African roots, is, as mentioned in Chapter I, detrimental to economic development. In traditional Africa, "whereas full-time specialization in craft production or trade is relatively rare, the specialist in government is quite common. . . . It is perhaps not going too far to assert that the *emphasis* in African systems of stratification is primarily political." (Fallers, p. 119.)

capacity for this extreme of individualism and personal dedication to an economic aim. (Hunter, p. 325.)

THE POSITION OF WOMEN

The position of women in African society is another important influence on economic development. In the farming tribes, women are by custom the cultivators of the food crops grown for home consumption. However, when cash crops are added, the men assume the main responsibility. As these are frequently new crops, grown in a new way, by men who have no long tradition of husbandry to fall back on, it is not at all surprising that the men are more receptive to advice and, consequently, that these cash crops are more efficiently grown. (See below, chap. v.) (This factor may also explain why the cattle-raising tribes, where the men traditionally looked after the herds, progress in moving into a money economy by upgrading and selling cattle is so much slower than in the agricultural tribes.)

As in practically all underdeveloped areas (it was true in the early years of the United States), the position of women is such that when school space is available but limited, boys get priority. (The Chagga in Tanganyika and, according to Dr. Hilda Kuper, some tribes in South Africa are exceptions.) And in general the women keep in closer contact with the countryside and the slower, rural way of life. Women either spend more time in the country on visits or may actually be left there to cultivate the farm while the husbands work in the city. They are more apt, therefore, to preserve traditional customs and remain conservative. Even in West Africa where women are active in trade and may frequently travel, their lack of education and their conservatism prevents the economy from getting the kind of impulse to growth that similar activity performed by men would impart. Félix Houphouet-Boigny, President of the Ivory Coast, in a most perceptive remark, is reported to have said that the time necessary for Africa to catch up with the West is "three generations of mothers."

The African tradition that as a man succeeds he takes on additional wives becomes a detriment in urban life; it is perhaps the most important cause of failure of shopkeepers in Tanganyika. The wives of a shopkeeper compete to see who can get the most goods and money out of the shop for her own use. Unfortunately, only in rare cases in East Africa will a wife be educated enough to be able to run the shop on her own—though there are cases of a man with several wives using them to run a chain of shops. (Mhina, p. 9.)

ECONOMIC RATIONALITY

It was a cardinal tenet of some European "old hands" in Africa that Africans do not behave in an economically rational fashion. Of course, there are very few persons anywhere in the world who behave as a completely rational "economic man," and those who do are often insufferable; the question is really whether Africans are sufficiently motivated by economic considerations to make economic policy meaningful. The answer by economists has been unanimously "Yes." Whenever African economic behavior has seemed irrational to the outside observer, it has seemed so because of an insufficient understanding of the major forces in the African environment influencing his behavior. As a matter of fact, agricultural schemes and industrial incentives in industry that have failed in Africa often did so because the African farmers or workers figured out what would pay them best more accurately than the people who set up the schemes.

The accusation of economic irrationality is usually couched in the terms that giving the African higher prices for produce or higher pay for work does not result in greater effort or more regular work—that better prices or wages may, in fact, result in lower output since the African will get the sum of money he wants more quickly. In actual fact, this phenomenon of the "target" worker (the worker who works to acquire a given sum of money to buy a given set of goods and is not interested in earning more) is not new. It was first identified in Western Europe when the European countries were beginning their industrialization. Max Weber described it as follows:

> A peculiar difficulty has been met with surprising frequency: raising the piece-rates has often had the result that not more but less has been accomplished in the same time, because the worker reacted to the increase not by increasing but by decreasing the amount of his work. . . . [The worker] did not ask: how much can I earn in a day

if I do as much work as possible? but: how much must I work in order to earn the wage, 2½ marks, which I earned before and which takes care of my traditional needs? (*The Protestant Ethic and the Spirit of Capitalism.*)

In economic terms, this phenomenon is a backward-bending supply curve for labor—i.e., the supply of labor called forth by a higher wage at a certain point bends backward and decreases instead of increasing with an increase in wages. But such behavior is completely rational. When what an individual wants to purchase with money is limited, when he has satisfied all these wants, and when the need to save money for unknown needs in the future either is not yet felt or is satisfied, it is quite understandable (and economically sensible) to stop work sooner and enjoy more leisure when the pay rate goes up. And, in fact, this happens quite frequently in highly developed societies when people's incomes for some reason shoot up more rapidly than their wants grow.

When Africa was being opened up to the outside world, the need for laborers to build railways or ports often grew more rapidly than the Africans' desires for goods bought with money. Consequently, until World War I in most parts of Africa, the governments tried to force Africans to work through direct compulsion or by imposing a head tax paid in money and so forcing the African to go out to earn the money. Indeed, such measures were still quite prevalent up to World War II—the Congo-Ocean railway in Equatorial Africa was built in this way—and in Portuguese territories until very recently. Where governments were unwilling to engage in such practices or felt they would not be effective enough, laborers were recruited outside of Africa—such as the Indians who were brought in to build the Kenya-Uganda railway and to work on sugar estates in Natal, or the Chinese who were recruited for the gold mines on the Rand in South Africa.

The backward-bending supply curve for labor is no longer a major concern in Africa, however, as far as the over-all supply of labor is concerned. (In those areas where shortage of labor is still experienced, as in parts of Liberia or the Portuguese territories, it is more probably due to wages being kept too low to attract a sufficient supply of labor than to wages being too high.) There are several forces operating: the level of income an African earns when remaining on the land, the level of wages necessary to induce him to leave the land and the amount of money that is his target income, and the number of individuals affected by these forces. As far as the individual African worker is concerned, the amount of wage labor he is willing to do tends to be inversely related to changes in village income and to changes in wage rates in the exchange sector. In the early years, once a worker got the sum of money he wanted, he quit. Now, a target income becomes more and more remote as an individual's wants increase in number and variety; it is of little significance to the "committed" workers in urban areas, who no longer move back and forth between the land and wage employment.*

In short, the shape of the aggregate labor supply curve—giving the total labor supply at each wage level—depends on the net outcome of two contrary changes accompanying each wage rise: changes in the number of people induced into wage employment; and changes in the average time each man spends at work. In the early days, the curve probably tended quite soon to turn backward: an increased wage induced only a few new laborers into employment and encouraged many already there to cut short their stay. In present-day Africa, this is no longer true: an increased rate stimulates more men to emigrate to paid jobs and leads far fewer to reduce their time in paid employment. When one remembers the great extent to which Africans move from country to country to get work, it is most unlikely that for any given country for any long length of time the aggregate labor supply would decrease when wages are raised. (Berg, pp. 468-92.)

In general, these remarks apply to African farmers too: if income rises more rapidly (due to rising prices or extraordinarily good crops) than the farmer acquires new wants, his labor supply curve will bend backward at some point. Normally, with the passage of time and the spread of education, formal and informal, however, this point

* An important factor in increasing the supply of labor in many areas has been the "push" from the rural areas resulting from the increased difficulty of attaining a desirable livelihood on the land. This may be due to the growing pressure of population on the land, given present levels of agricultural techniques and organization, accentuated in some parts of southern and eastern Africa by the forcible restriction of agriculture to confined areas in the "reserves." The pressure is also increased by the persistence in parts of Africa of "cattle culture," which leads to overgrazing and spreading poverty.

becomes less and less relevant. But in many areas in agriculture, unlike wage labor, the backward-bending supply curve may still be relevant to economic policy. If a worker quits, it is possible to find another worker; but if a farmer does not want to pick the last 10 per cent of his cotton crop, the crop is that much smaller. And, it will still be true in most areas that not knowing just where the bending point is will be a handicap in forming agricultural policy.

The Colonial Inheritance

The existing economic structures of the African states were influenced, shaped, and sometimes created by colonial regimes and their relationships to the metropolitan powers. The export trade and production, the systems of transport, the commercial, financial, monetary, tax, fiscal, and administrative structures—all were created during Africa's colonial period and have not been greatly modified since. It would be easy to criticize much of what was done or undone in the colonial period from the purely ideal standpoint of what the governing powers *should* have accomplished, especially if one applies present-day criteria. But, on the same basis, the policies applied to the European populations by their pre-war governments were scarcely better. There is no country in Africa, moreover, that suffered as severely from a laissez-faire colonial power as Ireland did, for example. In the main, it is practically indisputable that most of the lands of Africa that were formerly colonies are considerably richer materially as a result of their colonial heritage.

THE CIVIL SERVICES

On the plus side, a number of nonmaterial assets were acquired that give most African countries some advantages over other under-developed countries elsewhere in the world—good systems of justice, good civil services, and a good tradition of civil-service behavior. Independent African countries have, with two notable exceptions, preserved independent judiciaries that administer the laws in an impersonal and reasonably equitable manner—certainly a necessary and favorable condition for economic progress. In all the African countries, quite obviously much more could have been done, if men had been wiser and more farsighted, to train Africans to take over the civil service. Nevertheless, the traditions of honesty and (relative) efficiency in government service is a valuable economic asset. The high prestige of the civil service in itself is also helpful, although this has its drawbacks, of course, in attracting too many of the able young Africans into the government and away from the rest of the economy.

This latter tendency is also reinforced by a most unfortunate legacy of colonialism—the very high salaries of ministers and top civil servants.

> It was inevitable that as local persons invaded the senior ranks of the service their emoluments should bear a close relation to those of their expatriate colleagues in the same or similar posts. This has had a distorting effect on the whole of the salary structure. Even where an expatriation or inducement element was introduced, the gap between the lowest paid and the senior service officers of local origin was very wide indeed and still remains unhealthily wide. (Adu, p. 21.)

(The United States, in its first years, suffered from a similar carryover of a colonial pattern of privilege and example. This was eventually eliminated by Thomas Jefferson, who, upon taking office, gave up his coach-and-four and other colonialist luxuries, and by Andrew Jackson's introduction of frontier frugality. African nations have yet to see their Jeffersons and Jacksons.) The result is that, whereas in the United States, for example, top civil-servant salaries are at the maximum only four or five times the average wages of an unskilled laborer, in Africa the ratio will be more like 30–50 to 1.

This "neo-colonialism" in top government salaries and prerequisites (houses, cars, travel allowances) swallows up an enormous share of government receipts (in the ex-French African countries, two-thirds of current government expenditures), thus reducing the amounts available for public investment or economic services connected with development. It also has an unfortunate impact on the economy generally. To begin with, it sets too high a standard of consumption and reduces savings available for investment. It also stimulates political unrest—always unfavorable for economic growth. High living standards of "expatriates" in the colonial period were in a way more tolerable, since the mass of people did not feel they could aspire to them; in the end, these unattainable standards and privileges were a factor in the demand for independence. But, when it is *Africans* who are driving around in Mercedes limousines, the mass of people more readily feel that they too should receive immediate and tangible benefits from their nation's independence and, when they do not, think of overthrowing the government. Such feelings were openly expressed in the Congo (Brazzaville) revolution in 1964, for example. Ready-made leaders for rebellion are already at hand in the "second generation"—the new university graduates who find that all of the "plums" have gone to men just a few years older than themselves, who are often less well qualified and who will not be retiring to make way for them for many years.

The School-Leaver Problem

The wage and salary structure left behind by the colonial powers is in large part responsible for a new and growing problem in Africa: the so-called "school leavers," usually young men who have had a certain minimum education (elementary or junior secondary) but who are unable to find employment with position and income to match their training. The problem is essentially that the wage and salary structure was set when the number of educated or partly educated people was very small, and the jobs that required trained personnel consequently paid well in comparison to what the mass of people earned in unskilled agricultural labor. (The salaries included a substantial element of quasi-rent, in other words.) With the rapid expansion in education, the number of people qualified for these few jobs has become a flood, but the wage and salary structure has not adjusted to the change, nor has the economy grown sufficiently or in such a way to absorb these people.

What happens, then, is that a youth who has gone to school with the expectation of getting a clerical position may prefer to remain unemployed for months or years, waiting for an opening to turn up, rather than to go back to farm work and miss the glittering prize of work in a white collar. Moreover, his family, who has made many sacrifices to send him to school, will regard him as a failure if after all that education, he becomes a farmer like his uneducated brothers.

This is not the first time this kind of unemployment has appeared in Africa. The so-called "poor white" problem in South Africa in the 1920's and 1930's was similar. During this period, as many as 220,000 "poor whites," one-ninth of the European population, migrated from the rural areas to the towns. Here, the difficulty was that the salary and wage structure for whites was much higher than for the other races in the Union of South Africa, and the jobs at the "white" level were considerably fewer than the number of "poor whites" now demanding them. The government eventually took action to support the "poor whites" at the higher standard of living they demanded, and, after a generation of rapid economic growth, the South African economy grew sufficiently to absorb and afford the "poor whites" at the higher income level. Certainly, by the middle 1950's, the "poor white" problem had vanished.

Nor is this phenomenon unique to Africa: Italy experienced a similar "sociological unemployment" during the postwar period, as peasants, principally from the south, moved from the country to the cities before regular jobs could be provided for them. Somewhat as in Africa, the city earnings were kept up above the real market price by trade-union and government action. In the Italian case, the number of men in the cities searching for jobs remained almost constant for many years, in spite of the fact that the expansion of the economy was making it possible to absorb more and more of them.

At present, in Africa, the number of men who can live in a town without regular work is in part determined by the number of opportunities there are for picking up odd bits of work or money, as was the case in Italy. In Africa, another, perhaps more important, factor is also at work: the responsibility the African feels for his brother, in the widest sense of the word. A man in the city, earning what is regarded as a good income by his relatives in the country, often finds himself having to support the unemployed relatives who come and live off him. He may continue to acquire dependents until his (and his immediate family's) average standard of living sinks to something like the average enjoyed by his rural relatives, or until he or his wife rebels.

Some measures are now being taken to narrow the great discrepancy in incomes between skilled urban and unskilled rural labor— from both sides of the gap. On the one hand, attempts are being made to improve agricultural productivity and raise agricultural incomes. On the other, governments are trying to be careful not to raise urban incomes still further where there is an oversupply of applicants. In Rwanda, Tanzania, Nigeria, and Dahomey, steps have been taken to try to cut the incomes of certain urban groups. To some extent, the general inflation now occurring in Ghana, Mali, and the Congo (Léopoldville) serves a similar purpose: the rise in prices helps to bring the real urban wage and salary structure into line with agricultural income, in a new relationship that is more appropriate for the new conditions of the economy.

EXCESSIVE EXPECTATIONS FOR PUBLIC SERVICES

The paternalistic attitude of the colonial administrations, particularly after World War II, also left behind the habit of expecting considerable benefit from free public services—free schools, free medical services, free roads, free water, free sewerage, free or subsidized electricity, and subsidized housing.

The colonial governments provided most of these for Africa's cities —usually at the expense of the agricultural population. But with the growth of the cities, and the quite legitimate political demand for the expansion and extension of these services throughout the land, it becomes financially impossible to maintain them on the uneconomic basis of the past. It is also economic nonsense to consume resources in subsidies rather than to use them for economic development.

Throughout the world, pressure for such services is present. The way it is kept in line with what is economically feasible is either to charge the economic price (as is the case in most places for electricity, water, and sewerage) or to hand over responsibility for the services to the *local* government concerned—in which case the citizens can make a direct choice between paying higher taxes (to get better education for their children, for instance) or using their money for other purposes. But, with the usual African centralization of responsibility for these services in the national government, this economic calculus does not occur so immediately and directly. Pressure for the services thus tends to lead the African governments constantly to increase their expenditures for them and to give lower priority to other investments that might in fact result in faster growth of the national income.

TECHNOCRATS AND MICRO-STATES

Two other legacies of colonialism also deserve mention, although extended discussion of them would lead far afield from the central subject of this book. The first of these is the colonial regimes' overemphasis on technocratic considerations.

"A colonial regime is essentially one of bureaucratic authoritarianism. . . . The public does not participate in the political process; it is 'administered' by a bureaucratic elite, which by the system's definition knows what is best." (Coleman, pp. 46–47.) Aside from the political implications of this state of affairs, there are important economic and financial implications. The colonial bureaucrats in the technical services were often themselves technicians—doctors in charge of health services, engineers in charge of public works, etc. When they were not, the "lay" administrators of such services inevitably tended to be overinfluenced by their views on appropriate standards and quality of services—to avoid losing the battle for control to them, or to mitigate their power. The result was that in much of colonial Africa, standards were set uneconomically high; too much money was spent on high-priced, well-equipped, expensive central hospitals, while rural dispensaries were starved of funds. Effective use of educational funds in many instances also suffered from the same attitude of "the best is none too good." African countries have as a consequence been saddled with high maintenance costs and overly high construction standards that they find hard to change.

In the French territories and to some extent in the British territories, civil-servant rule meant a lack of coordination among the services—each department jealously maintaining its prerogatives and rivalries. "The nomination of ministers to posts previously run by chiefs of service and directors has only reinforced these inconveniences. There is an urgent necessity for reasons of effectiveness and of economy, to regroup the ministries in relation to the development objectives, for example, a single ministry of rural development replacing advantageously the distinct ministries of livestock and agriculture." (Bérard, p. 40, *I.*)

Finally, there is what Léopold Senghor, President of Senegal, has called the "micro-state." Most of Africa's independent nations have populations of less than 3 million. The cost of maintaining a full-fledged governmental apparatus—with a full set of ministers, foreign representation, etc.—is, viewed objectively, an absurd waste of funds for these micro-nations. As for creating new industries, the size of the state should not in theory be a handicap, and, by organizing a multi-state customs union or free market area, it should be possible to build up markets of sufficient size to justify many new industries. In practice, however, the play of political forces makes the establishment of such larger multi-national markets almost impossible. And, where politics does not stand in the way, working out the details of, negotiating, and maintaining such arrangements entail an immense use of scarce economic, financial, and diplomatic talent—far better used for negotiations to secure aid, commodity-support agreements, etc. In reality, therefore, the political boundaries of the micro-states that break up Africa into many small market units are real barriers to the possibilities of economic development in Africa.

Selected Bibliography

ADU, A. L. *The Civil Service in New African States.* London: Allen & Unwin, 1965.

BÉRARD, J-P. *Planification en Afrique.* Paris: Ministère de la Coopération, October, 1962.

BERG, E. J. "Backward-Sloping Labor Supply Function in Dual Economies—The Africa Case," *Quarterly Journal of Economics* (Cambridge, Mass.), LXXV, No. 3 (August, 1961), 468–92.

BIESHEUVEL, S. *Race, Culture, and Personality.* Johannesberg: South African Institute of Race Relations, 1959.

CALLAWAY, A. "School Leavers and the Developing Economy of Nigeria," in R. O. TILMAN and T. COLE (eds.), *The Nigerian Political Scene.* Durham, N.C.: Duke University Press, 1962. Pp. 220–40.

COLEMAN, J. S. "The Character and Viability of African Political Systems," in W. GOLDSCHMIDT (ed.), *The United States and Africa.* Rev. ed.; New York: Frederick A. Praeger, for The American Assembly, 1963. Pp. 39–73.

FALLERS, L. A. "Social Stratification and Economic Processes," in M. J.

66 *The Economics of African Development*

HERSKOVITS and M. HARWITZ (eds.), *Economic Transition in Africa.* Evanston, Ill.: Northwestern University Press, 1964. Pp. 113–30.

FISHER, F. J. "The Sixteenth and Seventeenth Centuries: The Dark Ages in English Economic History?," *Economica* (London School of Economics), new series, XXIV, No. 93 (February, 1957), 1–19.

FORDE, D. "The Cultural Map of West Africa: Successive Adaptations to Tropical Forests and Grasslands," in SIMON and PHOEBE OTTENBERG (eds.), *Cultures and Societies of Africa.* New York: Random House, 1960. Pp. 116–38.

GERLACH, L. P. "Socio-Cultural Factors Affecting the Diet of the Northeast Coastal Bantu," *Journal of the American Dietetic Association,* XLV, No. 5 (November, 1964), 420–24.

HIRSCHMAN, A. O. "Obstacles to Development: A Classification and a Quasi-Vanishing Act," *Economic Development and Cultural Change* (University of Chicago), XIII, No. 4, Part 1 (July, 1965), 385–93.

HOSELITZ, B. F. *Sociological Aspects of Economic Growth.* Chicago: Free Press, 1960.

HUNTER, G. *The New Societies of Tropical Africa.* London and New York: Oxford University Press, 1962.

JONES, W. O. "Economic Man in Africa," *Food Research Institute Studies* (Stanford University), I, No. 2 (May, 1960), 107–34.

KATZIN, M. "The Role of the Small Entrepreneur," in HERSKOVITS and HARWITZ (eds.), *op. cit.,* pp. 179–98.

LEWIS, W. A. "Aspects of Economic Development." Paper presented at 1965 Council on World Tensions, African Conference on Progress Through Cooperation.

LYSTAD, R. A. "Basic African Values," in W. A. LEWIS (ed.), *New Forces in Africa.* Washington, D.C.: Public Affairs Press, 1962. Pp. 10–24.

MHINA, J. E. F. "African Traditions Which Affect Economic Development." Unpublished paper, 1965.

McGALL, D. F. "Dynamics of Urbanization in Africa," in Ottenberg (eds.), *op. cit.,* pp. 522–35.

ROBERTSON, H. M. *South Africa.* Durham, N.C.: Duke University Press, 1957.

ROBINSON, E. A. G. (ed.). *Economic Consequences of the Size of Nations.* (Proceedings of a Conference of the International Economic Association.) London: Macmillan, New York: St. Martin's Press, 1960.

SPIRO, H. J. *Politics in Africa.* Englewood Cliffs, N.J.: Prentice-Hall, 1962.

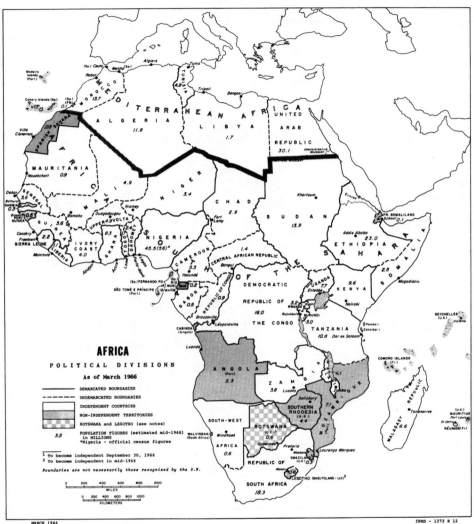

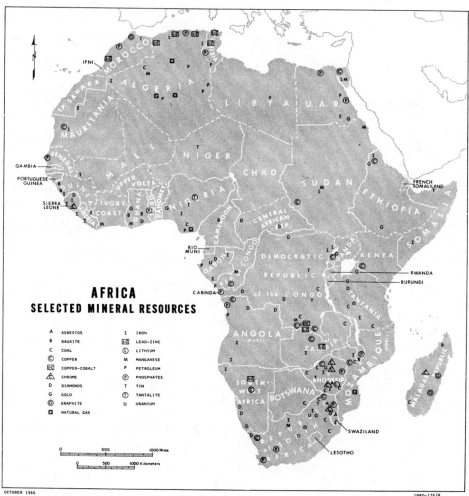

AFRICA
SELECTED MINERAL RESOURCES

A	ASBESTOS	I	IRON
B	BAUXITE	LZ	LEAD–ZINC
C	COAL	L	LITHIUM
©	COPPER	M	MANGANESE
K	COPPER–COBALT	P	PETROLEUM
⌂	CHROME	P	PHOSPHATES
D	DIAMONDS	T	TIN
G	GOLD	T	TANTALITE
G	GRAPHITE	U	URANIUM
⊡	NATURAL GAS		

0   500   1000 Miles

0   500   1000 Kilometers

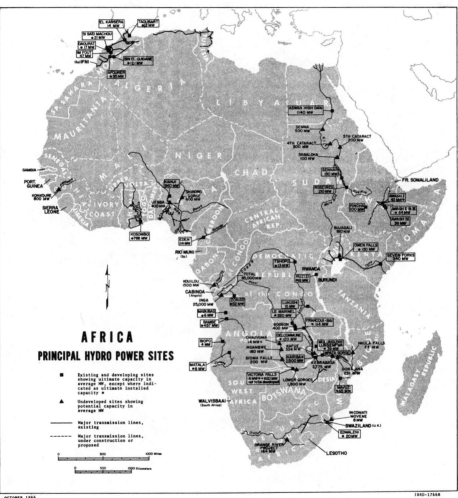

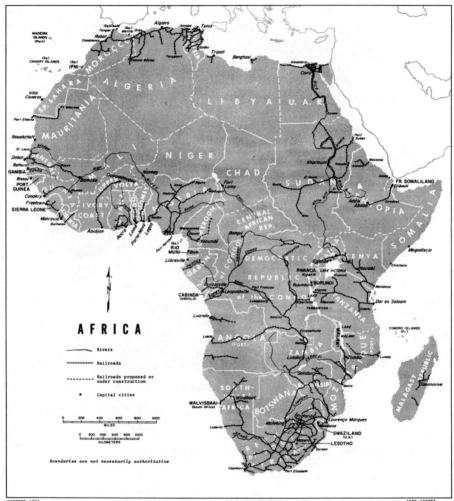

AFRICA

Rivers
Railroads
Railroads proposed or under construction
Capital cities

0 200 400 600 800 1000
MILES

0 200 400 600 800 1000
KILOMETERS

Boundaries are not necessarily authoritative

OCTOBER 1966

IBRD-1302R3

IV

Africa's Economic and Financial Position on the World Scene

*The colonial powers in fact abandoned
their empires in Black Africa with remarkable alacrity. Without wishing to
pretend to psychoanalyze this operation, one might well ask about the
motives: why was this disengagement
so easily accepted by the Belgians, the
Britons, and the French? . . . If the
European nations had considered Africa of vital importance, the transfer of
power would not have been so easy.*
RENÉ SERVOISE

The modern part of Africa is in many basic ways a part of the Western world and is particularly close to Western Europe. While Africa
is an important element in the origins of many Americans and
Brazilians and among many of the Caribbean nationalities, and
while Africa is an important influence in the cultures of these countries, Africa's main economic, cultural, and educational ties today are
with Western Europe. English and French are Africa's primary official and modern languages. African educational systems grew from a
European base, and European teachers are still an important, if not
majority, element; almost 50,000 African students are studying in

67

Western Europe (less than 10,000 in the United States, and an equal number, perhaps, in the nations of Eastern Europe, the Soviet Union, and China).

Still, while these relations with the rest of the world, notably Western Europe, are vital to Africa's well-being and development, to the rest of the world, economic relations with Africa, while valuable, are of comparatively little importance. Africa is of scarcely more than marginal economic significance for the United States, whose stake in Cuba or Central America, for example, has been a good deal larger. And, in today's world, with the enormous flexibility arising from the development, or possibility, of new techniques and synthetics, and with the prevalence of full employment and rapid economic growth in industrialized countries, it is hard to maintain that loss of contact with any one underdeveloped region would be disastrous for any industrialized country. The underdeveloped regions, indeed, have lost in relative importance in world trade during recent years, their share going from one-third of the total in 1950 to one-fifth in 1964. Trade with Africa amounts to less than 5 per cent of total world trade; West European trade with Africa is less than 10 per cent of total West European trade.

There is no doubt that loss of African supplies and markets would perceptibly affect the West European economy, but, on the whole, it could be taken in stride. No European country has the stake in sub-Saharan Africa that the Dutch had in Indonesia, for instance, nor has any European nation suffered in Africa that almost complete loss of assets and trade which the Dutch suffered in Indonesia, yet the Netherlands was never so prosperous as she has been since the "loss" of her empire and assets there. There is no reason to believe that the loss of trade with Africa or investments in Africa would cause greater damage to a European country than the loss of Indonesian trade and investments did to the Dutch.

As a matter of fact, it can be argued that, whatever the reasons for the extension of European domination over Africa during the nineteenth century, the economic history of the years since World War II has demonstrated that there were no *economic* reasons for the continuation of European colonial empires. The Marxist-Leninist idea that underdeveloped countries, including those of Africa, were vital to imperial powers as an outlet for investment no longer has

any real basis, even in theory. (See also chap. IX.) As John Strachey
has pointed out, Lenin's theory of imperialism was destroyed by
historical fact:

> There is not the slightest doubt that Lenin regarded the inevitability
> of a falling standard of life for the wage-earners and farmers within
> the highly-developed capitalisms as the thing which made the whole
> imperialist process inevitable. . . .
>
> He expressly states, although purely for the sake of argument, that
> *if* the standard of life of the wage-earners and agriculturalists could be
> raised at home, then the whole imperialist drive would no longer be
> inevitable. This neglected passage occurs at the beginning of his
> Chapter IV [of *Imperialism*]. . . .
>
> This passage is in some ways the most important in Lenin's book.
> For a steady increase in the standard of life of the masses and a rapid
> development of agriculture are precisely what *has* happened in, for
> example, both Britain and America. (Strachey, pp. 110–11.)

In short, the economic importance of Africa for the rest of the
world depends on its value as a trade partner, and, at present, this
value is not very great. This somewhat chastening fact is mitigated,
however, by several factors. The first is that Africa has a valuable
mineral and energy potential that may become of considerable interest to the rest of the world. (See below, chap. VI.) Secondly, the
African countries should become more valuable partners as time goes
on and their economic development continues—in absolute terms,
even if not relatively. Finally, bilateral relationships in any case are
not so important as they were prior to World War II. (See below,
chap. XI.) Since World War II, international economic and financial developments are more and more influenced by policy decisions
taken in multilateral economic and financial organizations. African
countries have made it a point to join the United Nations and the
U.N. specialized agencies, where most of these decisions are taken.
There, they have the opportunity to participate in decisions affecting
the world economy and, in turn, deeply affecting them. The changed
arrangements for association of the eighteen African countries with
the European Economic Community—from the original plan, where
Africans were not represented in the decision-making organs, to the
present one, where the associated African members have a full voice
—is another example of how Africans can influence the international

community and affect the impact the outside world has on their
dependent economies. (See below, p. 76.)

Aid and Trade

DEPENDENCE ON NON-AFRICAN CAPITAL AND PERSONNEL

Excepting South Africa, which is now able to finance her economic growth without help from abroad, sub-Saharan Africa still
depends on a flow of capital from the industrialized countries to
help in economic development. (See also below, chap. IX.) Funds
from non-African sources finance a very high proportion of capital
formation in Africa—over-all, according to the Economic Commission for Africa's estimates, half of Africa's total capital formation in
1950–57. This proportion has not decreased since, and in some countries, such as Upper Volta or Niger, it is nearer 100 per cent. In nine of
the ex-French territories, French aid was also needed to balance the recurrent budget at the time when independence was won (1960), but
by 1966 most of them no longer needed this. In Congo (Léopoldville), foreign aid continues to be necessary for the recurrent
budget. In most African countries, at least half and sometimes all of
the investment in the *public* sector is normally expected to be financed from abroad. But this is not unusual for small countries in
the development phase. In Sweden, from 1860 to 1890, more than
half of domestic net capital investment came from abroad; Canada
had the same degree of dependence in the early years of this century. (Kuznets, p. 38.)

A thorough and careful study made of the gross fixed investment
financed by public funds in the French-associated states (Mauretania,
Senegal, Mali, Upper Volta, Dahomey, Niger, Ivory Coast, Guinea,
Togo, Cameroon, Gabon, Congo [Brazzaville], Chad, Central African
Republic, Madagascar) for the period 1946–60 shows the following
over-all results: local funds financed $1.2 billion equivalent (304
billion C.F.A. constant francs of 1960) of gross fixed investments—
about 31 per cent of the total—with the remainder, or $2.575 bil-
lion equivalent (644 billion C.F.A. constant francs of 1960), financed
by *external* public funds (mostly from France). The local funds in-

cluded municipal budgets; special funds like road funds; port and rail authorities; and territorial and federal budgets when the old federations of West and Equatorial Africa existed. During this period, only $25 million was disbursed on aid received from the World Bank or the European Common Market Development Fund.

This high reliance on investment funds from abroad is unique to Africa among the major developing regions of the world. Elsewhere, investment funds from abroad may be important, but they remain a small proportion of the total.

In 1964, in very round numbers, the total of the gross investment made in sub-Saharan Africa (excepting South Africa) from domestic and external sources was around $2.5 billion equivalent, or equal to about 12 per cent of the area's over-all GNP of roughly $20 billion. (The former French territories conform to this pattern; they are also calculated to have invested an average 12 per cent of their GNP in 1960. [Bérard, p. 5, XIII.]) The total flow of financial resources from official sources from outside Africa in 1964 was around $1 billion equivalent, or 40 per cent of total gross investment. With private investment funds also included (on which there are no good aggregative data), the share of foreign-financed investment must have been more than half the total.

In South Africa, gross investment was also around $2.5 billion, or 25 per cent of a GNP of roughly $10 billion. While South Africa no longer requires capital from abroad to attain a satisfactory rate of economic growth, this "take-off" stage was only reached during the last eight years. Before that, South Africa's growth was aided by substantial investment from abroad, and the existing foreign-investment stake in South Africa was still valued at $4.3 billion in 1962.

Elsewhere on the continent, the countries that have largely financed their own development since World War II—Uganda, Ghana, Nigeria, the Sudan, and Zambia (formerly Northern Rhodesia)—were able to do so by taking advantage of favorable prices for their major export commodities to siphon off enough of the proceeds to finance most of whatever development they undertook. By 1964, however, Ghana, Nigeria, and the Sudan had stepped up the pace of development and other expenditures and consequently became much more dependent on foreign sources; Uganda and Zambia are still struggling with the problems of maintaining their previous momentum in investment and, while continuing to look abroad for aid, are not yet ready to put much more to good use.

In the amount of foreign assistance in the form of trained personnel, too, Africa is unique. In the public sector alone, sub-Saharan Africa had 35,000 foreigners, mostly French and English, in 1964—10,000 teachers and the rest in technical services. France alone spends some $130 million a year on this technical assistance. The English-speaking West African countries, the Sudan, Uganda, Mali, and Guinea, while they still need technicians, teachers, etc., now no longer depend on administrators from abroad. Other African nations will probably still need help for a few more years. Technicians and teachers will be needed for perhaps another ten to twenty years in most countries.

FOREIGN TRADE

The economic dependence on the export of a few primary com-modities is typical of underdeveloped countries anywhere in the world. But Africa is more involved in foreign trade than most other underdeveloped areas. Africa's money economy grew and still largely depends on output for export; it is therefore the progressive, growing part of her economy that relies on the rest of the world; the sub-sistence economy by definition has no concern with the outside world. The whole structure of modern African economies is shaped by their orientation toward foreign trade—the railways, the roads, the ports, the growth of the principal cities have been shaped above all by the foreign-trade flows or by the needs of production for export.

Over all of sub-Saharan Africa, exports average $20 per capita, con-siderably more than in underdeveloped areas elsewhere. The higher-income African countries tend to have the higher dependence on exports: Ghana and the Ivory Coast, for example, have per-capita export levels of around $50.

Sub-Saharan Africa exports about a quarter of its total GNP. Gen-erally, the poorer or slower-growing nations fall below this propor-tion, while the richer or faster-growing are above. In recent years, South Africa has run over 30 per cent; Ivory Coast, 33 per cent; Zambia, 40 per cent; Liberia, almost 50 per cent. On the other hand, Dahomey and Upper Volta run around 8 per cent, Ethiopia and

Chad, 10 per cent; Malagasy Republic and Niger, around 15 per cent; Senegal, Cameroon, Uganda, around 25 per cent.

The direction of trade to and from Africa has not radically shifted since the independence movement swept over the continent. French-speaking African countries still trade mostly with France, although Guinea and, to a lesser extent, Mali diverted trade to the Soviet bloc for a few years; the former English territories still find the United Kingdom their best trading partner, although they tend to have more diversified markets and suppliers than the French-speaking countries. Somalia still deals mostly with Italy, and Liberia with the U.S.; South Africa, Ethiopia, and the Congo (Léopoldville) continue to have a variety of markets and sources of goods, as in the past, mostly in Western Europe and North America. Imports into the Portuguese territories continue to be dominated by Portugal, but their exports go to a number of countries in North America and Western Europe.

Trade with Western Europe is consequently still the most important for Africa. Of sub-Saharan Africa's total trade (amounting in 1964 to $7.2 billion exports f.o.b. [including gold] and $6.8 billion imports c.i.f.), two-thirds is with Western Europe, 12 per cent with the U.S., 5 per cent with other African countries, and 5 per cent with Eastern Europe. No other primary producing area in the world is so heavily dependent on trade with Western Europe. Only about 40 per cent of the trade of all primary producing countries is with Western Europe.

By World War II, Africa had already become an important world producer of a number of commodities, and she continues to maintain or improve her position. Although her world position is strongest in minerals, she is principally an agricultural producer. Africa continues to produce around 90 per cent of the world's output of diamonds, two-thirds of the palm oil, sisal, and cacao; around half the manganese and chrome ore; one-third of the antimony and phosphate; and one-tenth of the wool. In copper, her output has climbed to over one-fourth of the world's total. According to figures cited by Sir Ronald Prain, Chairman of the Roan Selection Trust of Zambia, Africa's large copper producer, Africa's known reserves are estimated at about 60 million tons of copper content, or just under one-third of world holdings outside of the Soviet Union. African gold output has risen from 40 per cent of the world's pre-war output to about 70 per cent now; in coffee, her share in the world market has tripled and is reaching 30 per cent of the total.

Africa's dependence on exports of primary commodities makes orderly economic growth difficult, if not impossible. Prices of primary commodities are subject to wide swings, and consequently large fluctuations in income and activity throughout the economy occur:

Commodity	average yearly percentage deviation in price from trend, 1953–61
Sisal	24
Cocoa	18
Coffee	9
Palm kernels	9
Tea	7
Sugar	6
Palm oil	5
Cotton	5
Peanuts and peanut oil	4
Bananas	4

The strongest incentive to development in Africa has been provided by the demand for her mineral deposits. Diamonds and gold sparked and made possible the modern development of the Republic of South Africa; gold and copper initiated growth in the two Rhodesias, and Katanga copper in the Congo (Léopoldville). African mines attracted, and continue to attract, more outside capital than any other activity. It is largely to the exploitation of her mineral resources that southern and central Africa owes her new ports, railways, and towns. For the immediate future, the resources that are of particular interest to American and European capital are, in addition to water power, mostly minerals: bauxite, oil, uranium, manganese, and iron. Whereas in the past, mineral development occurred primarily in southern and central Africa, new sources have been located in West Africa, particularly in the former French colonies. This opens up for the first time the possibility of their more rapid development, financed to a greater extent from their own resources. (See below, chap. VI.)

BALANCE OF PAYMENTS

Data are not available to build up a proper over-all balance-of-payments account for sub-Saharan African countries. (In any case, South Africa is such a large part of the whole that to have meaningful figures at all, it should be dealt with separately.) But the following table, largely composed of "guesstimates," does bring out some interesting points. First, African countries on the whole appear to balance out in their trade account. It is their services and investment income payments that result in a deficit on current account which is matched by capital inflow. The capital inflow is, of course, largely from public funds—governments or multilateral agencies.

BALANCE OF PAYMENTS
AFRICA SOUTH OF THE SAHARA
(in billions of U.S. dollars
equivalent)

	1963		1964	
	South Africa	Other	South Africa	Other
CURRENT ACCOUNT				
Trade				
exports f.o.b. (including gold)	2.4	4.1	2.5	4.7
imports c.i.f.	−1.8	−4.1	−2.2	−4.6
Balance	0.6	—	0.3	0.1
Services and Invisibles				
investment income	−0.2	(−0.1)	−0.2	(−0.1)
technical assistance		0.2		0.2
other government		(−0.1)		(−0.1)
other	−0.2	(−0.6)	−0.3	(−0.6)
Total	−0.4	(−1.0)	−0.3	(−1.0)
Current Account, Balance	0.2	(−1.0)	—	(−0.9)
CAPITAL ACCOUNT				
bilateral official long-term financial flows		0.8		0.8
multilateral loans and aid		0.1		0.2
private investment, long-term	−0.1	(0.1)	−0.1	(0.1)
Total	−0.1	(1.0)	−0.1	(1.1)
Errors, omissions, reserves		−0.1	—	0.1 (0.2)

( ) = "guesstimates"

FOREIGN TRADE POLICIES

African countries fall into three main groups in their foreign trade policy: the Portuguese territories, juridically provinces of Portugal, the countries associated with the European Economic Community, and the others.

In the first—Mozambique, Angola (including the enclave of Cabinda), Portuguese Guinea, the Cape Verde Islands, and the islands of Sao Tome and Principe in the Gulf of Guinea—preference is given to Portuguese products through a high tariff preference and by quotas imposed on most competitive imports from other countries. Although Portugal is a member of the European Free Trade Area (EFTA) (comprising also the United Kingdom, the three Scandinavian countries, Austria, Switzerland, and Finland), Portuguese territories in Africa were not included in EFTA and did not benefit from the lower tariffs placed on industrial products from other EFTA members.

Countries in the third category in the main pursue nondiscriminatory trade policies. Great Britain, under her Commonwealth preferences policy, allows most primary products from African Commonwealth members to enter duty-free. Ghana, Nigeria, and the East African countries do not grant Commonwealth preferences in return; a few preferences have been granted by Gambia and Sierra Leone. The Federation of Rhodesia and Nyasaland did pursue a policy of granting substantial preferential treatment to British and other Commonwealth goods, and Rhodesia may continue this policy; Zambia and Malawi, however, may revert to the nondiscriminatory policy they pursued prior to the formation of the Federation. South Africa, since it left the Commonwealth in 1961, negotiated agreements with the United Kingdom to maintain part of its existing system of Commonwealth preferences, but these are gradually disappearing. South Africa's sugar quota of 150,000 long tons in the U.K. market, established under the Commonwealth Sugar Agreement, which was to have run to 1967, was terminated at the end of 1964.

A new Convention of Association linking the eighteen African associate members* with the European Common Market went into

* The former French territories, except Guinea—Cameroon, Central African Republic, Chad, Congo (Brazzaville), Dahomey, Gabon, Ivory Coast, Malagasy

effect on June 1, 1964, for five years. The convention extended and developed arrangements that had been made in 1957 to cover the then dependent overseas territories of the members of the EEC, when this came into being. Unlike the earlier agreement, however, the present system was freely negotiated between the African states on one side and the European Economic Community on the other.

The convention provides for a preferential trade zone between the EEC and the associated African states. When the convention is fully implemented (by 1969), there are to be no customs tariff or quota restrictions on trade among the African associates and EEC members. Provision is made, however, for the African states to be able to institute protection of infant industries by either tariffs or quotas, after consultation, as well as to establish customs unions and free-trade areas among themselves or with other states if such arrangements are in harmony with the association.

As soon as the convention went into force, the associated states acquired duty-free entry into the EEC for the bulk of their agricultural exports—coffee, cocoa, tea, pepper, vanilla, cloves, nutmeg, pineapples, coconuts. The EEC members' imports of these commodities, except for vanilla and cloves, are greater than the output of the associated African states, giving the latter a duty-free market for all of these products; and in this duty-free market, these products are protected against competition by tariffs levied on goods from other producers. While these tariffs were lowered when the convention came into force, they were still substantial:

Commodity	Percentage
Coffee	9.6
Cocoa	5.4
Pineapples	9
Cloves, nutmeg	15
Vanilla	11.5
Coconuts	4
Pepper	17

Duties on tea and tropical woods were suspended "temporarily" for all suppliers.

Republic, Mali, Mauretania, Niger, Senegal, Togo, and Upper Volta; the former Belgian territories—Congo (Léopoldville), Burundi, and Rwanda; and the former Italian territory of Somalia, now merged with former British Somaliland.

EEC states must also eliminate import quotas on associated states' products at the same rate as they eliminate them among themselves (in fact, the bulk of the tropical products were not subject to import quotas by the EEC members other than France); the associated states, in return, must eliminate quotas against imports from the EEC states too—this process to be completed in 1967.

For the former French territories, this creation of a preferential trade area with the EEC involves an expansion of the existing preferential trade treatment with France to include the other EEC members. At the same time, the preferential marketing arrangements they have enjoyed in France for some of their products are given up—in return, they get duty-free access to the entire Common Market area and, for many of their products, protection against competition from other producers in Africa, Latin America, or Asia (as well as some financial compensation.) *

This preferential treatment that the ex-French territories now lose was of substantial advantage to them. Peanuts and sugar had been guaranteed a good minimum price in French markets; palm oil and pepper were given preferential tariff rates; coffee and other products benefitted from quotas that limited imports from other markets to maintain a price that was often well above world market levels; cotton and other commodities received direct production subsidies. In addition, stabilization funds (*caisses de stabilisation des prix*) in the African countries concerned were able to borrow from a central French fund (*Fonds Nationale de Regularisation des Cours des Produits d'Outre-Mer*) whenever market prices fell below the prices set by it.

The additional foreign exchange secured as a result of this preferential structure amounted to as much as $60 million or $70 million annually—a substantial sum, especially for countries like Senegal, whose principal export crop, peanuts, was sold at some 75 per cent above world market prices in 1961.

Under the convention, these higher prices secured in France are to be eliminated by the end of 1967, except for bananas. (French

* Under the association convention, the Congo (Léopoldville) will have to give up the open-door commercial policy she followed under the Congo Basin treaties that originally created the Congo as a unit. The Congo has been given a three-year delay, however, in extending tariff preferences to EEC countries.

and Italian [providing higher prices for Somali bananas] marketing organizations were permitted to remain in this case.) In return, the EEC countries agree to provide $198 million in aid for production and diversification. In addition, aid for diversification was also agreed to for the four other associated African countries not a part of the French system:

Country	Amount of aid (in $ million equivalent)
Ivory Coast	46.7
Senegal	46.7
Malagasy Republic	31.6
Cameroon	15.8
Congo (Léopoldville)	15.0
Central African Republic	6.8
Niger	6.5
Somalia	6.5
Congo (Brazzaville)	6.4
Upper Volta	6.0
Chad	5.7
Togo	5.7
Mali	5.6
Dahomey	5.5
Burundi	5.25
Rwanda	5.25
Mauretania	5.0
Gabon	4.0
Total	230.0

It is almost impossible to judge whether this "compensation" for giving up the privileges of the special French marketing arrangements is adequate or not. With a notional capital/output ratio of 3 to 1, the capital required corresponding to an increase in output equivalent to the $60 million–70 million that the special arrangements were worth would amount to around $180 million–210 million. While most of the agreed-on aid will be in grants, some of it will be in the form of loans, so that the real benefit to the countries will be less. The capital/output ratio in practice may have averaged somewhere around 3 to 1 for the area as a whole, and the total compensation may be of the right order of magnitude.

In addition to this aid for diversification and production, the EEC countries also agreed to make available $500 million more in development finance. Of the grand total of $730 million, $620 million will be in grants from the European Development Fund (FED) of the EEC; $46 million in special loans from FED for investments (with maximum duration of twenty-five years, a period of grace on payment of amortization up to ten years, and a "favorable," presumably very low, rate of interest) where the economic yield of the project, and the capacity of the country to bear debt, justify making the money available on loan terms; and $64 million in loans by the European Investment Bank (made on conventional terms except that FED may subsidize the interest due up to a figure of 3 percentage points for loans with a maximum duration of twenty-five years).

This total of $730 million in aid is to be compared to the $497 million in grants to the African countries made under the first association arrangements of 1957–62 (which in practice were not all committed before 1964). It should also be noted that the figure reached represents a cut from the amount requested by the African states—$1.6 billion—and from the amounts that France and the Commission of the EEC estimated as necessary—$900 million–$1.2 billion.

Of particular importance to the relationship of the Common Market with the associated African states is the Caisse Centrale pour la Coopération Économique (Central Fund for Economic Cooperation), an autonomous French government agency. The Caisse Centrale is a key organization in the administration of French aid in the former French territories: it handles the financial operations of direct government aid; acts as a development bank in helping to finance large industrial and mining ventures (Comilog, Miferma, Fria, etc.); and sets up and helps to finance and manage local development banks making smaller loans and investments. It also administers the French Government–financed central commodity stabilization funds and, finally, in the countries where it operates, the financial operations of the Common Market's FED.

Another important aspect of the new convention is the increased emphasis given to technical assistance. Since, in Africa, development aid in the form of trained personnel is as vital as aid in the form of capital, this increased activity is particularly noteworthy.

The convention is not least important for the institutions it establishes for cooperation among the associated states and the Common Market. The convention establishes a Council of Association at the ministerial level, reporting each year on its activity to a parliamentary conference, to lay down the general pattern for financial and technical assistance among the countries concerned. Day-to-day administration is handled by a Committee of Association, consisting of one representative from each country; in formal votes, the eighteen Africans have *in toto* one vote, and the EEC members together one vote.

In short, the convention gives its associated African states preferential treatment for their exports to one of the fastest growing markets in the world; it provides them with a substantial volume of economic and technical assistance; and it attracts and concentrates the attention of Europe's rich, developed countries on this particular part of the developing world. There is little doubt but that it is of immeasurable economic benefit to the associate members.

African states outside the Association have so far suffered little direct damage from the preferential treatment given the associated states. But there is potential damage: the EEC-associated states have an inducement to expand production of protected goods more rapidly and so to exclude the products of other African states or force them to accept lower returns than their own producers can get, by having to sell either at lower returns within the EEC or outside in the world market. Even more important, perhaps, is the possibility that the Common Market will draw its associates' interest away from the rest of Africa.

In any event, some of the other African states, while not wishing to tie themselves closely to the Common Market, have concluded that some form of association would be desirable and have opened negotiations to that end. Among these countries are Nigeria, Uganda, Kenya, Tanzania, and, north of the Sahara, Algeria, Tunisia, and Morocco. The first to be successful was Nigeria, after almost two years of negotiations. In May, 1966, she completed negotiations to become an associate member of the EEC, but on a different footing from that of the other African associate members.

This agreement, coming into force in 1966, is to expire on May 31, 1969, at the same time as the Convention of Association which links the other African associate members to the EEC. It provides that most Nigerian exports will enter the Common Market on the same unrestricted basis as the exports of the other eighteen associate African states. Four of Nigeria's main agricultural exports—cocoa, peanuts, plywood, and palm products—will be subject to quotas based on the average of the last three years and enlarged by 3 per cent yearly. In return, Nigeria will grant a tariff preference of 2 per cent to a list of twenty-six European products—including wine, agricultural machinery, radios, and household goods. An alternative arrangement is open to the Nigerian Government, under which plywood would enjoy unrestricted entry into the Common Market countries and the import quotas for the other three Nigerian products would be raised by 6 per cent a year, in return for a preferential tariff of 5 per cent on the twenty-six listed products.

The agreement also provides that Nigeria will not discriminate in respect of the rights of Common Market countries to establish private enterprises in Nigeria and similar matters. Current payments on goods and services will be authorized by both parties to the agreement, but present restrictions on capital movements between the two areas will be maintained.

Because of Nigeria's wish to avoid any political association with the Community, the institutions to implement the agreement are expected to amount to no more than one meeting of a Ministerial Council each year.

The Nigerian success in reaching an agreement with the EEC, if it is followed by the other African states, may eventually lead to the establishment of a general preferential access to EEC markets for African goods without reciprocal preferences from the Africans. This would be of considerable help to all Africa in its economic development, but a detriment to other developing regions—except insofar as the African experience established a precedent.

Money and Banking

With a few exceptions, all African countries are members of European currency areas. Liberia, with its internal use of the U.S. dollar, is in a currency union with the United States. Ethiopia and

French Somaliland (largely because of close trade ties with Ethiopia) may be considered as being in the dollar area, although not
formally so. Guinea left the franc area when she became independent
in 1958 and has not yet made any new extra-African arrangements.
The Sudan, which used the Egyptian pound prior to independence in 1956, now has its own currency; although she is not
formally a member of the sterling area, she holds her reserves mostly
in sterling, her banking system is still largely British, and her exchange rates with other currencies are related to the exchange rate
with the pound sterling. Somalia is not formally a part of the lira
area but has mutual trade and payments preferences with Italy.
Participation of the Congo (Léopoldville), Rwanda, and Burundi
in the Belgian franc area ceased when these former Belgian territories
gained their independence, but a close relationship with Belgium's
central bank and financial institutions may well be re-established.
The Portuguese territories are part of the peseta area, although Angola and Mozambique have their own banks of issue (Banco de
Angola and Banco Ultramarino).

South-West Africa, the British protectorate of Swaziland (the
future Ngwane), Botswana (Bechuanaland), and Lesotho (former
Basutoland) are in the monetary area of South Africa, which issues
the currency for the whole area and administers payment and exchange controls. South Africa herself has had special and tenuous
relations with the sterling area since World War II: she holds
most of her reserves in gold and imposes controls over capital transfers to other parts of the area. She is associated with the London
capital and money markets and cooperates closely with London in
international financial matters.

The other independent countries of Africa are members of either
the French franc or sterling areas. Every African country holds its
foreign-exchange reserves principally in the European reserve currency of its area, carries out most of its foreign-exchange transactions through Paris or London, relates the value of its currency to
the franc or pound, and usually allows current and capital transfers to take place freely to the other members of its currency area.
The ties are particularly close in the French franc area; Mali and
Ghana are to some extent borderline cases—while transfers to them
from elsewhere in the franc and sterling areas, respectively, can take

place freely, they impose controls on transfers out, to other members of the areas as well as to the rest of the world.

An important part of Africa's connection with the European currency areas is the continuation of most of the banking connections established in pre-independence days. Aside from a few locally owned banks in Nigeria, South Africa, and the Sudan and state-owned commercial banks in Ghana, Ethiopia, Tanzania, and Uganda, commercial banks in Africa are all branches of European banks or are owned by European banks or European investors or, in a small number of cases, American or Indian banks. In recent years, some of the European branch banks have been converted into locally incorporated banks, or a new locally incorporated bank has been founded in the attempt to secure participation by local people. These new banks often represent a pooling of European and American banking interests with some local participation. In general, the degree of local participation, depending as it does on the number of Africans with money to invest or capabilities to contribute, is usually considerably below what the European or American banks would ideally wish.

No capital or money markets exist in Africa except for a rudimentary market in Lagos and Nairobi, a moderately developed one in Salisbury, and a more developed one in Johannesburg. In the main, Africa still depends on the money and capital markets of Europe.

CENTRAL BANKS

All the new nations of Africa, with the exception of Gambia and East Africa, soon after gaining independence set up their own central banks. (East Africa was more of a nominal than a real exception, since after the East African Currency Board moved from London to Nairobi, it assumed more and more of the functions of a central bank and in most of its activity was practically indistinguishable from most other central banks.) Tanzania broke away from the Currency Board in 1965, and its own central bank began operations in June, 1966. Both Kenya and Uganda consequently also decided to have their own central banks. The Central Bank of Rhodesia and

Nyasaland, created in the 1950's, was divided into three separate banks with the break-up of the Federation.

The former French territories preserved something more of a monetary link among themselves than did the former British or Belgian areas. They share combined central banks, as follows: the Banque Centrale des États de l'Afrique de l'Ouest for Dahomey, Ivory Coast, Mauritania, Niger, Senegal, Togo, and Upper Volta; the Banque Centrale des États de l'Afrique Équatoriale et du Cameroun for the UDEAC states (see chap. ii)—Cameroon, Central African Republic, Chad, Congo (Brazzaville), and Gabon; the Institut d'Émission Malgache for the Malagasy Republic. The currency of the first two central banks is called the franc CFA (Communauté Financière Africaine) and has the same value as the franc Malgache (i.e., on September 1, 1966, 50 francs CFA equalled 1 French franc).

These central banks each have an Operations Account with the French Treasury through which all its payments and receipts in foreign currency are settled. It can draw on this account as necessary (at penalty rates) to balance its international payments position at any time through an automatic, unlimited overdraft facility extended it by the French Treasury. There is French representation on the boards of the banks, which presumably should help to prevent any possible abuse of this privilege.

Guinea's and Mali's central banks do not have these close ties with the French Treasury. And, during 1960–65, neither country received the volume of effective aid that the other ex-French West African countries benefited from. Guinea, in fact, received as much (or even more) assistance from other sources, mostly nations of the Soviet bloc and China, as the other countries received from France. Unfortunately, this assistance was not accompanied by effective technical advice or applied to well-planned economic projects. The result, in spite of a large investment running well over 20 per cent of GNP, was a drop in per-capita national income. The central banks of Guinea and Mali also did not pursue the same moderate financial policies as did the other countries. By 1964–65, consequently, both countries were suffering from inflation, loss of external values of their currencies, and the necessity to adopt a full paraphernalia of external foreign-exchange and trade controls. Ghana, for somewhat similar reasons, was in the same kind of trouble by the end of 1965.

The fact is that central banks in Africa face a completely different environment and a completely different set of problems from those faced by central banks in developed countries. An African central bank can contribute to economic development by creating and nourishing the financial institutions needed for growth, by centralizing and managing the country's foreign-exchange reserves (both to economize on the need to hold reserves and to mitigate somewhat the fluctuations in export earnings), and by creating an objective, informal center for economic and financial research and advice for a government. In Africa today, it can do very little in the way of pursuing an independent monetary policy or of controlling the supply or price or availability of credit. The economic and financial dependence of the African economies on the rest of the world is so great that they would have to possess relatively enormous foreign-exchange reserves to gain much latitude in pursuing an independent monetary and credit policy. No African country possesses such reserves, and, consequently, if any tried to expand credit more rapidly than the rest of its monetary area, for example, it would soon find its foreign-exchange reserves exhausted and would be confronted with the need to backtrack directly or indirectly through foreign-exchange controls and, even, devaluation. The central bank is all-important as manager of foreign exchange, and as adviser to the government. As far as the management of money and credit are concerned, overambition is most dangerous.

In no country can one manage money while disregarding the outside world and the balance of payments. In Africa, this means that one has only a very narrow margin to operate in. The problem is that for a number of reasons monetary expansion in an underdeveloped country, particularly in Africa, results in a balance-of-payments problem with frightening rapidity. First, the internal flexibility in production that is present in a developed country is lacking. While there may be a surplus of unskilled labor at times, there is a shortage of complementary factors. In a developed country, if there is unemployment and you raise demand, the unemployed can be put to work with existing unused machines, or new machines may be produced—if the machines are imported and you do not have the foreign exchange to buy them, you can still make them at home;

they may not be as good or they may be more expensive, but you can still go ahead. In an underdeveloped country, if you cannot buy the machine from abroad, you cannot put the men to work.

This is true not only of capital goods but also of consumer goods. If demand is increased through monetary expansion, the immediate effect is to increase demand for imported goods, the marginal propensity to import being very high. For in Africa, the people in the money economy are most interested in imported manufactured consumer goods. Domestic production of such goods is small or nonexistent, and output in absolute terms can increase only very slowly. (On the other hand, the African goods exported, with a few exceptions, are not goods that are consumed in Africa, so that an increase in money demand does not directly reduce the volume of exports).

The United States of America did not create a permanent central bank until 130 years after the American Revolution. The African nations are now all equipped with central banks. These banks can contribute to economic development; they can also, if the temptation to create money out of thin air is not resisted, become a means to hold back or destroy the prospects of development. In only three cases so far—Guinea, Mali, and the Congo (Léopoldville)—has central bank policy had detrimental effects. The record is not too bad.

In order to help one another to cope with future problems and facilitate cooperation, the African central banks agreed in February, 1966, to organize an Association of African Central Banks, made up of the governors of the central banks and representatives of similar monetary institutions, such as a currency board where a central bank does not yet exist. Organizations with similar purposes in other parts of the world have been helpful in easing the way to solutions of international payments and problems and in encouraging central banks more effectively to promote good economic and financial policies. The creation of this organization at so early a stage in Africa's independent financial life is therefore a good augury.

Selected Bibliography

La convention de Yaounde. Brussels: European Economic Commission, 1965.

The Impact of the European Economic Community on African Trade.
(U.N. Economic Commission for Africa, E/CN14/29.) New York,
November 20, 1959.

INTERNATIONAL MONETARY FUND, AFRICAN DEPARTMENT. "The CFA
Franc System," *IMF Staff Papers*, X, No. 3 (November, 1963), 345–
96.

"Les investissements publics nationaux et extérieurs dans les pays franco-
phones d'Afrique tropicale 1946–1960." 2 vols. Paris: University of
Paris, Institut d'Étude de Développement Économique et Social
(IEDES), 1964. Mimeo.

JUCKER-FLEETWOOD, E. E. *Money and Finance in Africa.* New York:
Frederick A. Praeger, 1964.

KUZNETS, S. "International Differences in Capital Formation and Financing," in M. ABRAMOVITZ (ed.), *Capital Formation and Economic
Growth*. Princeton, N.J.: Princeton University Press, 1956.

LANGER, W. L. "Farewell to Empire," *Foreign Affairs*, XLI, No. 1
(October, 1962), 115–30.

LEDUC, M. *Les institutions monetaires africaines: Pays francophones.*
Paris: Editions A. Pedone, 1965.

MLADEK, J. V. "Evolution of African Currencies," *Finance and Development, The Fund and Bank Review*, Vol. I, Nos. 2 and 3 (September and December, 1964).

"La Nouvelle convention d'association entre Le Marché Commun et les
états africains," *Revue du Marché Commun*, No. 54 (January, 1963),
pp. 22–35.

PEARSON, S. R. and SCHMIDT, W. E. "Alms for AAMS: A Larger
Flow?," *Journal of Common Market Studies*, III, No. 1 (October,
1964), 74–82.

RIPOCHE, P. "Les Fonds européen de développement," *Les banques de
développement dans le monde* (extract). Paris: Dunod, 1964. Pp.
243–85.

———. "Le deuxième fonds européen de développement," *Les banques
de développement dans le monde* (extract). Paris: Dunod, 1965. Pp.
375–91.

RIVKIN, A. "Africa and the European Economic Communities," *Finance and Development, The Fund and Bank Review*, Vol. III, No. 1
(March, 1966).

SEN, S. N. *Central Banking in Undeveloped Money Markets.* 3d ed.;
Calcutta: Bookland Private, 1961.

SERVOISE, R. "L'Avenir économique des pays tropicaux." (SEDEIS
Supplementary Bulletin No. 828.) Reproduced in *Problèmes éco-
nomiques, la documentation française* (Paris: Institut National de la
Statistique), No. 780 (December 11, 1962), pp. 6–15.

STRACHEY, J. *The End of Empire.* London: Gollancz, 1959; New York:
Random House, 1960.

V

African Agriculture: Problems and Solutions

Mother Africa is a grand old lady; we may guide, persuade her—and even seduce her—but we cannot drive her.
FIELD MARSHAL SMUTS

The typical African is still a farmer or cattle herder. Ninety per cent of the African people live on farms. Almost two-thirds of Africa's exports are agricultural products, and these are the principal source of foreign-exchange earnings for all African countries except South Africa, Zambia, the Congo (Léopoldville), Sierra Leone, and Mauritania. These main exports are comparatively few in number, however—cocoa, coffee, peanut products, cotton, lumber, palm products, tobacco, sugar, rubber, sisal, tea, bananas, and hides and skins.

The key sector for economic development in most of Africa is still, therefore, agriculture. So far, only a few African countries have found and developed mineral resources, the only alternative way, at this stage, of earning foreign exchange. For most African countries, then, it is agriculture that must be depended on: to raise the standard of living of the people initially, to provide the minimum market necessary for manufactures to get a foothold, to earn the necessary foreign exchange to pay for imports, and to provide the revenues to finance needed government services. The improvement of agriculture must be the central part of any development program. How then can this task be done?

No simple answer to this question can be found in Africa. Although husbandry is one of the first skills acquired by man, to practice it well is still among the most difficult of achievements. Unlike manufacturing, the conditions of agricultural production—climate, soil, pests, diseases, the genetic qualities of plants and animals—are not easily controlled by man. (On the other hand, agriculture usually only makes minimal demands on such critically scarce resources as investible funds, foreign exchange, and high-caliber entrepreneurial talent, all of which are needed for industrial development.) Again, more depends on raising the level of productivity of the individual in agriculture, or his attitude toward work, or his power to make intelligent decisions than is true of the workers engaged in manufacturing. In agriculture, management has to be highly decentralized. All day long, the individual farmer or the worker in the fields must make managerial decisions—Should I plant this field this morning or weed that one? should I repair this fence or clean out that drainage ditch?

Rapid progress in agriculture can be achieved only by moving ahead on many fronts. If research has discovered the best fertilizer to use for a particular plant on a particular soil, it may be necessary also to develop the varieties that will respond best to it; to work out what changes in cultivation practices are necessary—such as planting more or less densely; to develop, perhaps, a different kind of weeding tool; and to change the times and methods of planting, weeding, and harvesting.

The problems facing the African countries in this respect, while difficult, are in fact similar to those confronted and solved by many presently developed countries. Industrialization in the United Kingdom, the United States, Australia, and Japan, for instance, was preceded in every case by the development of agriculture; it depended on and was able to build on agricultural incomes as a base. To achieve the necessary increase in agricultural incomes in Africa, changes have to be made in the kind of farming practiced over the centuries. Africans and African governments have already modified the old systems of farming or experimented with them in a number of ways, attempting to improve the standard of living and to develop the economy.

Nature

CLIMATE

Although Africa's chief livelihood depends on the land, she is singularly ill favored by nature. "About 92 per cent of the continent may be said to suffer from one or another climatic disability—surely one of the most important facts concerning Africa. . . . [Africa] presents a picture, as far as water is concerned, of plenty where it cannot be used and of paucity where it is most needed." (Hance, p. 15.) Forty per cent of the continent is arid or desert, another 20 per cent is semi-arid. In about three-quarters of sub-Saharan Africa, rainfall is scanty. Only 6 per cent of South Africa, for example, has sufficient rainfall to be fit for plowing. Around 20 per cent of the continent enjoys a savannah climate, with a long rainy and a short dry season; 8 per cent has a tropical rainy season of ten to twelve months. Rainfall fluctuates greatly within the year and from year to year; "average annual rainfall" means little when one year may receive three times as much rain as the next, or when it does not come evenly throughout a given season of the year but falls in torrents. The degree of variation even in a large river basin such as the Volta, which drains 40,000–50,000 square miles, is very great: at Akosombo, the flow at the peak is 125,000–350,000 cubic feet per second and only about 1,000 at the low.

But, while the African climate tends to be violent, and the sun is as often an enemy as a friend, the African heat and the absence of frost or winter over most of the continent favor the reproduction and growth of most species of life—whether animal, plant, or virus. If man ever learns to master the problems of the tropics, this could be turned to enormous advantage. On the present scale of research effort, however, it is unlikely that this potentiality will be fully realized in this century—but it is nevertheless there.

The forests of Africa are mostly restricted to woodland parts of the savannah—which have little in the way of commercially usable trees—and to the tropical rain forests, which do have major economic significance. What remains of the tropical rain forest begins in Liberia, stretches across to southwest Ghana, begins again in Nigeria, continues across Cameroon, Gabon, and the two Congoes to the plateau near the great lakes. There are also some remnants in the eastern part of the Malagasy Republic. It is primarily these tropical forest areas that produce four of Africa's most important exports: cocoa, palm products, timber, and rubber.

Soil

Little is known about how best to exploit and improve tropical soils. In general, these soils tend to be poor, due principally to the poor rock from which they were formed, because they contain little organic material. Except for the volcanic soils, African soils are generally derived from old acid parent rock which is poor in calcium and plant nutrients. The usefulness of the soils can also be easily destroyed. It may be true, however, that once the technique of the proper care has been found and applied, the soils will prove to be easily regenerated. There are already hints that this is so in a few experiments in restoring soil damaged by heavy erosion.

It took some time to learn that tropical soils are poor, for the evidence that springs to one's eyes seems to show that the soils must be very rich. Everyone who has traveled in Africa has seen fence posts that have taken root and started to grow, telephone poles that have put out branches. But nevertheless, tropical soils, even in the dense virgin forests, are usually thin and poor in fertility. In the forests, the plants and trees constantly return to the supporting soil—in the form of dead leaves, branches, and trunks—the elements they borrowed from it, so that equilibrium is maintained. But it is a precarious equilibrium, with very small reserves. If the tree or plant cover is removed, the thin layer of humus is soon exhausted or washed away with the first heavy rains.

Good soil is much like a complex living organism: its skeleton is made up of numerous tiny mineral soil particles aggregated into a firm and flexible structure. Intermingled with this skeleton are the organic substances, the "humus," which is the product of bacteria action on plant litter: in one pound of fertile soil, there may be 500 million fungi, 500 million protozoa, 10 billion bacteria, 400 billion algae. (Aside from their general function of creating humus, these organisms often have specific and essential functions. The successful establishment of the rapidly growing *pinus radiata* [Monterey pine] in forestry plantations in eastern Africa depended on bringing along with the seed from North America the particular fungus with which the tree roots have a close cooperative relationship.)

But for all these organisms to exist, the soil structure must be such that it can contain freely circulating air and water. In the tropics, it has to be protected against the heat of the sun, which would burn away the organic matter and kill the micro-organisms; and it has to be protected from the direct blows of the torrential rains, which would crush the structure of the soil, seal off the underlying soil from the air, and leach out the minerals or carry them so far into the earth that the plant roots cannot reach them. When the soil is laid bare and exposed to the elements, its temperature rises and the sun hastens the oxidation and disappearance of the humus; the big swings in temperature that occur in the tropics between day and night accelerate the mechanical disintegration of the soil; and the rains and the wind erode it. (Schroo, pp. 40–44.)

Tropical soils must, therefore, be protected against the sun and rain—by the existing natural vegetation, by cover crops, or by a thick mulch. Taught by centuries of experience, African farmers in some areas often plant in the same field three or four crops which mature at different times and so maintain a green canopy over the ground until the last is harvested. (This also provides a measure of security in the event one crop is lost.) Care has to be taken when introducing mechanical equipment to avoid plowing too deeply and burying the thin layer of fertile soil.

A peculiar transformation of the soil takes place in many areas of the tropics. When the forest cover is removed, silicate minerals are decomposed and leached out so that the proportion of iron and aluminum hydroxides is increased; the resulting soil is called laterite. In some areas, the percentage of aluminum hydroxide is high enough to lead to the formation of bauxite deposits, the raw material for aluminum, as in West Africa, and even of iron-ore deposits, as those

of Bukwe in Rhodesia, or Thabazimbi in South Africa. This helps
to explain why bauxite and iron are such an important factor in
Africa's economic potential (although most of the iron deposits in
Africa did not originate in this way). But if drainage is impeded
because the soil is crushed, the oxides may become iron-hard, and
the passage of tractors or other heavy implements will leave behind
unworkable soil. An instance has been cited by John Phillips where
plowing eighty acres of lateritic soil in central Tanzania wore 6
inches off the diameter of the 36-inch steel discs on heavy ploughs.

There are important exceptions to the poverty of soils in tropical
Africa. The first is the clay soil found in the alluvial plains—along
the coast, in the center of wide valleys, and, in particular, south of
Lakes Albert and Kyoga in Uganda, which is one of the few large
areas of fertile soil in Africa. A second main exception is the usually
very fertile volcanic soil, found in Rwanda, Burundi, western
Cameroon, Ethiopia, central Kenya from Mt. Meru extending
through to Mt. Kilimanjaro in Tanzania, the Poroto Mountains at
the head of Lake Nyasa, and Mt. Elgon and the Ruwenzori Mountains in Uganda. Finally, the forest soils of tropical mountains that
are high enough to escape the great heat found at lower altitudes
tend to be rich in humus and fertile. All in all, the African soils
vary greatly in quality. Variations from place to place are much
greater than in temperate-zone countries, where, moreover, over the
centuries, ploughing, manuring, fertilizing, and liming have built
up the quality of the soils.

One further comment must be made on Africa's soils: their
chemical make-up tends to perpetuate the shortage of proteins in the
African diet—a shortage that naturally has an impact on work
efficiency:

> As might be expected, tropical plants tend to be poor in nitrogenous
> constituents which must be manufactured from the precarious supplies
> in the soil. On the other hand they are relatively rich in carbohydrate
> which can be synthesized by the plant from carbon dioxide in the air
> and the abundant water. Sugar, manioc, rice, corn, and sweet potatoes
> are familiar examples of tropical foodstuffs rich in carbohydrate but
> relatively poor in protein. (Lee, p. 33.)

Much has been learned through intensive research efforts on how
to handle the soils for tree crops in order to improve output, but for

the annual crops this is not yet true. Since World War II, the experiments with fertilizer on tree crops have produced remarkably good results—in considerable gains in productivity and improved plants—but similar experiments on annual crops have so far had little success except in a few cotton-growing areas. Fertilizers are expensive, and little is known about what specific deficiencies need to be made good in tropical soils and how they can be made good. It took some twenty years to discover what trace elements (tiny percentages of minerals such as copper, cobalt, etc.) were needed in the Kenya soils to make it possible to raise non-African breeds of livestock successfully. Then, too, in areas subject to hard tropical rains, the fertilizer a farmer may put on the soil may go down the river with the next downpour, if the application is not done correctly.

COMPETITION FOR SURVIVAL

While the soils of tropical Africa may be poor, the climate favors reproduction and growth. (It is this that accounts for the fence posts that take root and grow.) The result is that life in Africa takes on an almost infinite multiplicity of species and sub-species, but with only a relatively few individuals of any one kind in any one place. Only a mixed animal population with varying demands can survive where the heat favors food growth but the supply of any one required food is limited. As a result, the competition for survival among the species is fierce and the evolutionary cycle most rapid. (It is not surprising that the human population in Africa was also sparse and widely scattered. For man to have survived in Africa, he had to beat off assaults from every quarter. The poet for the tropics is Henley and, above all, never Wordsworth.)

This central fact of the tropics—fierce competition for survival and survival depending on dispersion—has large economic implications. Tropical lumbering, for example, is a quite different kind of operation from temperate-zone lumbering. In the tropics, there may be only one or two trees of a particular kind, mahogany for instance, per acre; the lumberer is engaged in an activity that is more like hunting than mass production, and costs go up. Another, even more important, effect is that it is extremely difficult to grow a concentration of any particular plant or animal. There is a good chance that among the surrounding multiplicity of species there is at least one present or potential enemy of the crop or animal. The enemy may be a microbe, a virus, an insect, an animal, a bird, or even a plant. Defense against it is an essential part of any major innovation in agriculture in the tropics. For once that enemy discovers the new growth, it will flourish at the expense of its food, until there are only a few individuals of either kind, living in precarious coexistence. (Similar problems, but on a lesser scale, confront agriculture in the temperate zones also. In Great Britain, for example, potatoes can be grown on the same land only one year in seven; in Utah, sugar beets require a four- or five-year rotation; tomatoes should not be planted in the same place two years in succession—all this to avoid the concentration and build-up of disease organisms.)

Africa is littered with the ruins of projects that neglected this factor. The British Colonial Development Corporation's million-dollar chicken-raising scheme in Gambia was completely wrecked by disease killing off the chickens by hundreds of thousands. The Richard Toll rice-growing scheme in Senegal has not yet coped successfully with the hundreds of thousands of weaverbirds (Quelea) that descend on the paddies each year when the rice is ripe. Sorghum, a basic cereal over much of Africa, is also attacked both by weaverbirds and by the purple-flowered witchweed, which feeds on its roots. (This weed has now found its way into the southern United States.) The problem of the weaverbirds is so great that a special bird-control officer was assigned to Bornu Province, in northern Nigeria, to try to destroy their nesting places with gasoline and bombs. During the 1961 season, an estimated 100 *million* nests were destroyed in this way—with two birds per nest, this would mean about 200 million birds were killed.

The need for constant research and defense measures is well illustrated by the history of wheat-growing in Kenya. Lord Delamere, who introduced wheat into Kenya before World War I, spent almost ten years trying to grow wheat successfully—his first crops were destroyed by wheat rust—and finally succeeded in finding a rust-resistant wheat. During the 1950's, however, a super-virulent black stem rust succeeded in breaking through again and scientists had to develop a new kind of wheat to resist it. (McKelvey, p. 329.)

The enormous variety of species in Africa also includes bearers of animal and human diseases. There is no question but that disease in Africa is a major factor holding up development. The diseases that affect animals (in particular, the trypanosomiases carried by the tsetse fly, but also the tick-carried East Coast fever, rinderpest, etc.) prevent Africa from utilizing its vast stretches of savannah for a major meat-producing industry. An example of the difference the presence or absence the tsetse fly can make is the experience of Buruli County, in Uganda: in 1945, when the tsetse fly was present, there were 144 cattle in the county; in 1961, after the fly had been eradicated, the county was raising 46,000. (Masefield, p. 96.)

Traditional African Farming

SHIFTING CULTIVATION AND SUBSISTENCE FARMING

Over the centuries, the inhabitants of most sub-Saharan Africa established a method of cultivation to meet the conditions confronting them—"shifting," or "semi-nomadic," cultivation, the same solution that peoples in other tropical countries have found.

The most important factor determining the choice of a particular system of cultivation is the character of the soil, which establishes the ratio between the length of time the soil can be cultivated with satisfactory results and the length of time it must be left alone to enable fertility to be restored. On the best soils, and where the climate is also favorable, it is possible to have almost continuous cultivation, or at least a fallow of only one year or two after three or four years of cultivation. The closest approach to continuous use of land in Africa is on the volcanic soils of Mounts Kilimanjaro and Elgon and the rich soils of Buganda, where plantains and bananas are permanent crops.

At the other extreme, there are weak, leached soils which "may require twenty-five years or even more to regain a brief fertility after two or three years of cultivation. Between these extremes there is an almost complete range of gradations, so that it is very difficult to say where shifting cultivation begins and ends." (Allan, p. 6.)

The cycle of shifting cultivation is roughly as follows: the men of the village, clan, or family clear the land; trees or bushes are cut down, branches are cut off, and the trees and branches are burned on the soil to be cultivated. The land, thus enriched by the ashes, is then cultivated by the women. (In some cases, in Zambia and the southern Congo, wood is collected and burned primarily to have the wood ash enrich the soil, not incidentally, as in other areas, where the main purpose is to clear the land.)

> The spectacle is very typical: a few tall trees, either protected by taboo or considered too difficult to fell, are still standing, witnesses to the former forest splendour and also precious seed-bearers for future vegetable recolonisation; everywhere the stumps are standing, and between them the soft iron hoes of the women scratch the ground to make it produce a few crops of bananas, manioc, or sweet potatoes. Here and there, dotting these primitive fields, the untidiest in the world, are the blackened trunks that have not been properly burned. . . . Two or three years, sometimes four, of this exposure of the soil to the sun's rays and to the rains, are enough to deprive it of its fertility, and then the village waits for the signal from its old men and its witch doctors to depart to a new site suitable for temporary occupation. The abandoned clearing is then reconquered more or less rapidly by the forest, and this recolonisation, depending upon the nature of the sub-soil, the degree of deterioration, and the extent of the clearing, is more or less complete, or, in other words, the secondary growth forms an assemblage perhaps as rich as the forest previously cleared by the cultivators.
>
> When sufficient land is available, the semi-nomadic group, under the leadership of its chiefs, makes ten to fifteen shifts before returning to a spot formerly occupied by it. This forest land, left uncultivated for thirty to fifty years, usually has its soil restored sufficiently to allow it to withstand a fresh cultural occupation under conditions not more harmful to it than those obtaining before; that is to say, if allowed the same period of rest, it is capable of a fresh regeneration sufficient to allow still another revolution of the cycle. (de la Rue, *et al.*, pp. 171–72.)

The chosen farming areas of course become smaller and smaller in relation to increasing populations. Consequently, the periods of "bush fallow" must get shorter and shorter and the productivity of the soil declines. This problem has already begun to arise in eastern Nigeria where, for tribal or other reasons, the people cannot easily move into new areas.

Even if enough land is available, major improvements in the farmers' standard of living are practically impossible in this type of farming—it is superb for survival but only at a bare existence level. Shifting cultivation has also meant, in many parts of Africa, but not all, that one of the main advantages of agricultural over a nomadic life—the growth of a settled community—is not attained. (In Rwanda, people live in one place and cultivate the surrounding plots in rotation. But this is possible because the volcanic soil is sufficiently rich; it is more impracticable elsewhere.) However, in a few instances, the people had no choice but to remain permanently in one place even though the soil did not encourage permanent cultivation. This was the case, for example, of the Kara, on Ukara Island in Lake Victoria, and of the Hill Pagans in northern Cameroon, who were kept out of the lowlands by their enemies. In these instances, the people had to invent a method of permanent agriculture to survive, and they did. The Hill Pagans terraced the hillsides with stone walls, rotated their crops, kept cattle for manure, collected weeds to make compost, and used these, wood ash, and night soil to maintain the fertility of their fields. All this was much more laborious than shifting their location, but there was no choice.

Most farming in Africa is still subsistence farming—that is, the farmer produces mainly to feed himself or herself and family. More than half the agricultural output in Africa south of the Sahara is consumed on the farm. Now an agricultural economy consisting of subsistence producers is bound to be poor and nonprogressive: the producers are isolated from other economic influences; the mechanism through which small producers cooperate with the rest of the economy—that is, the market—is missing, and the inflow of innovations and ideas accordingly limited; specialization, an important means of growth in productivity, is absent, since it can develop only to the extent that exchange takes place.

It is possible that the transition from subsistence to market agriculture is the single most important economic change taking place in Africa today. Four main stages of this change-over can be differentiated. Examples of the first stage—completely self-contained subsistence production—are already very rare; perhaps they exist only in the Kalahari and Sahara deserts. There are still many communities in the second stage where the opportunity to sell a small surplus above immediate subsistence requirements occurs largely unintentionally. The production of a small surplus is, in fact, a normal result of subsistence agriculture in an average year. Since the farmers' lives depend on the food they produce, they must plant, if possible, an area large enough to ensure sufficient food even if the season proves to be a poor one—otherwise they are faced with starvation. In a normal year, therefore, this insurance will result in a small surplus, which, if a market is available, will be marketed. In this way, subsistence agriculture slips easily with time into the next stage.

In the next stage, a marketable crop is deliberately introduced, but the main emphasis is still on subsistence production. Most African farmers in south, central, and eastern Africa and in the savannah regions of West Africa are in these middle two categories. In the fourth stage, production for the market predominates. The cocoa farmers in Ghana and in the Western Region of Nigeria, and the coffee producers of Buganda, have by and large reached this last stage.

In the main, the cash crops produced in Africa have been for export, while the subsistence food crops have entered very little into the market. With the growth of cities, however, food crops to sell in the cities are becoming more important. In fact, over much of Africa, there has been a drop in the price level of locally produced foods over the last ten or fifteen years—indicating a very great elasticity of supply over time. This seems to contrast with the experience in many other underdeveloped areas: in Africa, an increase in urban demand for foodstuffs usually calls forth an increase in supply from the countryside; but in India, an increase in demand for food in the cities often results not only in a rise in prices but in a drop in supply. This kind of backward-bending supply curve, which occurs rarely in Africa in this particular way, is due to the farmer-supplier using part of his increased income from the raised prices, in the form of increased consumption of his own food crops and so putting less on the market. The absence of this phenomenon in Africa not only testifies to the great elasticity of supply of African foods, but—which is the same thing in another form—also shows that Africans by and large get enough to eat.

AGRICULTURAL WORK PATTERNS

Like all peoples, the African farmer does not fit into a single mold but, as in most national and cultural groups, it is possible to ascertain some dominant behavior and attitude characteristics.

First of all, the African farmer is not really a peasant and does not behave like one, being much more open and receptive to change. While he is interested in economic and social security and, therefore, in land as a means to achieve that security, he does not have the deep emotional ties a peasant has to a particular piece of land or to agriculture as a way of life. The African farmer has readily moved from one area of land to another and is still ready to move at any time. He is also generally ready to go off and become a wage-earner if this will pay better.

The absence of a peasant mentality in African farmers is not wholly a benefit. Going along with the "business approach" that regards land as something to be exploited is the desire for a quick return. With insufficient heed to the long-term results of such exploitation, the land is "mined" rather than cultivated. The lack of a peasant commitment to the land also means that the farmer mixes farming with other occupations—being a school teacher, a trader, or an artisan. The full productivity of a farm may never be attained, even though the individual may maximize his income in the short run by engaging in this wide spectrum of activities.

Most African farmers also still place a high priority on "leisure," and this continues to inhibit the growth of their money income. It is true that "leisure" is rather a misnomer, since what they desire is rather time to engage in a wide range of traditional tribal activities— the administration of tribal justice, initiation ceremonies, discussions of tribal affairs. This priority has some economic basis in the traditional economy: the necessary food crops could be grown by the women alone; there was no particular gain in growing a surplus since it could not be sold nor could much of it be stored. It made sense, therefore, for the men, like the ancient Athenians, to devote much of their time to public affairs. (It is the same pattern, in fact, that leads the middle-class American woman, who now increasingly finds herself free from the necessities of work at home, to devote herself to civic causes and politics.)

In present-day Africa, this pattern often results in a decision not to put in more labor when that labor gives more income but at a sharply diminishing rate of return. This accounts for the widespread practice in many cotton-growing areas of Uganda, Kenya, and Tanzania of leaving the last 10 to 20 per cent of the cotton unpicked. Also, as his income rises, the farmer will often spend part of the increase to hire labor to do work that he and his family are well able to do.

The African farmer is interested not only in the level of his return but, and especially, in the security of the return. With his and his family's lives at stake, he will depart from tried and true practice only when he is convinced that the new practice is absolutely safe. It may be possible to show that if he plants his crop each year at a certain time he will get better average returns, but if this includes the risk of crop failure in *one* year, he will prefer to adjust to the variable rainfall in Africa, minimize his risk, and plant the crop over a number of days.

In the same way, the cattle herder may find that he maximizes security and income by building up his herd as much as he can during the good years, and then sells off or loses cattle in the bad years (getting some benefit from the hides and meat). He may find this more sensible than restricting the number of cattle to an average or minimum he can carry in good years and bad. There is evident here, in addition, a conflict between what is most sensible for the individual to do and what is most sensible for the group as a whole to do. If there are a large number of competitors for scarce grass, and the individual herder cannot rely on the others to behave "sensibly" and so restrict the total number of cattle to the optimum carrying capacity, then he, like the others, will try to increase his own cattle as much as possible, even though this will mean that the land is overgrazed.

Another adverse impact of the high priority placed on security is the slow development of trade in food in the rural areas. Every farm tries to grow its own basic food supply. Over much of Africa, this quite natural tendency was reinforced by requirements laid down by the colonial regimes: that every farmer grow a famine reserve— usually in the form of manioc, which can be kept by leaving it in the ground; that every district try to be self-sufficient in food supplies at all costs (e.g., the policy followed in Uganda). This second policy is still regarded as unquestionably a desirable one by most independent governments in Africa. Many development plans take for granted that if a district or a region is a "food-deficit" area, action must be taken to encourage more food production there. The same is true on a national level; countries like Senegal and Sierra Leone spend a great deal of time and energy trying to persuade people to grow food crops rather than, in the one case, growing peanuts for export, or, in the other, digging alluvial diamonds—even though the latter activities clearly pay far better.

This desire for security, in addition to the government policies that reinforce it, has several adverse results. First, it tends to ensure that crops grown for market sale are and will remain grafted to subsistence production, slowing down the transition to a market economy. Second, cash crops tend to remain, as they began, mainly for export, since the development of a local market for food crops is discouraged, restricted to the still very small urban centers (and even here, people try to and are encouraged to grow their own food).

In short, this means that specialization in both cash export and local food crops is prevented or hindered—hence, productivity all around is held down. Not only is the farmer held back from specializing, but the best use cannot be made of the different special ecological potentials. Take two areas, for example, one especially suited to grow coffee, and the other to grow maize. If maize is grown in the coffee area, the coffee output will suffer, since the cost of growing maize in an unsuitable area may be very high. As for the other area, it may not even be able to grow coffee at all. Its inhabitants are condemned to a low standard of living—growing maize only for their own consumption and with no cash crop to enable them to buy other commodities.

Development of trade among farmers should also promote the diversification and improvement of quality in the African diet. This may not happen automatically, however. Research in western Nigeria has shown that "Nigerian parents were wealthier in villages that specialized in cocoa production but their children suffered a greater incidence of nutritional disorders than those in villages where corn, plantains, cassava, and yams formed part of the agricultural system." (McKelvey, p. 326.) The need to *purchase* food to diversify a diet in such circumstances apparently has still to be learned.

The traditional African division of labor between the sexes is often another decisive economic factor. Where the tradition is still strong, the family is virtually split into two separate enterprises, and its labor force is not considered as a single one.

There are a number of adverse consequences from this situation:

the woman—who is responsible for providing the family's food by her agricultural labors, regardless of her husband's income, but who is permitted to keep any money earned from selling food not needed for the family—will resist switching any land that she cultivates to cash crops if she will receive no benefit from the cash income. (The husband is responsible for and collects the income from cash crops grown for the market.) And she will be reluctant to contribute her labor to his crop and he to hers. At crucial periods, therefore, the best use of labor may not be made. Since handling cattle is man's work, the use of ox-drawn plows in food production by women, even where it is feasible, is held up. One difficulty, which threatened the viability of the small-holder tea-growing scheme in Kenya in 1964, was that wives of the farmers in the scheme found it profitable to pick tea leaves, sun-dry them, and sell them for cash themselves, thus reducing the amount of good tea properly plucked and sent through the regular organization to the factory for processing. When the tea was properly plucked and processed, proceeds were higher but the husbands got them.

The division of labor between the sexes is gradually changing in Africa. With time, these problems will no longer recur. In some areas, a great desire to educate the children (school fees may absorb as much as 50 per cent or more of a family's cash income) has been one of the most effective forces bringing husband and wife to work together to earn money from cash crops.

It is probably the absence of ambiguity about the role of husband or wife on the farm that explains the otherwise curious fact that certain farms run by women are "progressive" show places of the agricultural-extension officers. In these cases, the woman running the farm is a widow or a wife whose husband is away for long periods; she is therefore getting the full benefit of the returns and tries to maximize them by seeking and following the extension officer's advice. There is, in short, no problem of different elements of labor and income, and the farm is operated as a single management unit.

Indeed, there are an increasing number of "progressive farmers" in Africa—in most countries and most communities. More and more African farmers are receptive to new ideas and willing to experiment with them. The outstanding characteristic of these farmers is that they have had the kind of experience which broadened their horizons and increased their knowledge or skills—outside the tribal environment, whether in a clerical government job or a paid job in private or public enterprise. Even serving as a soldier, a policeman, or prison guard helps to instill a disposition to listen to the agricultural officers and to create better work habits. In Kenya and Zambia, working on a non-African farm or farming alongside a non-African farm provided useful lessons. Work as a trader or artisan also seems to give not only a broader horizon but useful managerial experience, especially in handling money. Formal education too, whether or not it included training in agriculture, seems to result in this receptivity to change.

Work experience outside the traditional environment also very often serves as a means to accumulate capital to invest in farming by the purchase of better farm tools and equipment. (This, incidentally, is a highly important kind of investment that often escapes inclusion in the national accounts' estimates.) As a matter of fact, one of the first ways in which Africans tried to raise their incomes was to combine part-time wage-labor with existing farming procedures. This is the basis of the prevalent "migratory labor" system in Africa, which also derives from what I would call "sociological underemployment" arising from the division of labor between the sexes on the farm. If men, for example, regard clearing new land for cultivation as man's work and the actual work of cultivation as women's work, then the men may be underemployed in the periods when no new land has to be cleared. A man can maximize his income by then going to work in industry or mines, returning home to clear new land when this is necessary. Of course, there may not be sufficient jobs to absorb all of the men who would periodically want them, and sociological underemployment may continue to persist for this reason. The costs and time involved in the men getting from their farms to the job opportunities in industry or mining may also be considerable; or the men may not know of jobs available hundreds of miles away, and this may inhibit movement and prevent this cure to underemployment. But, except early in this century when industry and mining were first beginning in Africa, and except in very special circumstances today, the latter factor does not appear of great importance; on the contrary, it is remarkable the obstacles and the distance the average African man will overcome to get to an available job.

The extent of this migratory labor in Africa is quite startling for those accustomed to labor patterns in other continents. The economies of Upper Volta, Mali, Niger, Malawi, Lesotho, the gold mines of South Africa, much of the industry in southern central and eastern Africa, the sisal plantations of Tanganyika, the large coffee farms of Uganda, the Gezira scheme in the Sudan, the cocoa farmers of Ghana and of western Nigeria, the peanut farmers of Senegal, and the cocoa and coffee farmers of the Ivory Coast—all participate in this migrant labor system.

While migrant labor was probably necessary at one stage of African development, with time it has become clear that the gains have been exhausted and further progress depends on a different kind of development. With the migrant moving back and forth between the money economy and the farm, he is unable to increase his productivity as an industrial worker or as a farmer but becomes stuck on a plateau of relative inefficiency in each case. And, the costs in terms of time and energy wasted in shuttling back and forth are very high. But, on the other hand, as I have said, the migrant worker does acquire the potentialities and the capital required to become a "progressive farmer," if the farming structure to which he returns permits it (i.e., if there is the possibility of becoming a permanent settled farmer).

Land Tenure

Wherever it is possible to establish permanent farms with a settled farming population, the traditional land-tenure systems may become an obstacle to economic progress. All of Africa's local variations on the communal or tribal land-tenure system are based on the assumptions that land has no scarcity value and that the right to use it depends on membership in or consent of the community as a whole. As long as population was relatively scarce and the primitive method of shifting cultivation prevailed, there was no cause to change this system; in fact, any attempt at fundamental change would have been futile and rather silly. But when permanent farms became possible and are economic, a change does become necessary to give the farmer permanent rights to the land he is cultivating.

To increase a permanent farm's output, it is necessary for the farmer to invest labor and capital—to build up the quality of the soil, to improve the drainage by digging ditches or leveling or changing the slope of the land, to protect the crops and stop wind erosion by planting trees as windbreaks, building fences, etc. For the farmer and his family to undertake all this, they must feel that they have security of tenure for themselves and for future generations. In addition, the farmer needs capital for implements and for seasonal requirements of seed, fertilizer, insecticides, etc. Economically, it makes sense to borrow, if necessary, for such short-term productive purposes as well as for capital improvement. But to borrow, the farmer needs good credit; the best collateral is the pledge of land; so, for this too, individual ownership of land is essential. The individual farmer and his family must also have every incentive to work hard both to increase current output and to improve the farm for future output— and this is provided by farm ownership (which is why most schemes of collective farming fail, whether the Pilgrims' in the Plymouth colony or the Russians' on the steppes).

(It is possible that with highly advanced agricultural development, such as in the United States, where the soil is known thoroughly, and the application of fertilizer can control fertility, the supply of water from rainfall or irrigation is reliable, the characteristics of plants are well known, and techniques of mechanization have been perfected, farming can be handled like factory production. In such conditions, professional managers and a wage-labor force or even well-organized collective farmers might be as efficient as single-family farming. These conditions certainly are not applicable to Africa today or for the next generation.)

In recent years, the spread of cash crops and the growth of population is giving an economic value to rights in land, whether the traditional system is ready to recognize it or not. As the East African Royal Commission put it in a 1955 report:

> Increased African production requires a new conception of land rights and tenure. For, as land becomes one of the factors of production for the market, with the consequent division of labor and specialization of production which its use as a factor of production in the market economy entails, two fundamental changes occur: (*a*) the land becomes valuable as a specialized factor of production, and (*b*) an in-

creasing proportion of the population becomes less directly dependent upon the land and is able to find new income-earning opportunities in other directions, opportunities greater than those which occupation of the land itself can offer them. Indeed, a rise in income per head in the community as a whole presupposes such a diversification of economic activities, either by increased diversification on the land itself, or by increased specialization in occupations divorced from it. A tribal community which is economically isolated from the market cannot introduce these changes. (East Africa Royal Commission, pp. 48–49.)

Frankel, a member of the Commission, has gone so far as to say:

It is clear that the root cause of the economic backwardness of various African territories, as well as of the native areas in the Union [of South Africa], lies in the failure to modify customary control of land occupation and tenure, which has prevented the emergence of land use and ownership compatible with modern forms of commercialized production in a money economy. The failure to make of the land a viable economic factor of production has condemned the peoples on it to eke out a precarious subsistence. (Frankel, p. 7.)

While individual ownership of land is often an economic step forward, it must be recognized that so fundamental a change as a shift to individual land tenure can and should be made only when conditions are ripe for it. The World Bank's Economic Survey Mission to Uganda identified the following major necessary preconditions: a relatively high density of population; use of land to grow cash crops, thus the imputation of money value to land; and a growing rate of litigation over land rights, showing that these are acquiring growing value. In addition, it is important that the program not be imposed against the wishes of the population affected.

So far in Africa, the greatest progress in this direction has been made in Kenya. (See below, p. 110.) But conditions were quite favorable there to begin with: by the early 1950's, virtually all the land of the Kipsigis tribe had been enclosed into individual holdings—a movement started by the younger men in defiance of the elders. To carry out programs for individual ownership in the African areas, existing customary rights were surveyed and adjudicated, farms were laid out on the new basis, and new freehold titles issued. In resettlement areas where Africans were acquiring former European farms, the new settlers obtained freehold title from the very beginning.

In Uganda, the *mailo* land in Buganda (arising out of the Uganda agreement of 1900, which allocated land to the leading Buganda in square-mile blocks, hence *mailo*), while held by individuals, has certain limitations on it: it cannot be sold to non-Africans, which has hampered its use as credit collateral; and, perhaps even more important, its full economic exploitation has been restricted by the existence of squatters with certain customary rights. But, even with these handicaps, the *mailo* land has aided a more rapid economic growth in Buganda than has occurred elsewhere in Uganda without it.

In Ghana and southern Nigeria, the increase in cash crops and the growing scarcity of good land for such crops has led to the evolution of *de facto* individual ownership in the cash-crop areas. As this is an unplanned evolution, it has involved a great deal of litigation over the various rights to use of the land, as well as to the appropriation by chiefs of formerly communal land. In brief, individual ownership of farms is occurring essentially through the rather costly process of adjudication by courts on individual cases.

In the lands of the former French empire in Africa, the French Government had recognized two kinds of property rights: customary rights under tribal law; and freehold title acquired by registration of land granted, conceded, or purchased. In 1955, a law was passed under which the customary rights were confirmed, and the machinery for transforming these rights into individual property on request was simplified. The same arrangement has been carried on in the independent French-speaking states. Essentially, therefore, there is no legal obstacle to Africans shifting to freehold tenure whenever the land begins to acquire sufficient economic value to justify going through the whole procedure of survey and registration. This process has evidently not gone very far, however, except in the most economically advanced nations—that is, in the Ivory Coast and Senegal—and in some of the *paysannat* schemes set up before independence. René Dumont has, on the other hand, pointed out that under this law the chiefs have been able to cede exploitation rights to other people—expatriates or African strangers—who have set up plantations manned by migrant workers in areas like the Ivory Coast or eastern Cameroon while the local people have drawn incomes from this without work and without inducement to work. (Dumont, *False Start in Africa.*)

Permanent Farms and Cash Crops

TREE CROPS

One important means by which it has become possible for African farmers to settle permanently on a farm they in large part pioneered themselves—that is, the development, where conditions are suitable, of tree crops. The main crops involved are cocoa and the oil palm in West Africa; coffee in many countries, but particularly Uganda and the Ivory Coast; and, in the last few years, tea, mostly in East Africa. Tea (in Malawi and Uganda), bananas (in Somalia, Cameroon, and the Ivory Coast), oil palm in Congo (Léopoldville), and rubber (in Liberia and the Congo [Léopoldville]) are also grown on plantations. The cultivation of these tree crops largely bypasses many of the problems of arable agriculture I have mentioned earlier. The plants in such cases, shading and protecting the soil (although sometimes additional shade cover is still necessary), come close to achieving the equilibrium with soil and climate of the original forest. The farmer is able to have a settled farm on which he can apply the results of research and improve his methods, and so increase his productivity and income. In tropical Africa, the tree-crop farmers have been most successful in improving their lot; the other farmers sometimes have at best merely held their own.

OTHER SCHEMES

The most ambitious schemes to reorganize farming on the basis of permanently settled farmers are found in Kenya and in the Land Husbandry program of Rhodesia. In both of these countries, large tracts of land—because of altitude, rainfall, and soils—are suitable for permanent mixed farms—that is, farms using a rotation of crops and the manure from the livestock to help to maintain and restore fertility. In both countries, also, European farmers and governments over some fifty years came to learn how temperate-zone farming techniques had to be modified to be successful under local conditions. In both countries, also, trained agricultural officers or experienced farmers were available to help African farmers with new methods. Many African farmers took advantage of the work experience on European farms or of living next to European farms to acquire new techniques.

Under the Swynnerton scheme in Kenya, begun in 1954, about 2.5 million acres (around 300,000 farms) in the Central, Rift Valley, and Nyanza provinces were laid out in permanent individual farms and farmed on the basis of plans and other advice from the agricultural extension services. (This area comprises about one-quarter of the high- and medium-potential agricultural land held by Africans in Kenya at the time.) This program is being extended to other parts of Kenya, where conditions are favorable—that is, where the soil and climate permit such farming, where there is local demand for it, and where land settlement officers are available. Since 1961, however, the main emphasis in Kenya has been on several settlement schemes, totaling around 1.25 million acres, on farms formerly owned by Europeans. These schemes, progressing on the whole quite successfully with the help of the former owners, are to be supplemented by an additional scheme taking over another 2 million acres of European farms. These, however, are to be farmed on a new, untried cooperative basis rather than by individual farmers, which, if it goes ahead, is much less likely to succeed. (See above, p. 107.)

The Land Husbandry program in Rhodesia, begun in 1951, has so far been less successful than the schemes in Kenya. It undertook to reorganize all of the land set aside in the African reserves into individual farms. While well-worked-out in concept, the program cannot be considered an economic success—partly because it was restricted to the less desirable land (it did not include land reserved to Europeans), and partly because in many tribal areas the available land was insufficient to create economically viable farms and the farmers were not granted full freehold title to the land. Moreover, the African political leaders did not accept the program, and the cooperation of the African farmers themselves was thus reduced. Furthermore, the industrial economy of Rhodesia, largely due to political developments of 1962–66, did not grow fast enough to absorb the farmers who were theoretically to leave the land and become industrial workers, thus permitting the remaining farmers to acquire economically sized farms. As a result, the program virtually stopped by the end of 1962, by which time the grant of the rights to farms had covered less than 50 per cent of the arable and 40 per cent of the grazing lands.

In countries where the natural conditions do not appear suitable for mixed farming, several other promising experiments have been tried—in the Congo, a particularly promising one called the *paysannat*. The *paysannat* was a system of farming under which farmers were settled along a road on plots laid out adjacent to one another in strips perpendicular to the road. These strips were subdivided into fifteen or twenty sections. The farmers were to practice a kind of rolling rotation, moving down the strips with particular crops section by section, from year to year, leaving the sections behind in bush fallow. As various sections would be growing identical crops at the same time, it was possible to experiment with mechanical cultivation or harvesting going across the strips at right angles. Some 200,000 families had been settled on such schemes by 1960 when the schemes collapsed due to the chaos that accompanied independence in 1960. (The extension workers who were needed to keep the scheme going also then departed.)

In other parts of French-speaking equatorial Africa, other attempts were made during the 1950's to establish settled farms, similarly called *paysannats*. After a number of failures, a certain degree of success—as in the Niari Valley in the Congo—was achieved by carefully selecting sites with the best possible soil and communications, and by investing considerable amounts in roads, housing, schools, and dispensaries. Among the most successful schemes are those based on tree-crop plantations.

In Zambia, a system of rotating areas within a single farm is being tried, with considerable success, on what amounts to a pilot-project basis. There are some areas in Zambia where mixed farming on the Kenyan or Rhodesian model might be successful.

Government Programs

Aside from the question whether such basic transformations as the change to permanent farming and the shift from communal to individual land tenure are carried out or not, there is much that can be done to increase output. In general, government programs to increase agricultural output in the existing agricultural structure can be subdivided into two main categories: those which alter the infrastructure and environment in which the farmer operates; and those which require changes in the way the farmer himself operates. The permanent-farm schemes of course involve both types, but in areas where natural conditions or the farmers are not ready for these, much potential growth can be realized from programs of the first type. Building roads to open up new areas, providing better water supplies, spraying crops, controlling locust breeding places and locust swarms, providing selected seed or seedlings—all are examples of exogenous programs to improve agricultural productivity.

The output of a crop often hinges on the labor supply at a crucial time—at planting, weeding, or harvesting. But the labor available at these stages may be reduced by unavoidable calls on the time of the farming population; in particular, having to go long distances for water, for the household or livestock, or for fuel wood. New wells or boreholes, and new roads, by reducing the time that must be taken away from work in the fields can thus lead to an increase in output even with no change in traditional farming methods.

The U.N. Special Fund's International Anti-Locust Organization since 1959 has systematically tracked down and destroyed, in their breeding places and in flight, locust swarms that would otherwise have destroyed the crops upon which millions of Africans depend. And for most cash crops, it has become established practice for public organizations to provide selected seed or seedlings, thus making it possible, with an adequate organization for agricultural research, to upgrade the quality or yield.

All these programs can be carried out by government or other organizations without necessarily calling on the farmer to improve his own management techniques. So far, they have been more manageable and successful than programs to improve actual agricultural skills. But it is on this second that the continuance of a rise in African income ultimately depends.

What is the most effective way of inducing a change in agricultural techniques and having it spread through a group?

The most effective way known so far is to pick out the individual farmers ("master" or "progressive" farmers) who have shown or appear to have the potential to be innovators and to give them special help, credit facilities, and other services to enable them to forge ahead. (See *The Economic Development of Uganda*, pp. 125–202.) But unless effective extension services work with these "progressive farmers," much of the opportunity to make substantial gains in agriculture in Africa will be lost.

AGRICULTURAL EXTENSION SERVICES

The key governmental instrument for transforming African agriculture is the extension service. Unfortunately, when the colonial powers departed, the services they had established were still in their infancy. Paradoxically, while political independence has improved the African farmers' receptivity to the services' advice, the departure of "expatriates" before Africans had been trained to replace them has weakened the effectiveness of the services.

An agricultural extension service has essentially three tasks to fulfill: to diagnose the real agricultural and economic problems of the farmer; to devise measures to solve them; and to persuade the farmers to take the necessary action.

Not enough is yet known about the conditions facing the African farmer. There are very few areas, for example, where all the main soil types and how they respond to varying treatments are known. Still less is known about different micro-climates; what may be the best plant variety and best system of cultivation in one area may be completely wrong for a village ten miles away.

In addition to technical ignorance, there is an even greater lack of knowledge of the economics of the African farm. The agricultural extension services have been and are primarily concerned with technical problems, and have concentrated on the yield to be gotten out of a piece of land. The African, on the other hand, thinks in terms of the return on his labor. If he can get more return from a given expenditure of labor by cultivating additional land than by intensifying cultivation on a given piece of land, he will do so, even though the yield per acre is not high. An example of this point was a program in Sukumaland administered by the trusteeship government of Tanganyika before independence in 1961. The agricultural officers tried to persuade the farmers to raise their cotton yields and avoid erosion by tie-ridging their fields to conserve water and avoid run-off. At the same time, new land was made available to the tribe through a program of clearing out bush, eliminating the tsetse fly, and providing water supplies. The Sukuma, comparing their advantages, preferred to expand into the new area, and the program of intensified cultivation was a failure. The same experience has been repeated in other parts of Africa. When people emigrate from areas where the distribution of human and livestock populations makes intensive agriculture desirable to areas where pressure on the land is less intense, they revert to extensive agriculture. Similarly, if to avoid soil erosion takes too high a cost now in relation to the return over the next few years—or if it is possible to move on to new land instead— it is useless to try to persuade farmers to expend labor on anti-erosion works.

It is also necessary to know where the real bottlenecks are in the allotment of time to specific agricultural tasks. Usually the most critical factor affecting the size of a crop is the timing of the planting; but a farmer's failure to observe the recommended planting dates is usually due, not to stubborn conservatism or laziness, but to an inability to cope with the work load, given the tools available or, as we have discussed before, a desire to maximize security rather than output. It is useless to tell farmers to plant immediately upon the advent of rains, for instance, when they have been unable in advance to break the hard dry ground with their work hoe or ox plow, or when they must interrupt the planting in order to cope with weeds in fields that were sown earlier.

The second big task for the agricultural extension services, once the farmer's main problems are understood, is to find the answers to them. This is primarily the task of applied research. Insufficient research was done in the past (although there are outstanding exceptions, such as the work done at the Cocoa Research Institute in Ghana, the Oil Palm Research Institute in Nigeria, and the Rice Research Institute in Sierra Leone), and, unfortunately, even less is being done in the era of independence. Earlier British Colonial Development and Welfare grants to research, for instance, have not been carried on in full measure by the new governments in the English-speaking countries. And, in all of newly independent Africa, the departure of the career "expatriates" has not been offset by the entry of Africans, nor are the new short-term contract officers who have replaced the career officers in some areas likely to be as effective as the men who gave their lives to research in Africa.

The final and crucial step is in getting the farmers to accept and follow the extension services' advice. Here, the outlook has become brighter in recent years. In the past, tribal societies emphasized conformity to established customs and practices and deference to established authority, particularly to the elders. This discouraged any serious deviations from the accepted way of doing things and made the "progressive farmer" an object of suspicion and hostility, unless he himself happened to be a person of authority in the society.

During the colonial period, the Belgians in particular and the British in some areas gave preference, when educating the Africans to chiefs and sons of chiefs, in this way attempting to get influential leaders of the next generation on the side of change. When the various colonial territories became independent, nationalist leaders, parties, and movements took the "progressive farmers" as their own and made them status-holders. In Malawi, the contrast is particularly striking: before independence the progressive farmer was often regarded as a pariah; since independence, he has often been singled out as a success symbol for the other farmers. The new favor with which the progressive farmer is viewed should have a good effect on the level of productivity in many African countries—as long, of course, as the nationalist movements do not become dizzy with success and try to leap forward further than knowledge of and conditions in the environment permit.

In some cases, reliance on individual farmers to move ahead of the group is unsatisfactory, and it is necessary to work with an entire rural population to achieve any success at all. In the cotton-growing area of Kenya's Central Nyanza, progressive farmers discovered that if they followed advice and planted cotton before planting maize and sorghum, these latter crops, when grown by farmers who did not follow the new schedule, harbored and encouraged the multiplication of cotton pests which attacked the cotton. Further, the progressive farmers got their cotton crops in early, but if the rest did not, the gins would not be open when they harvested and they would have to store the cotton in the interim.

Also, it is necessary for everyone to pull up and burn cotton stalks after the harvest; if some do not, the remaining stalks will harbor pests into the next season.

In central Africa in the mid-1950's, the cotton-boll worm appeared. For some years in Rhodesia, this wrecked the promising development of cotton as an additional cash crop on African and European farms. In what was then Nyasaland, however, the boll weevil was defeated by all the farmers simultaneously switching the season—reversing the time of planting and harvesting. Such a program could not be carried out in Rhodesia, reportedly because the Agriculture Department was not able to secure the voluntary cooperation of the European farmers.

AGRICULTURAL CREDIT

Adequate agricultural credit systems are essential to the rapid development of agricultural output. Credit is needed to give a farmer the capital he needs to increase output in advance of the time necessary to finance himself through building up his savings. Properly used, capital helps the farmer to achieve an output surplus sufficient not only to repay the borrowed capital and the interest on it, but to give him something beyond this to add to his income.

The only safe way to provide credit to farmers who are still deficient in managerial ability is in combination with managerial assistance—that is, the credit must be supervised by informed professionals who can ascertain that there is a proper need for the credit, that it will be spent on what it was secured for, and that it will be used to secure higher output. To safeguard the extension services' day-by-day relationships with the farmers, however, the services cannot get involved in loan repayment collections. Cooperatives, when properly administered, have proved to be an excellent alternate device for the allocation and collection of credits. So far, however, there have been few good examples of credit programs in African agriculture. The most successful ones have followed these general principles.

So far, commercial banks have not been very helpful in meeting the credit needs of African agriculture. In most areas without land titles, they are practically barred from even trying. In any case, they have difficulties in assessing the credit needs of small farmers and in controlling disbursements of loans, and have dealt more successfully with the larger commercial farmers and the cooperatives. It may be that they will be able to work out ways to finance members of cooperatives. In most countries, however, it is fairly certain that some sort of government credit agency is needed.

COOPERATIVES

Farmers and governments alike (particularly in Tanzania) have had enough experience with cooperatives to show that they can be an important means of agricultural development in Africa. Cooperatives fit in well with the existing social structure; they are naturally most successful when based on existing kinship or social groups, so that both the members' feeling of identification with the organization and the management's feeling of responsibility to the members are encouraged.

Cooperatives have done well in Africa in buying, bulking, grading, storing, and the simple processing of their members' produce. But it is yet to be demonstrated that cooperative farms, where the land is farmed in common and the produce is shared, can be operated successfully. Farms where some of the operations are performed for all the members—i.e., mechanical plowing of all the fields—but where the produce of the individual plots goes to each individual farmer might well be successful in appropriate circumstances.

The continued, successful operation of cooperatives appears to require government supervision, inspection, and audit of accounts, as well as government advice on management. This service again was badly hurt by the exodus of "expatriates" after independence. Another problem is the pressure applied by some governments, including Tanzania's, to proliferate and expand cooperatives more rapidly than available personnel can ensure a reasonable chance of success. In spite of such temporary problems, however, cooperatives should be one of the strong points in the expansion of African agriculture.

LARGE-SCALE SCHEMES

So far in this chapter, I have mentioned primarily programs and policies for increasing the output of existing African farms. Even the schemes in Kenya, though they involved hundreds of thousands of farmers, were well grounded on either existing African farms or on formerly European farms settled by African farmers. But a number of governments now believe they must decide whether to try to increase the national output by improving, helping, or even reorganizing existing farms or by undertaking large-scale schemes for the development of unutilized or underutilized land—between concentrating on and trying to increase production within existing areas of agricultural production, or putting resources into large-scale agricultural projects such as resettlement or irrigation schemes.

There is no easy answer for a government faced with this decision, although theoretically it is just a matter of comparing the yield of investment in alternative projects (including both private and social costs and benefits in the calculation). Unfortunately, not enough of the elements are known to demonstrate clearly what the answer should be. Under these circumstances, the large schemes, with the greater risks of loss, are a dubious choice. There is a tendency, just the same, to prefer them—in part because they are more spectacular and make a greater effect in a development plan, and in part because when they succeed, it is easier in these schemes to demonstrate the benefits deriving from government action than when the benefits are scattered over the mass of a farming population.

It was for reasons such as these that the British Government decided to launch the ill-fated scheme costing some $80 million to increase the supply of peanuts in Tanganyika, rather than to help Nigerian farmers to increase production and improve the marketing arrangements for their groundnuts. The White Paper advocating the Tanganyika scheme said: "No significant increase in the present output of oilseeds can be achieved . . . by the existing methods of peasant production. Nothing but the most highly mechanical agricultural methods, on a vast scale never previously envisaged, will result in any appreciable amelioration of the present disastrous food position." (*A Plan for the Mechanized Production of Groundnuts*, p. 18.) It is obvious, with hindsight, that if only a small fraction of the money wasted on the groundnut scheme had been used in Nigeria to improve rail transport, peasant production of groundnuts would have been increased by more than the Tanganyika scheme hoped to achieve.

The Tanganyika scheme was only the most notorious of a number of failures of this kind in various parts of Africa. Another example is the South Busoga development scheme started in Uganda in 1947 to use mechanical cultivation to increase food supplies for Jinja, where it was anticipated that industrialization would create a demand that the small African farmer could not hope to supply. By 1954, the scheme had to be written off as a complete failure, while the farmers demonstrated that they could meet all increased demands for food without major difficulty.

The same seductive attractions of large-scale schemes are enticing some of Africa's independent governments today. In the Western Region of Nigeria, the 1962–68 development plan provides for large-scale settlements of young farmers—200 farmers per 5,000–7,000 acres, with each farmer debited with a capital cost of £2,400 to be repaid over fifteen to twenty years. In Tanzania, a large number of village and settlement schemes are planned, although not one has yet been proven successful.

One type of large-scale scheme of particular importance is concerned with irrigation projects. With a climate favorable to reproduction and growth, there is a good possibility of developing a prosperous farming community, *if* an adequate supply of water can be assured and applied to soils whose characteristics are thoroughly understood. Wherever a good supply of water can be found in the arid and semi-arid regions of Africa, irrigation is a possibility worth exploring. So far, however, only the large Gezira irrigation scheme in the Sudan has successfully overcome the sociological and administrative obstacles. (See below, p. 121.) The Office du Niger scheme in Mali, the Richard Toll scheme in Senegal, and the Mweya scheme in Kenya, to name only the most conspicuous, have not shown any outstanding economic success. In 1965, the Office du Niger, after some thirty-five years of existence and an investment of around $180 million, was not yet paying its way currently, much less providing any return on capital.

It is clear that, for a large-scale project to be successful, a great deal must be known about the natural conditions; a pilot project should be operated for some years to discover the practical answers to the challenges they present. But governments are often too impatient to move as slowly as necessary. Secondly, a sufficiently large cadre of skilled agricultural technicians and extension agents is needed to provide guidance and control for the mass of farmers involved. But governments have been unwilling to wait until one develops. Thirdly, it is important to assign responsibility for preparing and administering the scheme to a quasi-governmental entity, outside of and independent of the regular governmental administration—on the example of TVA, or the Gezira Board. Finally, the farmers must be ready to accept and follow the advice proffered. Again, farmers have frequently not been ready to adopt new methods wholesale, and the government is unwilling to be tough with those who will not.

With these difficult major conditions for success, it is not surprising that at this time in Africa and for some time to come, the most practical and economic approach to achieving a sizable increase in agricultural productivity and output would be to enhance the efficiency of the existing agricultural economy, not in attempting large-scale transformation projects. Unfortunately, the unhappy experience of the past is cheerfully overlooked, and it is a rare development program in Africa that does not include substantial investment in large-scale untried transformation, "resettlement," or "mechanical cultivation" schemes.

THE GEZIRA SCHEME

The Gezira irrigation and cotton-growing scheme is an outstanding exception to the record of failures of large-scale projects in Africa. Due to good management and some good luck, the Gezira scheme was able to avoid most of the difficulties that ruined other such projects. To begin with, of course, the Sudanese had many centuries' experience with irrigation from the Nile. The actual idea for this scheme dated back to a 1907 pilot irrigation project for water pumped from the Nile, a project handled by a British company, the Sudan Plantations Syndicate, which was already farming in the Sudan. This project was successful and was gradually expanded with more pumps until, in 1925, the Sennar Dam was completed and gravity irrigation became possible. The project was then expanded rapidly to new areas. In 1950, the Sudanese Government took over the concessions, and the management was taken over by the Sudan Gezira Board, an autonomous public authority, whose personnel had been trained over the preceding twenty-five years. With some 2 million acres now under irrigation, the scheme is still expanding. The completion of the Roseires Dam will, under the Nile waters agreement with Egypt, permit the Sudan to use more water— and thus both bring more land under cultivation and intensify production of already cultivated land.

The Gezira scheme is operated on a partnership basis: the government provides the water and the land, which has been purchased or rented (if necessary, compulsorily) from the original landlords; the board administers the scheme and does the research, allocates the tenancies, supervises and finances the tenants, mechanically cultivates the land, provides cotton seed and fertilizer, undertakes pest control, transports gins, and markets the cotton; the tenants provide the labor. The net proceeds of the cotton sales are divided among the tenants, government, and board in the ratio 44:40:10. Of the remaining 6 per cent, 2 per cent goes to the local government, 2 per cent is spent on social development by the national government and 2 per cent goes into a Reserve Fund held by the board against the possibility of a crop failure (until the fund reaches a certain point, after which it will go to the tenants). The land is under cotton only a quarter or a third of the time, depending on the area; other crops raised belong in their entirety to the tenant. In recent years, the tenants have numbered around 75,000, their average annual share about $500; the board also employs directly 10,000 workers and there have been in addition about 250,000 laborers working for the tenants. The government gets 5–15 per cent of its total revenues from the Gezira scheme directly, and probably an equivalent amount indirectly from import taxes levied on goods bought by consumers whose incomes derive from it. The Gezira is responsible for around 8 per cent of the Gross Domestic Product of the Sudan and around 16 per cent of the product of the modern sector; it is the source of 35–40 per cent of total foreign-exchange earnings. Over the last fifteen years, the direct return to the government on its investment in the Gezira has averaged 20 per cent per year.

The Small Farmer vs. the Plantation

During the colonial period, the issue of whether a particular country should develop its agriculture on the basis of plantations or small farms came up at different times, and was as often as not decided as much on political or social grounds as on economic grounds. The alternatives are still posed today.

Prior to World War I, the British colonial office, for example, in considering a request by Unilever to establish oil palm plantations in Nigeria, decided against plantations, because they did not want to create a large landless agricultural proletariat, and Unilever moved to the Belgian Congo instead. This was the origin of the vast Huileries du Congo Belge plantations, still important today.

At present, the principal plantation products are rubber in Liberia and Congo (Léopoldville); oil palm in the Congo; sisal in Tanganyika and Kenya; sugar in Uganda, Kenya, Tanganyika, Mauritius, and Natal; bananas in Cameroon, Somalia, and the Ivory Coast; tea in Malawi and Uganda; coffee in Kenya, Ivory Coast, and Angola; the coconut palm in Mozambique.

The newly independent nations of Africa are now free to reconsider the methods they want to employ for agricultural development. There seems to be a tendency to experiment: Nigeria and Ghana have begun to try out plantations or the equivalent of plantation systems; Tanzania and Kenya are trying small-holder production of what were formerly plantation crops. Social and political considerations probably justify the bias toward small-farmer production, if this is an economic alternative. It provides a more even distribution of income and power and avoids the concentration of wealth and power in a small group, whether private or public. Economically too, small farms can be said to have a number of advantages over large-scale production: their owners have a stronger incentive to work harder themselves and to work their families; the innumerable managerial decisions that must be taken day by day, hour by hour, are hard to organize by a management having to deal with large areas and many workers, etc. Farming in Africa is exactly the opposite of large-scale factory output, where conditions can be completely controlled and the cycle of production is set and repetitive. It is not surprising, consequently, that for production of most crops in Africa, plantations failed when in competition with small farmers.

Yet, plantations have been successful in competing with small farmers in raising certain products where the following advantages are critically important: command of a large amount of capital, greater technical knowledge, better work discipline where timing of operations is important, greater knowledge of and better trade contacts with foreign markets. Throughout the world, indeed, smallholders have been least successful in production of tea and sisal.

In sisal, for example, the minimum scale of feasible operation is already very large. The decorticator, the machine that strips the sisal fiber out of the leaf, has a minimum economic capacity of around 1,200 tons annually—requiring an area of 2,700 acres (1 ton of fiber per acre per year over a productive period of 4 years, 3 years to come to maturity): mature sisal, 1,200 acres; immature, 900; annual planting, 300; fallow, 300. Second, sisal requires a precise, well-timed transport organization. Only 2 to 5 per cent of the leaf yields fiber, and it is therefore necessary to transport to the processing machines a great weight of what is essentially waste in order to get a small amount of product; this processing has to be done within forty-eight hours of cutting to prevent the plant juices from becoming gummy; the waste materials must then be discarded. Large amounts of water, too, are needed. Consequently, one has what amounts to an industrial operation—large-scale organization of transport on a tight schedule to feed a large unit.

In tea, the decisive matter is taking very good care of the tea plant, plucking the right leaves at the right times, and getting the leaves to the processing plant quickly. For successful growing of tea, it is necessary to inculcate and to maintain a rather high level of skill and rhythm of work.

In principle, it is not impossible to organize even the main "plantation" crops on a small-holder basis. The government, or a cooperative, or a private enterprise could handle the processing and marketing part of the operation. The crucial point is the technical and sociological level reached by the farmer—whether he is able to maintain sufficient self-discipline to perform his part of the operation or not. If the farmers in a particular country or area have not yet reached this level of development, small-holder production of crops that requires it will fail.

Plantations can be much more than instruments of agricultural output. They could be a center for radiating modern techniques into the surrounding economy: a place where the local population was taught skills and habits of methodical work, and acquired supervisory experience. In short, a plantation could be, like a mining development or a large-scale industry, a nucleus for development of the whole economy.

In actual fact, this has not yet happened in Africa. In the past, this was because the plantations, while depending on African migratory labor, reserved the key jobs for non-Africans; Africans received little or no training and acquired few valuable skills. Today, the governments tend to eliminate existing plantations for anticolonialist reasons (exceptions are in Tanzania and Uganda, where the sisal and sugar plantations are used as centers from which development can spread), rather than to use them as a place to create and train skilled African workers and managers. It would be better to keep these golden geese than to kill them.

Marketing Boards

Another important institution in African agriculture is the marketing board. Marketing boards, or *caisses de stabilisation*, were set up during or after World War II to control the marketing of some of the most important export crops in a number of countries: cocoa in Ghana and Nigeria; coffee in Ivory Coast, Uganda, Kenya; cotton in Uganda and Nigeria; peanuts in Senegal and Nigeria, etc. There were a number of reasons for doing so, some of which were not completely formulated at the time and some of which may have been quite contradictory. In some cases, the boards were designed to maintain purchases of the farmers' crops at a time when world markets were closed because of the war; in other cases, the boards were designed to eliminate the middlemen in the sale of crops and to provide stable prices for the farmers. Generally, however, as world prices went up in the postwar period, the prices received by the crop-growers in the English territories did not follow suit; in the

French territories prices received tended rather to exceed what the world market price would justify. Some of the differences between the world market prices and the prices paid to the farmers by the marketing boards was set aside in price reserve funds, parts of which were later taken over or borrowed by the governments for development plans. (Part of the export proceeds was also directly taken by the governments in the form of export taxes and used to finance capital and current expenditures.)

In the early postwar years, there was some justification for the policy of building up large price reserve funds, in that the supply of commodities the farmers could buy was limited anyway, and giving them extra money would simply have resulted in their bidding up prices against themselves. But, once this first period of scarcity was over, the issue was clearly joined. As the East African Royal Commission and a number of economists pointed out in sharp criticism of the marketing board policy, economic development would progress faster if the African farmers received the full benefit of the higher prices, than it did with the government's use of the money: (a) in benefiting from the higher prices, the farmers would have made greater efforts, producing greater output of the commodities concerned; (b) the farmers would have saved more, and used the funds to develop, improve, and even transform their farms; (c) the higher purchasing power in rural areas would have stimulated other forms of economic development—African traders and backyard industries; (d) the marketing boards insulated the farmer from world market prices, hindering the development of an entrepreneurial sense and leading the farmer to believe that the way to change low prices was to put pressure on the government; (e) government expenditures, both current and capital, were enabled to increase rapidly, through the higher availability of funds to the government (much of the money went into assets, such as educational and research assets, with a very slow yield; but much was probably wasted in extravagance).

This is a formidable indictment. Unfortunately, no thorough research has been done either to prove or to disprove these points. There is some possibility that research will throw light on the main point of whether higher incomes for farmers do have the beneficent results claimed for them—by making a comparative study of the results obtained in Ghana, where a policy was followed of taxing cocoa producers quite heavily, with that in some of the ex-French nations, where France made part of her aid available in the form of prices above what would be justified by world market prices. Not all economists agreed, or agree, with the main critique of the marketing boards as given above. In view of the lack of any real data, one's attitude to what the marketing boards accomplished or did not accomplish is largely a matter of judgment. The World Bank Economic Survey missions of Nigeria and Uganda, after making as thorough an assessment as they could of the policies followed and their results, concluded that on balance the way the export proceeds were used did contribute effectively to the national development. In Nigeria, the mission said, "On the whole, the operations of the Marketing Boards have benefited the producers of the controlled crops and the Nigerian economy in general." It pointed out that under any stabilization scheme, a period of rising prices is the time for the formation of reserves. Setting relatively low producer prices greatly mitigated the severity of inflationary pressures at a time when no other machinery for anti-inflationary action existed. And the accumulated stabilization reserves were large enough not only to assure producers the direct benefit of reasonable and relatively stable prices for many years, but also to enable the boards to lend large sums to the government for development purposes. A recent study agreed with this conclusion:

> Can it be said that the uses to which the trading surpluses earned by the Nigerian Marketing Boards were put were superior to those to which the peasant farmers would have put them had they been given the opportunity? Since a much larger proportion of the increase in peasant income would have been consumed than that which was actually consumed out of Marketing Board trading surpluses, the rates of return on peasant investments would have had to be much greater than those on Marketing Board ones if peasant uses of the funds in the aggregate were really to have been considered superior. The disposition of Marketing Board surpluses may not have been perfect, but the rates of return from their investments in research, roads, agricultural schemes, universities, modern manufacturing plants and so forth are unlikely to have been any lower than those on housing, sewing machines, land clearing and the other small-scale outlets for

peasant funds discussed above, let alone so much lower as to offset the difference between consumption ratios. It can therefore unambiguously be stated that Nigerian development has been aided through the device of channelling a portion of its export earnings via the Marketing Boards away from the producer to other (governmental) decision-makers. (Helleiner, p. 603.)

In Uganda, the World Bank survey mission of 1960–61 felt, the marketing boards and export tax arrangements had made a useful contribution in financing a large growth of the infrastructure and of most of Uganda's modern economy outside of agriculture; in view of the very high prevailing cotton and coffee prices, the predominant position of these two crops in the Uganda economy, and the fact that Africans were exempt from income tax, the government had no choice but to tap this tax source. But it is also true that the export tax introduced an element of inequality: cotton and coffee growers became subject to a rather heavy tax burden while the producers of other crops and livestock paid no similar tax.

A similar practical conclusion is advanced for most developing countries:

> For an underdeveloped country that is seriously trying to achieve economic progress, the requirements for investible funds and government revenue seem certain to outstrip the supply except in those countries which have large earnings from petroleum or mineral exports or particularly favorable access to foreign capital. The sheer size of the agricultural sector in an underdeveloped country points to its importance as a source of capital for over-all economic growth. (Johnston and Mellor, p. 348.)

It is now generally agreed that marketing boards and *caisses de stabilisation* should be regarded as multi-purpose institutions, not merely as stabilization devices. In general, the stabilization sought is of the national income, not necessarily of the price paid to producers. In some cases, it is possible to act to stabilize the national income by using the marketing board resources elsewhere than to increase prices to producers. The boards also perform useful technical and commercial services for the small farmers, protect them against collusive buying by middlemen, and often finance effective technical aids to production.

Selected Bibliography

ALLEN, W. *The African Husbandman*. New York: Barnes & Noble, 1965.

CLAUSON, G. *Communal Land Tenure*. (Agricultural Studies No. 17.) Rome: Food and Agriculture Organization, 1953.

DUMONT, R. *Afrique Noire, Développement Agricole*. Paris: Presses universitaires de France, 1962.

———. *False Start in Africa*. London: Andre Deutsch; New York: Frederick A. Praeger, 1966.

EAST AFRICA ROYAL COMMISSION. *1953–55 Report*. (Cmd. 9475.) London: H. M. Stationery Office, 1955.

The Economic Development of Nigeria. Baltimore, Md.: The Johns Hopkins Press, for the International Bank for Reconstruction and Development, 1955.

The Economic Development of Uganda. Baltimore, Md.: The Johns Hopkins Press, for the International Bank for Reconstruction and Development, 1962.

FRANKEL, S. H. "The Tyranny of Economic Paternalism in Africa," supplement to *Optima* (Johannesburg), December, 1960.

GAITSKELL, A. *Gezira*. London: Faber & Faber, 1959.

GOUROU, P. *Les Pays Tropicaux*. Paris: Presses universitaires de France, 1947.

HELLEINER, G. K. "The Fiscal Role of the Marketing Boards in Nigerian Economic Development 1947–1961," *The Economic Journal*, LXXIV, No. 295 (September, 1964), 582–610.

JAVABU, N. *Drawn in Colour*. London: John Murray, 1960; New York: St. Martin's Press, 1962.

JOHNSTON, B. F. "The Choice of Measures for Increasing Agricultural Productivity: A Survey of Possibilities in East Africa," *Tropical Agriculture* (London: Butterworths, for University of West Indies), XLI, No. 2 (April, 1964), 91–113.

JOHNSTON, B. F., and MELLOR, J. W. "The Nature of Agriculture's Contribution to Economic Development," *Food Research Institute Studies* (Stanford University), I, No. 3 (November, 1960).

JONES, W. O. "Food and Agricultural Economics of Tropical Africa," *Food Research Institute Studies*, II, No. 1 (February, 1961).

———. "Increasing Agricultural Productivity in Tropical Africa." Paper presented at Nyasaland Economic Symposium, 1962. Mimeo.

LA RUUE, E. A. DE, BOURLIÈRE, FRANÇOIS, and HARROZ, J. P. *The Tropics*. New York: Alfred A. Knopf, 1957.

LEE, D. H. K. *Climate and Economic Development in the Tropics*. New York: Harper & Bros., for the Council on Foreign Relations, 1957.

MCKELVEY, J. J., JR. "Agricultural Research," in R. A. LYSTAD (ed.),

The African World: A Survey of Social Research. New York: Frederick A. Praeger, 1965. Pp. 317–51.

MASEFIELD, G. B. "Agricultural Changes in Uganda: 1945–1960," *Food Research Institute Studies,* III, No. 2 (May, 1962), 87–124.

PHILLIPS, J. *Agriculture and Ecology in Africa: A Study of Actual and Potential Development South of the Sahara.* London: Faber & Faber, 1959; New York: Frederick A. Praeger, 1960.

——. "Certain Criteria for Application to Large-Scale Irrigation Projects in the Developing Countries." Unpublished paper, 1965.

——. *The Development of Agriculture and Forestry in the Tropics: Patterns, Problems, and Promise.* London: Faber & Faber; New York: Frederick A. Praeger, 1961.

"A Plan for the Mechanized Production of Groundnuts in East and Central Africa." (Cmd. 7030.) London: H.M. Stationery Office, 1947.

POGUCKI, R. J. H. *Land Tenure in Ghana.* Accra: Lands Department, 1957.

RAEBURN, J. R. "Some Economic Aspects of African Agriculture," *The East African Economic Review,* V, No. 2 (January, 1959), 45.

SCHROO, H. "The Three Pillars of Agriculture in the Tropics," reprinted as "Soil Fertility" in *Weekly News* (Nairobi), No. 2005 (July 17, 1964), pp. 40–41.

THOMPSON, V., and ADLOFF, R. *The Emerging States of French Equatorial Africa.* Stanford, Calif.: Stanford University Press; London: Oxford University Press, 1960.

VAN DER HORST, S. T. "Africans on the Land," review article, *The South African Journal of Economics* (Johannesburg), XXXIII, No. 3 (September, 1965), 237–47.

WICKIZER, V. D. "The Smallholder in Tropical Export Crop Production," *Food Research Institute Studies,* I, No. 7 (February, 1960).

WILDE, J. C. DE. *Experiences with Agricultural Development in Tropical Africa.* Baltimore, Md.: The Johns Hopkins Press, for the International Bank for Reconstruction and Development, to be published 1967.

WORTHINGTON, E. B. *Science in the Development of Africa.* London: CCTA and Scientific Council for Africa South of the Sahara, 1958.

YUDELMAN, M. *Africans on the Land.* Cambridge, Mass.: Harvard University Press, 1964.

VI

Mineral Development

*The dynamite works get into production and deliver to
the miners who blast, the mule drivers, engineers and
firemen on the dinkies, the pumpmen, the rope riders,
the sinkers and sorters, the carpenters, electricians and
repairmen, the foremen and straw-bosses,*

*They get out the ore and send it to the smelters, the
converters where by the hands and craft of furnace
crushers and hot blast handlers, ladlers, puddlers,
the drag-out man, the hook-up man, the chipper, the
spannerman, the shearsman, the squeezer,*

*There is steel for the molders, the cutlers, buffers,
finishers, forgers, grinders, polishers, temperers—*

*This is for the sake of a jack-knife in your pocket or
a shears on your table.*

CARL SANDBURG, The People, Yes

The exploitation of mineral resources has been and will probably
continue to be, for at least the next decade, the only rapid way open
to some African countries to bypass the slow and laborious process
of economic growth through agricultural development. (In Chapter
VII, I shall attempt to demonstrate why industrialization in most
of Africa will probably also continue to be slow and halting, especially in the countries that do not have mineral resources.) Under
present conditions in Africa, only through the development of min-

131

eral resources can a state multiply its export earnings, national income, and government revenues within a few years.

In general, a successful new mining complex requires bulk transport facilities, and leads to new railways being built, which, while not so efficient as highways in opening up new country, do provide transport facilities that help agricultural producers to find a way to markets. Further, the export of minerals requires a port, to which general cargo wharves can be added and other exports thereby promoted. Mines also require an infrastructure of other public services: the Kariba power project on the Zambezi River, built in the late 1950's and completed by 1960, was necessary at that particular stage because of the growing demand for power from the Zambian copper belt, which could no longer be met economically by thermal plants burning imported coal from Southern Rhodesia or America. Mines provide, lastly, an enclave of modern technology in the empty spaces of Africa where Africans can be trained, learn to improve their productivity, and move into the machine civilization.

If large enough, the mining sector is often an effective leading or propulsive sector of the economy: it provides a direct demand for manufactured products: the incomes it generates stimulate demand for consumer goods; and, through the multiplier process, it tends to raise output and incomes generally in the economy. In some cases, mining groups not only engage in the industrial processes of mining proper, like refining, but move on into other industries. (In Australia, the iron and steel producer BHP was initially a mining concern. When its zinc mine ran out, BHP looked around for something else in which to invest its organization and capital, and, deciding that Australia was ready for a modern iron and steel industry, set to work to create one—now among the most economic in the world.) In Zambia, the British South Africa Company (BSA), the Anglo-American Corporation, and the Roan Selection Trust joined to finance and subsidize the first modern (and first tolerable) hotel in the capital city of Lusaka as a means to encourage other foreign investors. BSA also financed several trucking concerns. In Rhodesia, Anglo-American was involved in creating a fertilizer industry and a ferro-chrome industry.

The modern economic development of South Africa was, of course, sparked by the discovery of its mineral wealth—beginning with the discoveries of diamonds at Kimberley in 1867 and of gold on the Witwatersrand in 1886. Mining required, and the income derived from mining made possible, the railways that opened up the whole country; financed the government and its aid to agriculture; provided the market and stimulus for industrialization; and earned most of the foreign-exchange income of the country. Even though today mining is no longer South Africa's dominant economic activity, it still earns the foreign exchange to pay for the imported machinery, fuel, and raw materials that South African manufacturing requires.

In Zambia, the output of the copper, lead, and zinc mines, valued at around $400 million a year, furnishes about half the Gross Domestic Product; the mines provide almost all the exports and nearly three-quarters the government revenue to finance both current and capital expenditures. The Congo (Léopoldville) also now produces about $400 million of minerals a year; Nigeria, $200 million; Liberia, $150 million; Southern Rhodesia, Ghana, Sierra Leone, and Mauritania, $50–$80 million. In Mauritania, the new Miferma iron-ore mine is such a large part of the economy that in 1962, when its development was at its height, gross investment was at the absurdly high level of 70 per cent of GDP! Angola, Gabon, and Tanganyika produce $20–$30 million a year, and Kenya, Uganda, Rwanda, and Swaziland about $10 million.

Obviously, not all countries can use mining as a propulsive sector. This depends first and foremost on having and finding exploitable minerals; second, in exploiting them; and, finally, in ensuring that the general development of the country benefits as much as possible from the mineral development.

Unfortunately, even though there is still much to learn about the geology of Africa, it is already certain that the useful mineral deposits are unevenly distributed—some countries are likely to be very fortunate and some comparatively poor in mineral resources. Apart from South Africa, already a success story in this regard, Gabon and Nigeria clearly possess the mineral potential that, if used wisely, makes successful and rapid economic development possible. Gabon already possesses manganese and uranium mines under exploitation; oil output is expected to reach 2.5 million tons by about 1968; and the very rich Mekambo iron-ore deposits will sooner or later prove economic. Oil wells in Nigeria are now rapidly being drilled and brought into production. From a negligible oil output in 1958, output reached 4 million tons in 1963, 6 million in 1965, 13 million in 1966; 18 million are forecast for 1967, and around 40 million for 1970. Nigeria's large natural-gas resources have not yet found a market but will certainly do so. Then there are other nations whose mineral production, while not so spectacular as Gabon's or Nigeria's, still provides a solid volume of export earnings as a developmental base: Mauritania, Guinea, Sierra Leone, Liberia, Congo (Léopoldville), Zambia, Angola, and Rhodesia. Ghana could move into this group if she does not frighten off possibilities of exploitation of her bauxite deposits; she now exports manganese, diamonds, and, in a somewhat less solid position, gold.

The Search for and Exploitation of Minerals

By now, the major features of the geology of Africa are known, but, aside from a few areas like the Witwatersrand in South Africa and the Katanga-Zambia copper belt, most of the continent has not been investigated in great detail. In any case, mineral wealth is hard to assess even in areas (like the United States) where a very great deal is known about the geology—as the experience of the 1950's showed, in the many discoveries made of rich uranium deposits feasible for mining that occurred when a determined effort was made by governments to encourage prospecting for that element. And the chances of finding minerals have been increased in recent years with the improvement in prospecting methods due to new techniques of geophysics and geochemistry. These are particularly important in Africa, where direct geological research is difficult and expensive, due to the forest cover or the sand or laterite overburden in many areas.

The "mineral solution" to development in any one area of Africa should not be ruled out of hand. While blind optimism is foolish, one can also go far wrong in being pessimistic about mineral resources, as can be seen in the following remark from a book written in 1952 by a deservedly noted geographer: "The conditions favoring the accumulation of oil in quantity, in folds among the sedimentary rocks on the margins of great sedimentary basins, do not exist in

Africa." Within ten years, oil wells in the northern Sahara were producing 51 million tons of oil annually, and production is now over 100 million tons! And south of the Sahara (mostly in Nigeria, Gabon, and Angola), oil output is expected to reach around 50 million tons by 1970, conceivably 100 million tons by 1975. Quite clearly, the chances of finding a particular mineral vary from area to area—oil is not likely to be found in the Pre-Cambrian rocks of inland Cameroon, or a diamond pipe in the Niger Delta. But, as the demand for particular minerals grows in the world, there is a good chance that different regions of Africa will be discovered to possess minerals sought in economically exploitable quantities and conditions.

Whether a particular deposit is "exploitable" or not depends on the economics of its possible use. The iron mountains near Fort Goraud, in Mauritania, have been known since the 1920's but were uneconomic to exploit until the 1950's. A 1962–66 World Bank study (financed by the U.N. Special Fund) on the transport costs of getting iron ore from the mountains of eastern Gabon to the sea will determine whether the Mekambo deposit is presently exploitable or not. Again, developments during World War II and after, when techniques of moving large volumes of materials at low cost were revolutionized, have improved Africa's chances. Materials that once could not be feasibly mined because of prohibitive costs of transport are now able to compete. (These techniques are applicable not only to Africa. For example, in the last few years they have made it possible to open up vast new iron-ore deposits for exploitation in the vast wastelands of western Australia.)

The combination of improved methods in prospecting and in exploitation have underlined the fact that there is no such thing as an absolute scarcity of mineral resources in the world; there are only costs involved in finding exploitable new deposits. All the continents of the world have many usable mineral resources. All other things being equal, which deposit in which continent is developed will depend first on which is known, and on the general environment in which the mining operation will have to take place. High on any government's list of economic priorities, therefore, should be continuing study of and search for minerals.

There is little justification for the theory governments express occasionally that exploitation of a mineral resource should be held back on the ground that it is "a wasting asset." When there are so many possibilities of finding a good mineral deposit elsewhere in the world, a government or company that sits on a resource too long may find in the end that it has no value. By the time it was finally decided to exploit the Tonkolili iron-ore deposit, in Sierra Leone, for example, it was no longer feasible—other iron-ore deposits in Africa and Australia had been discovered in the meantime that were much more economic. If South Africa had hesitated in 1950 and 1951 to make contracts to sell its uranium from the gold-mine tailings, she would have never succeeded in doing so, since interest in them would have vanished as richer resources were discovered in North America. With modern technology, moreover, it is always possible that some invention or process will alter the whole economics of an industry, and of the kind and quality of raw materials it needs. If a resource is already being exploited, it may be able to continue to compete; if it is not, interest in it may disappear.

Before the search for minerals can begin, there are certain prerequisites that must be filled. The nation must have appropriate mineral-resources legislation which provides security to the mining enterprises, exploration incentives, and a suitable institutional framework. It is useless to invite prospectors into the country if, when they wish to follow a promising lead, they have to negotiate with every petty chief to get access to the land.

Aside from these conditions, and aside from direct government support of research on the country's basic geological structure and mineral wealth, an important contribution can in many cases be made by the mining companies themselves and by individual prospectors. The creation of conditions encouraging both prospectors and the large mining companies to search for minerals is often the best line of action for governments to take. This is shown by the cases of Canada, Australia, and South Africa.

In fact, a government that can capture the interest of one of the large mining companies or groups in its country has an asset of great value. Any mining group will give priority in its search for minerals to the country where it is already operating, to take advantage of economies of scale for the existing organization. And a routine part of the on-going mine operations is the continuous establishment of new reserves by drilling, which often results in the discovery of new minerals as well as in additions to the knowledge of the country's geology. Finally, while there are certainly outstanding exceptions, the large mining companies or groups nowadays are in the main very conscious of their responsibility to aid in every way in the development of the countries in which they operate. This does not mean that hard bargaining with them is no longer necessary, but it pays off best when coupled with the recognition that most of these groups are willing to go beyond their immediate economic interests to help the national development. The initiatives taken by the Roan Selection Trust group of companies in Zambia to finance agricultural research on the Kafue flats; in breaking the color bar in the mines; in making, together with the Anglo-American Corporation, what was in essence a grant contribution of $28 million toward the financing of the Kariba power project as well as a large loan of $56 million for the same purpose; and in financing secondary school construction in the Copper Belt—these are all examples of an enlightened policy a government can hope to encourage.

The large mining groups are in addition an important channel for bringing foreign capital into Africa. The international private capital markets have largely dried up for Africa. (See below, chap. IX.) The one section of the investment community that is still willing to take risks is that composed of the mining investors. The international groups that have entered Africa, particularly since World War II, are among the most important in the world; maintaining their interest in the future development of Africa, as against other continents, should be among the top economic-policy priorities of African governments. This is a matter of economic pragmatism and not of ideology. Most African governments have been well aware of this: the lead was in fact taken by such ideologically sensitive leaders as Sekou Touré in Guinea and Nkrumah in Ghana, who encouraged aluminum producers to invest in the development of their resources.

Also, as noted earlier, a mining group often will branch out into other activities. And the indirect influence of these mining complexes must also not be underrated. Their educational value, in affecting Africans moving from an age-old subsistence agriculture into a world of modern technology, is bound to be profound.

(While small mining operations do exist in Africa, in general, as seems to be true of other underdeveloped areas, profitable mining evidently requires large mining groups. This is probably due to the fact that mineral deposits in Africa are usually found far from the coast or in such difficult terrain that only a large-scale operation has hopes of making a go of the enterprise.)

A major problem in the exploitation of any African nation's mineral resources nevertheless continues to be the negotiation of the terms with the mining group or groups involved. While most mining corporations may take a long-term view of their interests and be conscious of the need to give a fair share of the benefits to the country concerned, this does not obviate the need for hard bargaining on the part of the government. All mining groups are not equally enlightened, for one thing. In any case, a government that drives a hard bargain is not so repelling to potential investors as one that does not keep its side of a bargain once it is made and harasses a concern by changing the conditions under which it must operate.

The African countries now have at their disposal a variety of aids in their negotiations that were not available or as easily accessible in earlier eras. A study of a proposed project by the U.N. Development Program (formerly Special Fund) or World Bank (granted under certain circumstances, e.g., possible World Bank participation in the financing) can provide a completely objective analysis of the project, including the basic financial parameters involved. The World Bank study of the Volta Project, for example, gave a basis for Ghana's negotiations with private aluminum companies on the smelter they were to build to use power from the Volta Project—analyzing as it did what the financial impact would be of different sizes of smelter, different rates charged for the power, etc. And the World Bank also advises on matters such as whether a consulting firm a country is thinking of appointing is suitable. There are also other sources of such help: an oil-producing country can take advantage of the technical information that has been acquired by the Organization of Petroleum Exporting Countries (OPEC) over the years; the Economic Commission for Africa and the United Nations have both made comparative studies of mining legislation in various countries.

In short, there is no reason why an African government confronted with a large international mining group need feel handicapped. A government should be able to secure the full benefits available to it from mineral exploitation and need have no inferiority complex about or resentment against "enclave investment."

Africa's Minerals

In the past, the main African minerals of any economic importance were gold and diamonds. Indeed, gold—an African export since time immemorial—has become more and more a primarily *African* commodity. South Africa's share of world production outside the Soviet Union has been steadily increasing and was, by 1966, at $1 billion a year, about 65 per cent. (The Soviet Union, the world's second largest producer, may have an output of $200–$300 million— far below that of South Africa.) Rhodesia, Ghana, and the Congo (Léopoldville) together produce under $100 million. Africa also produces 95 per cent of the world's diamonds—Brazil and the Soviet Union being the only other significant producers. Diamonds are a leading South African export, and the South African de Beers Company, with its related companies, still controls the world diamond-selling monopoly. Diamonds are Sierra Leone's main export and a significant one for the Congo (Léopoldville), Ghana, South West Africa, and Angola. They also figure in the export earnings of other countries such as Tanzania, Guinea, and the Central African Republic.

Copper became an important African export between the wars. It is now the main export (with around 800,000 tons a year) of Zambia, second only to the United States in production, and is also important in the Congo (Léopoldville), which produces more than 300,000 tons. Uganda's copper output, only about 2 per cent of Zambia's, is still its most important mineral export. Among other minerals, most of the world's cobalt comes from the Congo, Zambia, and Morocco; manganese from Ghana, South Africa, Congo (Léopoldville), and Gabon, which provides about one-fifth the world's supply; half the world's chrome ore, one-third of vanadium ore, and one-fifth of its asbestos come from South Africa and Rhodesia. The uranium for the world's first atomic bombs came from a mine in Katanga which has since been exhausted. South Africa was an important world producer of uranium from gold-mine tailings during the 1950's but has since decreased in importance as lower-cost sources were found in the United States and Canada, Gabon is probably the main source for France's uranium at the present time. Africa is also believed to have some 60 per cent of the world's thorium reserves (of over 0.01 per cent oxide content)—mainly in South Africa, Madagascar, Malawi, Nigeria, and East Africa.

One African mineral that has recently become of major significance is iron, which became economically important after World War II as the steel industries in Europe and America outran their raw-material base. Before World War II, the United States was self-sufficient. Now, with its highest-grade ores used up, it must look to Canada, Latin America, and Africa for at least one-quarter of its present consumption. In Europe, Great Britain has depended on imported ore since the 1930's; the Common Market countries used to be self-sufficient, but by 1960, they were importing 28 per cent of their total consumption, by 1965, 40 per cent.

Iron-ore deposits have been known, mined, and processed into iron in Africa for centuries. Most of the large, economically exploitable deposits of today were discovered in the last fifty years and, with the markets opening up for them, large-scale mining began essentially after World War II, with the major expansion in the 1960's. A brief account of the development of some of these may bring out more clearly the pattern mineral development in Africa takes.

Iron ore was discovered in West Africa about sixty years ago near Conakry, in Guinea, during the building of the Niger railway. Systematic study of the deposits was made before World War I and after, but the ore, with less than 50 per cent iron content, could not be exploited and marketed economically until the 1950's. Under a million tons a year is now exported from the port of Conakry (which can only take ships of under 25,000 tons). In Sierra Leone, iron ore of 56 per cent iron content, was discovered by the government's Geological Department at Marampa, within forty miles of Freetown, one of the best natural harbors in Africa (which can handle ships of 35,000 to 40,000 tons). It was therefore economic to exploit, and in 1933, the Sierra Leone Development Company, formed by private Scottish investors (Baird's) to develop the deposit, became the first exporter of iron ore from West Africa. The mine now has a capacity of more than 2.5 million tons a year. Another deposit, Tonkolili, about 100 miles from the sea, has ore of around 56 per cent iron content but with high moisture and alumina content. After an intensive study, the company concluded in 1962 that the competition from better ores in other African countries would not allow an economic return on the $90 million or so that would be required to build the railway and ore-mining installations necessary.

In Liberia, the Bomi Hills deposit was first reconnoitered in the 1930's by Dutch interests, they could not find sufficient financial backing to undertake development. In 1944, the U.S. Geological Survey, working with the Liberian Government, thoroughly explored the deposit, and in 1949, L. K. Christie, who founded the Liberian Mining Company to develop the deposit, got the needed support from the Republic Steel Corporation to begin mining. Three other deposits were also explored and are now being exploited by other interests.

The largest and, now, most important of these is the LAMCO–Joint Venture, exploiting the Mount Nimba deposits, which lie at the point where Liberia, Guinea, and the Ivory Coast meet 170 miles from the sea. The deposits go across the border into Guinea. LAMCO–Joint Venture, with an investment so far of around $300 million, is the largest single mining project undertaken in Africa up to the present time. The project is financed by a partnership of the large Swedish company Grängesberg (75 per cent of the total) and Bethlehem Steel (the remaining 25 per cent). In 1955, the Swedish Government had bought Grängesberg's holdings in the Swedish Lapland iron-ore mines and Grängesberg, looking around for a new source of iron ore and having the money to invest, came to Africa. The LAMCO project includes the development of the mine (with known ore reserves of about 250 million tons of around 66 per cent iron content), construction of a U.S. standard-gauge railway (4'6", compared to Africa's standard gauge of 3'6"), and the artificial harbor and port of Buchanan (which can handle 60,000-ton ships). LAMCO is currently planning to build a $50-million plant at Buchanan to concentrate the ore further into pellets before export. In 1966, the capacity of the Nimba mine was raised to 10 million tons a year. With the other mines, Liberia's total iron-ore exports in 1966 are thus expected to be around 17 million tons, making it the largest producer in Africa and the third largest exporter in the world.

Other important African iron producers are Mauritania, with an output in 1966 of roughly 6.5 million tons, Guinea, Senegal, Angola, and Swaziland. Rhodesia converts its iron ore into pig iron for export and sells it mainly to Japan. Tunisia, Algeria, and Morocco have also been exporting ore for years. Altogether, Africa now exports around 35 million tons of iron ore annually, and provides from one-fifth to one-quarter of Western Europe's iron-ore supplies.

Of the other African countries, the most important *potential* iron-ore exporter is Gabon, with its Mekambo deposit of around 800 million tons of proven ore of 60 per cent or higher iron content. This deposit is, however, 400 miles from the sea, near the border with the Central African Republic; the magnitude of the investment required, and the engineering problems of building a railway from the deposits to the coast, across the whole jungle width of Gabon, will undoubtedly delay exploitation until well into the 1970's. Guinea has two large deposits but also well inland—one in the Mount Nimba area, which might be developed in conjunction with the Liberian one. Undeveloped iron-ore deposits are also present in Ghana, which may become accessible with the creation of the new Volta Project lake; Nigeria, where plans are under way to use them for a domestic industry; Dahomey, Mali, Niger, Togo, Cameroon, Congo (Brazzaville), Zambia, Tanzania, Somalia, Ethiopia, and the Sudan. Most of these are still insufficiently proven, have too low iron content, or are still too inaccessible to good harbors to be serious contenders for development over the next five to ten years.

It must be remembered, however, that since World War II, the search for new sources of iron ore has not been restricted to Africa. Canada has become a major exporter to the United States and Great Britain. Both Brazil and Venezuela have also become large-scale exporters. And, within the last few years, billions of tons of high-iron-content ore have been found in western Australia. These finds have coincided with the continued trend to huge super-ore carriers of upwards of 100,000 tons, which, if ports can take them at both ends of their voyage, reduce the cost of transport so much that Australian ores may be able to compete effectively in any market. To stand up to Australia's competition, the African ores may also have to be transported in the huge ships, which means added large investments to create the necessary harbors and ports. In this connection, Australia's proven political stability gives her an intangible advantage which may weigh heavily with corporation managers who must decide where they should commit hundreds of millions of dollars in one sizable lump of investment.

The mining of bauxite, the raw material for aluminum, the fastest growing nonferrous metal in consumption, is another potentially very important African industry. For, so far as is known, Africa has the largest and best unexploited reserves of bauxite in the world. (At the current rate of use, known bauxite reserves in the Western Hemisphere may be exhausted within twenty or thirty years. There are possibilities of more reserves in the Western Hemisphere, and large reserves, competitive with those of Africa, have been staked out in the last few years in northern Queensland, in Australia. Nevertheless, Africa remains in a favorable competitive position, all else being equal.) In addition, Africa possesses the greatest and most economic unutilized hydro-electric potential in the world. (See below, chap. VIII, p. 177.) With sufficient political stability, she therefore has the basis for one of the world's largest centers for aluminum production.

At present, bauxite ore is exported from Guinea, Sierra Leone, and Ghana; and in Guinea, the first stage in the process of transforming bauxite into aluminum has been developed for some years, with a large plant at Fria, in operation since 1956, converting bauxite into alumina at a rate of 500,000 tons of alumina a year. In Edea, in Cameroon, the first aluminum smelter in Africa is already producing 50,000 tons of aluminum annually. In Ghana, an aluminum smelter owned by the American Kaiser and Reynolds companies with an initial capacity of around 115,000 tons should begin production in April, 1967, using electric power from the Volta Project. It will be the biggest smelter in the world outside North America.

Production of phosphate for fertilizer in Africa is also important—until recently, mostly in North Africa: in Morocco (the world's second largest producer, at 9 million tons a year) and Tunisia. Since World War II, rich deposits in Togo, have been developed and more than 500,000 tons were exported in 1965, making phosphate one of Togo's main exports. Senegal has also become an important exporter. Rich deposits have also been discovered in the Spanish Sahara (estimated at over 1 billion tons), and plans for full-scale exploitation have been made for 1968–69, if the $200 million needed to build a railway, port, etc., can be found. Rich potash deposits have also been found in the Congo (Brazzaville) in the course of a search for oil. Exploitable potash deposits are known in few countries of the world (mainly the United States and France), and the growing need for it in fertilizer production means that there could be a bright future for the Congolese deposits.

African Mining Companies

The important mining groups operating in Africa are still few, most of them are in southern Africa, where mineral development first occurred on the continent. The richest of these groups is probably the Anglo-American Corporation of South Africa, Ltd. Anglo-American is mostly owned in South Africa and the United Kingdom; American shareholdings are negligible. It has large interests in gold and coal mines and in electrical manufacturing and chemicals in South Africa; it manages the Wankie coal mine in Rhodesia and has some industrial interests there too; in Zambia, it controls the lead and zinc output at Broken Hill and more than 60 per cent of the output of the copper belt. In partnership with Imperial Chemicals, Anglo-American owns the largest explosives manufacturer in the world—African Explosives. Anglo-American is also closely associated with de Beers, the diamond monopoly interests of South Africa marketing the bulk of the world's diamonds, which also has an interest in and manages the Williamson diamond mine in Tanzania.

The Roan Selection Trust (RST) controls the mines producing the other 40 per cent of Zambia's copper. RST is largely owned by American, British, and French investors; American Metal Climax (AMAX) of New York is the largest shareholder. AMAX also has interests in Tsumeb, a lead-zinc mine in South-West Africa and, along with other companies, in the new Palabora copper mine being developed in the Transvaal.

The British South Africa Company, organized by Cecil Rhodes, which administered both the Rhodesias until 1923 and 1924, continued to own all the mineral rights in Zambia to the eve of that country's independence in October, 1964. It continues to have interests in some of the other mining operations in the former Rhodesias, and in some industrial and transport companies. It is closely allied with Anglo-American through having some important directors and stockholders in common.

Tanganyika Concessions, Ltd., which has nothing to do with Tanganyika, was organized in 1889 and was given the right systematically to prospect the Katanga. When Union Minière du Haut-Katanga was organized in 1906, it was a pooling of the interests of Tanganyika Concessions, the Société Générale of Belgium (Belgium's leading financial group), and the Comité Spéciale du Katanga (the concessionaire group which had been given the right to administer the Katanga by the Congo Free State). Tanganyika Concessions now owns about 15 per cent of Union Minière and 90 per cent of the Benguela Railway Company, which owns the rail line that runs from Katanga through Angola to the sea. Among its major stockholders are understood to be Anglo-American, the Société Générale, the Belgian Banque Lambert group, and Lazard Frères of France.

The principal interests in Katanga are all, then, closely associated with the Société Générale through the latter's shareholdings and financial guidance in the Union Minière, Forminière (the foremost producer of industrial diamonds in the world), and the BCK (Bas Congo–Katanga) Railway, which serves the Katanga and the power companies. The main shareholders of Union Minière—which produces around 300,000 tons of copper, 8,000 tons of cobalt, 180,000 tons of zinc concentrates, and various other metals in smaller quantities such as cadmium, germanium, etc.—are the Democratic Republic of the Congo, which now owns 18 per cent of the shares and has a voting power of 24.5 per cent, Tanganyika Concessions, the Société Générale, and the Katanga Company. (*The Economist* [London], June 19, 1965, p. 1453.)

The Consolidated African Selection Trust and its sister company, African Selection Trust, own the diamond mines in Ghana and Sierra Leone. They are related to RST in Zambia through the British Selection Trust (organized by Sir Chester Beatty), as well as to the Tsumeb Corporation in South West Africa, AMAX, Bikita Minerals (lithium) in Rhodesia, and several gold-mining ventures in South Africa.

Union Carbide, an American concern, operates chrome mines in Rhodesia and the manganese mine in Ghana. Other large American iron, steel, and aluminum companies have an interest in African minerals. Republic Steel has interests in the Liberian Mining Company. Bethlehem is not only part of the group exploiting the Mount Nimba deposits in Liberia but holds interests in the eventual development of the Mekambo deposits in Gabon. U.S. Steel is a principal shareholder (with French interests [Mokta-el-Hadid] and the French Government's Bureau Minier, charged with mineral exploration and development in Africa) in the Comilog manganese mine in Gabon.

Of American aluminum companies, Kaiser and Reynolds are owners (90 per cent and 10 per cent, respectively) of the large new Valco aluminum smelter in Ghana; Olin Mathiesson is a partner in the 500,000-ton Fria alumina plant in Guinea (responsible for some two-thirds of Guinea's total foreign-exchange earnings); and Harvey Aluminum has the concession for the rich Boke bauxite deposits in Guinea originally held by Aluminium Ltd. of Canada through its French affiliate, Bauxites du Midi. The large French aluminum concern Pechiney is also a partner in Fria, as well as the owner of the first aluminum plant constructed in Africa, the 50,000-ton smelter at Edea, in Cameroon.

Selected Bibliography

COLLIER, J. L. "West Africa and Its Iron Ore: the Present and the Future." Unpublished paper, School of Advanced International Studies, Johns Hopkins University, 1966.

KIMBLE, G. H. T. "The Mineral Realm," in Tropical Africa. New York: The Twentieth Century Fund, 1960. Pp. 289–370.

KUN, N. DE. "The Mineral Resources of Africa. Amsterdam: Elsevier, 1965.

McKINNON, D. "Minerals, the Key to Progress in Africa," Optima (Johannesburg), XIII, No. 2 (June, 1963), 73–81.

MOUSSA, P. Les Chances économiques de la Communauté franco-africaine. Paris: Colin, 1957.

OSTRANDER, F. T. "The Place of Minerals in Economic Development." Address to the Council of Economics, American Institute of Mining, Metallurgical and Petroleum Engineers, Dallas, Texas, February 27, 1963.

OSTRANDER, F. T., and KLOMAN, E. "The Corporate Structure of Rhodesian Copperbelt Mining Enterprise." Unpublished paper, August 31, 1962.

PRAIN, SIR RONALD. "Copper and its Place in the World," *Horizon* (publication of Roan Selection Trust), April, 1964, pp. 22–28.

PRÉ, R. "Problems of the African Mining Economy," in E. A. G. ROBINSON (ed.), *Economic Development for Africa South of the Sahara.* London: Macmillan, 1964. Pp. 588–608.

A *Review of the Natural Resources of the African Continent.* Paris: UNESCO, 1963.

STAMP, L. D. *Africa. A Study in Tropical Development.* New York: John Wiley; London: Chapman & Hall, 1953.

WOLFE, A. W. " 'The Team' Rules Mining in Southern Africa," *Toward Freedom* (Chicago), XI, No. 7 (January, 1962), 1–3.

VII

Industrialization

Aside from the Republic of South Africa, no African country has taken more than the first steps leading to industrialization. South Africa, however, already produces a quarter of its GNP in manufacturing, and the addition of mining, which is also highly mechanized, brings the total to around 40 per cent. She is, in fact, beginning to move into the final stages of industrialization—the production of capital goods and equipment for her industries. Insofar as such comparisons are valid, she is now at roughly the same stage of development as Italy was before World War II. Like the Italy of that period, but even more so, she still has large sections of her population that derive little benefit from the modern economy.

Outside of South Africa, only Rhodesia, Kenya, and the Congo have as much as 10 per cent of GNP derived from industry. These are essentially the countries that had a large inflow of private foreign direct investment and non-African technicians into industry after World War II. All the rest, including Senegal and Ivory Coast (which also have had sizable inflows of private foreign investment), Cameroon, Ghana, and Uganda (which have made good beginnings in industry) still show less than 5 per cent of GNP derived from industry. In Nigeria, where a sizable list of enterprises can be drawn up, industry's contribution to GNP has been in the neighborhood of 1 per cent.

Although industry plays a relatively unimportant part of total

GNP, in many countries there are already a number of small enterprises of many kinds. These include, first of all, food-processing industries producing for the local market: flour mills, bakeries, soft-drink plants, breweries, and even distilleries. Building materials are produced in most countries—bricks, cement, window-frames, paint, etc. Shoes, cigarettes, textiles, and other consumer goods typical of the first stage of industrialization are also widely produced in West Africa—in Senegal, Ghana, and Nigeria, for example.

The impact of the automotive industry has been felt throughout Africa. Among the first industries to be considered feasible in many countries are tire re-treading and the making of simple spare automobile parts. And, as the number of motor vehicles has increased, it has begun to be economic to import them in components and to have the final stage of assembly in the country. Truck-assembly plants have opened in Ghana and Nigeria, for example, and automobile assembly plants in Rhodesia, Zambia, and Kenya.

Then too, with the growing markets for gasoline and oil, the large oil companies have become concerned to get a stake in them, although it is clear that for a long time to come not more than one oil refinery per country will be economically justifiable. The desire to be the company owning that one refinery is usually very strong and has tended to outweigh the consideration that, at present, hardly any African market outside of South Africa, Nigeria, and the East African common market is large enough to justify an economic size of refinery (roughly 1 million tons of annual through-put). Stimulated by the demands from the governments and the particular competition from Italy's government-owned oil company, E.N.I., the large international oil companies in the early 1960's raced to be the first to build the refineries—a race made possible by their large capital resources and their experience in coping with political risks in all parts of the world.

The result is that refineries have been built all around the coasts of Africa. In 1962, there were four refineries south of the Sahara, two of which were in South Africa; in 1965, there were eighteen built or under construction, fourteen outside of South Africa. Hardly any major port is without its refinery, usually one which is below the optimum minimum size. Still, only one (in Tanzania) was below 500,000 tons capacity, and, in most cases, the additional cost resulting from building a small refinery is not too great to be borne, given the long-term benefits that Africans will get from becoming trained in the refinery's highly technical and complex operation. For the oil companies, with long experience in operating and developing countries, have definite policies favoring local training and aid to local enterprises.

Small iron and steel mills have already been built in Rhodesia, Kenya, and Uganda; Nigeria is likely to have one before 1970. But the potentially most important African metal industry is aluminum. (See above, chap. VI, p. 143.) With an output of 50,000 tons in Edea, Cameroon, and a smelter of 115,000 tons in Ghana, Africa is just beginning to exploit its potential in this regard.

The Goal of Industrialization

The desire of most African governments to try to industrialize their nations as rapidly as possible is essentially well based. Unfortunately, the range of possibilities open in the immediate future is not very great. Industrialization lies a considerable distance off in the future for most African countries. But this does not obviate Africa's need to make as much progress toward this goal as possible. It is only in manufactured goods and services that human beings appear to have almost limitless wants; it is only in these fields, therefore, that nations can count on demand rising at the same pace with or faster than the rise in incomes—i.e., demand for manufactures is income elastic. Although these figures depend on many factors, it is significant that, from 1948 to 1962, while the value of exports of industrialized countries increased at an average rate of almost 7 per cent yearly, the value of underdeveloped countries' exports did only half as well, increasing at 3.5 per cent per year. One study on industrial growth and world trade concluded that, looking ahead to 1970–75, the developing countries' exports of primary products (other than oil) are unlikely to rise more than two-thirds as fast as the total real incomes of the industrial countries. (Maizels.) As income growth in the African countries in particular is closely related to export incomes, this means that the already large gap between their incomes and those of the industrial countries is likely to increase not only absolutely but relatively. (A widening absolute gap is inevitable in any case: a 1 per cent increase in American per-capita GNP is more than $30; if African per-capita incomes grew at a rate of 10 per cent a year, which they do not, this would be an increase of $10 [assuming a per-capita income of $100]. Even with a 10 per-cent increase in African per-capita income and a 1 per-cent increase in American incomes, the absolute gap would continue to widen yearly.)

African countries at present export mainly agricultural products, and most of these are foods—coffee, cocoa, bananas, edible oils. Over-all and in the long run, demand for food follows Engel's Law— that is, as income rises, the proportion of it spent on food declines. (As a rule of thumb, the long-term income elasticity of demand for primary foodstuffs can be taken as below 0.7.) Even within this context, there is considerable opportunity for some food producers to prosper. With a rise in income, demand for a "superior" food can be elastic over a considerable range, as consumption of it increases at the expense of an "inferior" food. That is, consumption of chocolate will increase at the expense of sugar candy, meat at the expense of potatoes or bread. There is also the possibility of changing habits or new habits resulting in an increase of consumption of a particular food occurring more rapidly than the increase in population or even income, e.g., the jump in the amount of coffee drunk in the United States when the coffee-break became a widespread habit during and after World War II. Again, if a nation is exporting a food with only a slowly growing demand, it can still, by winning a larger and larger part of the market, improve its GNP more rapidly than the over-all demand position for its products would seem to permit. And, in fact, many African countries since World War II have done just this—at the expense of Asian, particularly Indonesian, and Latin American producers of tropical products. Similarly in the nineteenth century, American development was greatly aided by American grain producers taking over much of the European market from European farmers.

But, while a country can do quite well for a considerable time by taking advantage of these possibilities, for the food producers as a group the fact remains that their over-all market position will ultimately hamper their attempts to improve their standards of living; certainly it will hamper them in any attempt to catch up and keep up with the developed countries.

Producers of industrial agricultural products—e.g., raw cotton—and minerals confront similar fundamental problems. Again, total demand for these products does not rise as rapidly as incomes in the industrialized societies. For one thing, while no one has expounded it as yet, there is an industrial law equivalent to Engel's Law, which would read: As the value of a particular manufactured product goes up with its further improvement, the proportion of total cost represented by the raw materials used tends to go down; in other words, the higher the price of a manufactured good, the more likely it is that the high price represents the cost of the manufacturing process or the value added to the raw-material components. The automobile or airplane of today uses more raw materials than that of yesterday, but the raw materials are a smaller fraction of the total cost.

Further, with the rise in incomes in industrialized societies, the proportion spent on services goes up, and services use little if any raw materials.

Another set of causes holding down the rate of increase of demand for raw materials stems from the progress of technology: many technological improvements are directed to economizing in the use of raw materials; another main objective is to produce inexpensive synthetic substitutes for raw materials. The process that made it possible to tin-plate steel with tin only a molecule thick, for example, prevented any substantial growth in the demand for tin for a good decade and more; synthetic fibers cut into the demand for cotton and wool, etc.

As in the case of the market for foods, these various factors bear unequally on different products and different countries. In particular, there is the possibility that an underdeveloped country can take the market for minerals away from a developed country as the latter's richest deposits are exhausted, become unable to meet the growth in demand, or even prove to be uncompetitive with newer and richer mines. The exhaustion of American and European iron-ore mines and their inability to meet growing demands, for example, has led to widespread interest in African iron ore in the last twenty years. This excellent possibility of winning away from the industrial countries a larger share of the growing market tends to make minerals in particular a potential propulsive sector for many countries in Africa.

Whatever the main product a country exports, however, whether food, agricultural raw materials, or minerals, that country is likely to find that its export earnings are far more vulnerable to price fluctuations than is the case with countries that sell a variety of industrial products. Even though there has been no major international depression since World War II, and though there is not much likelihood of there being one, prices of primary products have fluctuated much more than those of industrial products as a group. The Sudan, for example, found the prices of its exports dropping by almost 60 per cent in the period of 1956–58; Ethiopia's products dropped by 21 per cent in 1957–58. In 1962, the world's coffee producers sold a quantity of coffee half again as great as their 1954 sale, but their exchange earnings dropped by one-third. With the heavy reliance African economies now have on the export sector, the magnitude of such fluctuations presents major problems to the government and people. This alone is a powerful reason for trying to increase industrialization as much as is economically possible, so as to mitigate the vertiginous ups and downs in the economy.

Some theorists hold that, over the long run, terms of trade develop adversely against primary producing countries. But they usually overlook the fact that the quality of the industrial goods whose prices they are comparing over the period has changed. The price of an industrial good may have gone up, but the service it renders may be quite different from that formerly given by the commodity; i.e., a pound of copper now is essentially the same as a pound of copper was in 1914, but an automobile of today provides a more comfortable and carefree ride than the auto of 1914. The phonograph of today may cost more than the gramophone of yesteryear, but the music reproduction is infinitely superior. It is true that over most of the period since World War II, the terms of trade have tended to move adversely against the primary producers, but not in comparison to the pre-war period. From 1948 to 1962, for example, the *volume* of exports from underdeveloped countries increased by 4.5 per cent yearly, while the *value* increased by only 3.5 per cent yearly. Meanwhile, of course, the prices of the manufactured goods these countries purchased not only did not go down but in fact went up.

There is another series of reasons for favoring industrialization. As I have tried to make clear in earlier chapters, progress in agriculture is bound to be slow in Africa. Too much is still not known as to the best methods of improving tropical farming and of changing the attitudes and increasing the productivity of subsistence farmers. In industry, on the other hand, a great deal of the necessary skill and technology is easily transferable from the advanced countries to Africa: there is little real difference in the technical processes of textile manufacture between a factory in Europe or in Uganda. The catch is, of course, that this presupposes the use of or the importation of scarce entrepreneurial talent, skilled workers, and capital. Difficulties arise if reliance must be placed on the local supplies of these factors, which are very scarce or non-existent.

The Problems of Setting Up Industries

There are many self-reinforcing constraints on getting industries started in any underdeveloped country. Probably the most important and dangerous one is a market that is too small. Most of the nations of Africa have a monetary gross national expenditure of $200 million equivalent or less, and the per-capita money income is usually not more than $50–70; the size of the internal market is therefore quite restricted, and the amount and variety of goods bought are likewise limited. The kinds and sizes of industries that would have a sufficient market to justify consideration of establishing plants is therefore also very small. (This assumes that a new industry would be afforded the usual protection given to infant industries to allow them to get started, but also that the country would not impoverish itself by overprotecting industries that stand no reasonable chance of becoming viable and able to meet foreign competition.)

Now since the size of the market in most African countries depends primarily on the incomes of farmers, who make up the overwhelming mass of the population, it follows that, as stated by the Uganda Economic Development Committee in 1958, "the most effective steps which can be taken to secure development of manufacturing industry in Uganda, paradoxical though it may seem, are steps which will have the effect of increasing agricultural production. The committee *recommended* that Government's economic strategy should be determined accordingly." In a World Bank report of 1962 on the economic development of Uganda, the essence of the policy recommendations remained the same (although there was a subtle change in emphasis): that "everything that is administratively and economically feasible be done in the next five years to increase output in manufacturing, mining and agriculture. . . . It is quite obvious, however, that in spite of doing everything possible in manufacturing and mining, the main opportunities for economic growth in Uganda in the next five years are in agriculture."

These forces, of course, are self-reinforcing. As manufacturing and towns grow, the internal market for agricultural products also grows. The internal market can then gradually provide more and more of the propulsive impulse that export markets still provide in Africa.

The chances for successful industrialization obviously will increase (up to a point) as the market area increases. There is, of course, the possibility of manufacturing for export to the growing markets of the industrialized countries. Unfortunately, for most African countries this solution is out of the question at this time. For their manufactured goods to compete successfully on even terms in the industrialized countries, a degree of skill in design, of uniformity in quality, and of response to market conditions is required that is beyond reach. Even South Africa, with over a generation of industrial experience, has not yet been able to export manufactured products successfully in any appreciable volume outside of Africa. The penetration of the markets in industrial countries on any scale is tending to become more difficult, rather than easier, as the varieties of commodities produced and consumed there depart further and further from the simple goods a country embarking on industrialization is able to produce.

The trend in industrialized countries toward more complicated capital-intensive production may, however, open up the market for simple, cheap, mass-produced commodities (the kind Japan used to produce but is now abandoning) for those developing countries that are able to produce them. To enter this market, Africa must be able to compete against Taiwan, mainland China, Hong Kong, and India—all of which are likewise interested in and penetrating these markets, and all of which have a head start in terms of number of entrepreneurs, trained technicians, and skilled and semi-skilled labor. However, if increased African political unity results in some intra-Africa economic cooperation, African countries may be able, by protection of their markets, at least to win them from competing Asian producers.*

Local political federations, customs unions, free trade areas or industry-preference agreements among a number of African countries, on the other hand, would unquestionably facilitate and speed up industrialization—certainly for the area concerned as a whole, although the economic benefits for a given individual state might be slight or even negative. A tariff area as a whole will benefit industrially from protection since protection may encourage the development of industry and so enlarge the size of the market that it justifies the original decision to set up the industry. And, the social benefits of new industry—in the form of trained workers and entrepreneurs, and in terms of the boost it gives to the indigenous economy—may be great enough to warrant imposing a tariff that permits the industry to operate at a private profit.

But the benefit from tariffs may on the other hand be unevenly distributed. A customs union that joins together a relatively developed and a relatively underdeveloped country will benefit the former; Country A, which already has more industry than Country B, has considerable advantages in attracting still further industrial investment, some of which might not come into the area at all in the absence of the larger market provided by the union but some of which might have been located in Country B if the union had not existed (in which case Country B could have raised a tariff to protect the industry from Country A's competition).

Jacob Viner, in his authoritative work on customs unions, regarded the common market in East Africa as a good example of how a customs union worked to the detriment of the less developed part of the union—i.e., Tanganyika and Uganda, vis-à-vis Kenya. The East African Fiscal Commission (Raisman Commission), in a report of February, 1961, and the World Bank's economic survey mission to Uganda in 1962 also examined the East African common market from this standpoint. They agreed that the East African common

---

* The foregoing applies to sub-Saharan Africa. North Africa, Tunisia in particular, has the potential, in uniting European enterprises and indigenous labor (already considerably skilled, through centuries of artisan work and through experience in European manufacturing enterprises), to produce and compete successfully in European markets.

market had resulted in special benefits to Kenya, and that there should be some special compensation to Kenya's partners in the market to offset it. (The East African common market has been considerably weakened recently, largely under pressure from Tanzania, which has been even less successful than Uganda in offsetting the "natural" pull of industry to Nairobi.) The Raisman Commission felt, however, that Uganda and Tanganyika had received some benefit from an "over-spill" of Nairobi's development, and that the amount of compensation needed was therefore limited. The Bank's mission, on the other hand, was not able to find any such benefits, pointing out that any increase in demand for Uganda's agricultural products in Kenya that might have come from higher incomes (due to industrialization) was prevented from resulting in larger sales by various impediments that Kenya put in the way. In the long run, Uganda could gain from a demand for Ugandan labor in Nairobi, but this had not yet occurred. In addition, she had to pay more for certain goods when a protective tariff led to a shift in purchases from imported goods to ones from Kenya. (And she also lost the revenue from the import duty.)

The Bank mission did not recommend abandonment of the common market, however. Uganda may eventually benefit from increased inter-territorial trade when Kenya removes some of the obstacles she has created to the sale of Uganda's agricultural products in Kenya. And a unilateral attack on the common market would jeopardize the common services from which Uganda gains so much. Finally, the mission pointed out, however, Uganda will find it difficult to share fully in the benefits of economic integration without a substantial degree of political integration, which would make it possible to share such benefits more equitably.

With the Federation of Rhodesia and Nyasaland—made up of the present states of Rhodesia, Zambia (formerly Northern Rhodesia), and Malawi (formerly Nyasaland)—a customs union and a political federation were created at the same time. The economic benefits of this union have been studied closely, most notably by Hazlewood and Henderson. Their basic conclusion was that the Federation did contribute to economic development but not as much as some analysts have implied. The contribution it did make was due mainly to the fact that government expenditures and investment were higher than they would otherwise have been, since tax revenues from the copper belt in Northern Rhodesia were used for the Federation as a whole, whereas otherwise they would have reduced or eliminated the Northern Rhodesian Government's need to borrow. Most of the advantages accrued to Southern Rhodesia, which, as the region most attractive to investors, probably drew industries that without the common market might have gone to Nyasaland or Northern Rhodesia. In addition, tariff changes were made to the detriment of Nyasaland consumers but in the interests of Southern Rhodesian industry. Since Nyasaland was not able to set tariffs to protect industry from Southern Rhodesia's competition, this may also have kept her industry from developing—a trend that could have been offset with a policy of other inducements to industry, but this was not done.

The main advantages of the Federation for Nyasaland were that she received more government revenue and that employment opportunities for Nyasas in the Rhodesias increased.

It cannot be taken for granted, then, that a particular country will or will not benefit from participating in a common market, customs union, or federation. The answer must depend on an economic analysis within the framework of the political and constitutional decisions that determine how the economic benefits can be distributed.

It should be noted, though, that the economist may look at the problem of the federation from two different points of view. From the vantage point of a particular country, he may conclude that a proposed federation is against its interests. On the other hand, from the vantage point of the development of Africa or the particular area of Africa involved, he may legitimately conclude that it is economically advantageous. Similarly, in any consideration of the allocation of revenues and expenditures within a federation, an economist advising a constituent part of the federation can legitimately propose a transfer of revenues from the richer to the poorer sections, while, on the federal level, he might advise that the over-all economic interest in achieving rapid growth of Gross National Product required concentrating on the development of the already richer section. (This also applies, of course, to multiracial countries, where there is no necessary coincidence between policies that result in the most rapid growth of total gross national product and those that raise the standard of living of a particular race most rapidly.)

There is also always the possibility of the Africans attacking the problem of how to develop industrial production at both ends of the manufacturing–trade–distribution process—by taking, at one end, materials they produce and processing them further before export, and, at the other, by completing the last stages of manufacture on commodities they import. If a given raw material or product is reduced substantially in weight or size through processing, there will be an added advantage in lowered transport costs if it is processed on the spot or in the country of origin; and, at the other end, if a manufactured commodity is bulkier than the materials of which it is made—such as furniture, or assembled cars and trucks, there may be advantages in lowered transport costs here too if the last stages of assembly or finishing are done in or close to the ultimate market. In both cases, it helps if these steps in the production process are labor-intensive—i.e., if wages are a high proportion of the production cost. For, with low-cost labor in the developing country, the savings in wage costs can then be added to the savings in transport costs (assuming that the labor is sufficiently productive to ensure that low wages mean low costs).

A lot of progress has already been made in Africa in the first type of "nibbling" at the process of industrialization, and further movement down the production process should be possible as time goes on. Copper, for example, is no longer exported as ore but in the form of blister and, in recent years, more and more as electrolytic copper—that is, as practically pure metal. Gold, too, is refined on the spot. Iron, manganese, and chrome are still exported mainly in the form of ore, although processing into ferrochrome is becoming important in Rhodesia. Rhodesia also successfully exports pig iron rather than iron ore. African cotton is always ginned and separated into cotton fiber and cotton seed before being exported, and the next steps, spinning the fiber into thread or even weaving finished fabric and processing the seed into cake and cotton oil, are becoming economically feasible in some countries.

Whether further processing of raw material is economically feasible or not depends not only on the productivity of the local labor force—the technical skills available, etc.—but even more on how the processing will affect transport costs and the costs of the next stage in the production process. Processing electrolytic copper into copper wire before exporting it, for example, would not reduce the weight or save any significant amount on labor costs, and it would add, because of more awkward packing sizes, more to transport costs than could be saved by the processing.

At the other end of the industrial process, similar considerations apply. It is cheaper to import tin plate for cans in flat strips than to import the cans, which take up a lot of space. The same is true of lumber vs. furniture and of metal components vs. car and truck bodies. As time goes on and African markets grow, it will become more and more economic to make the parts for such finished goods; this process has already gone far in South Africa.

Other Industrialization Problems

Many of the difficulties that African countries face in industrialization are common to the rest of the world. The following report could just as easily be a story of an African factory, and every weakness mentioned is typical of ones found in African industries:

POST MORTEM ON A FURNITURE FACTORY

The National Seating and Dimension Company was started in 1962 as a way to help industrial development of the area. It bought the newest and most modern equipment and got the bulk of the finance on favorable terms from the government. It created more than 100 jobs but never paid its way and was closed in November, 1964.

Among the difficulties it experienced was bad management. At one point administrative control was so bad that a load of damaged or imperfect parts, though labeled plainly as scrap, was shipped out to customers as good products. Products often came unglued when received by customers.

Holding and finding key personnel was another problem: the supervisor of maintenance for the milling machines, the production manager, and the general manager left and were not immediately replaced. The company failed to procure sufficient working capital to carry it over the difficult teething period. The secretary of the corporation blamed "a few union troublemakers" for bad labor morale. Finally, he mentioned a thought that haunts the . . . officials who are trying to inject new life into the region—that Appalachia's people do not want to work. (Ben A. Franklin, "First Plan to Aid Appalachia Fails," *The New York Times*, November 25, 1964, pp. 1, 24.)

The difficulties faced by this factory in Appalachia, in the United States, and similar difficulties faced in Zambia, Mali, and Tanzania, are due to the same lack of experience; they are all soluble with patience, effort, and time. The techniques for achieving success are by now well known. Entrepreneurs are developed: in part from the trading community, by the government encouraging (and sometimes pushing) them to convert to industry; in part from active and energetic individuals working for large foreign firms, by encouraging them to set up as parts suppliers or subcontractors; in part from skilled workers and foremen trained in public-works and railway workshops, by encouraging and helping them to set up on their own. Government industrial advisory services and industrial development finance companies are set up to aid small entrepreneurs with advice, guidance, and funds. Governments create industrial estates where many of the problems of new industries are already solved such as obtaining various governmental permits, land set aside for manufacturing, public utilities laid on,* transport facilities and often buildings provided. By various tax and financial incentives, governments invite foreign investors to enter the country, and encourage new industries by offering them protection from competing imports through tariffs, quotas, rebates, or subsidies—as may be justified. Then, the whole environment is made as encouraging as possible to industrialization— an atmosphere of political stability, government aid in the search for and encouragement of exploitation of natural resources, education and training programs for children and adults, etc.

* The availability of electric power, railways, or roads are often necessary preconditions for industry, but they are by no means sure-fire stimulants to it. Aside from a few industries that absolutely require it (the electro-chemical or electro-metallurgical industries, for example), cheap electric power is not a significant factor in the economics of most industries, reliability and adequacy of the power supply being more important, and most industries being able, if necessary, to generate their own power using diesel plants. The formula that industrialization is called forth by cheap electric power is much too simplistic, therefore, as Uganda found when she built a power project at Owen Falls in the early 1950's, which industry did not use to capacity for another ten years. The Russians made the same mistake when attempting to follow Lenin's famous dictum "Electric power plus Soviets equals Communism."

LABOR

There are a few specifically African problems in the matter of industrialization, however. There is first of all the problem of "non-committed" or migrant labor. (See above, chaps. III and V.) It is important to note that the experience during the beginning of the Industrial Revolution in Great Britain has not occurred in Africa. (Elkan, *Migrants and Proletarians.*) In England, the people from the countryside who settled in the cities as the new industrial proletariat were not farmers but agricultural laborers who had no property stake in the land. But this is true of most African wage-earners, and their economic calculus is consequently different. In most of Africa, existing land tenure and market arrangements do not give land *per se* a money value. The only way a man can secure benefit from his claim to land is by keeping his family on it and working it. Land provides social security against unemployment, sickness, and old age, but the individual cannot use it for these purposes if he does not preserve his claim to it. Thus, he himself has a constant incentive to quit an industrial job for (longer or shorter) periods to return to his family and land.

Given the prevalence of migrant labor, industries that need semi-skilled or skilled African labor find it difficult to become efficient and survive. In other words, progress in industrialization, like agricultural advance, may be closely related to the slow change in land-tenure systems and in the relationship of men to the land.

Very recently, a major change in this respect has occurred in some African countries (notably Ghana and Nigeria). The major earlier educational drive in these countries is turning out large numbers of "school-leavers" who would prefer clerical jobs but are unable to find them, since their number far exceeds the number of such jobs available. These school-leavers are reluctant to return to the country and are, therefore, soon ready and willing to become committed industrial workers. These countries are now findng themselves, consequently, with a ready-made proletariat available for employment and training in new industry. In Ghana and Nigeria, these potential industrial workers already number in the tens of thousands. Schools in other countries, where the increased educational effort came later—

Uganda, Kenya, Ivory Coast—are also now turning out thousands of soon unemployed school-leavers.

There is another special aspect to the labor supply problem in Africa which, while it is present in other parts of the world, is so important there as to seem peculiarly African. This is the infinite elasticity of supply of unskilled labor—or, more bluntly, the unlimited supply of labor. The parts of Africa that have developed modern economies are still so small in relation to the sea of subsistence activities that surrounds them, and the mobility (intra-national and transnational) of labor is so great that, within a reasonable wage range, the supply of labor can be considered virtually unlimited. What, then, determines the level of wages for unskilled labor?

Before World War II, Ida Greaves concluded that wages paid to an unskilled worker had to be high enough to overcome the strength of the tradition that binds him to customary tribal practices. (Wages, therefore, could be used by an anthropologist to measure the strength of tribal tradition.) In the 1950's, W. Arthur Lewis went further, and concluded that the floor, or minimum-level of wages paid was set by the subsistence income an African could earn on the land, while the ceiling was set by this income plus the necessary incentive to go into wage labor. (Lewis, "Development With Unlimited Supplies of Labour.")

Not all African governments have fully appreciated the implications of this analysis. For example, what happens if wage rates are raised by minimum-wage legislation, union action, or other influences above the wage "ceiling" as thus defined? Clearly the wage will then attract labor from the subsistence economy into the urban areas even after there is no longer any need for more workers. The result may be that the number of urban unemployed will increase until the average real income of urban wage workers is reduced (by their having to support some of their unemployed tribal brothers) or the capacity of the urban center to sustain the unemployed (housing limitations, police action, petty jobs available, etc.) is reached. Given the forces holding nominal wages up, the level of unemployment then would be like a pressure gauge, the exact level of which would be set by the pressure of the movement of people from the land into towns against the counter-pressure of the absorptive capacity of the towns. (See also above, chap. III, p. 62.)

Policies to bar foreign Africans and expel those who have been living in a foreign land for years, therefore probably do raise the average wage level of a nation's unskilled workers, by putting definite limits on the number of them available. Such policies have been enacted in Tanzania, against the Kikuyu from Kenya; by the Ivory Coast, against Ghanaians; by Gabon, against Congolese; by South Africa, against Africans from north of the Limpopo River; etc. However, these policies may retard the general growth of the economy otherwise by raising wage-costs and preventing the establishment of some industries.

NON-AFRICAN ENTREPRENEURS

Another problem which may be present rather more in Africa than in other developing areas is the presence of foreign entrepreneurs. In East Africa, most of the groups from which industrial entrepreneurs should logically emerge—in commerce, among skilled workmen and foremen—are non-African, mostly Asian, in origin; in West Africa, many of these people are Syrians, Cypriots, and Lebanese. In actual fact, this need not become a problem unless it becomes one politically. For industrialization is a snow-ball process: if an Asian creates a new industry in Nairobi, he is not reducing but, in the long run, augmenting the opportunities for other (African) industrial entrepreneurs. Problems develop only if governments and politicians, continuing an existing non-African bias from commerce, in trying to encourage African entrepreneurship believe they must do so by discouraging non-African entrepreneurs.

LAND TENURE

Another specifically African problem is, like some of the labor problems, related to the land-tenure situation. In some countries, the communal land tenure may make it difficult for infant industries to secure the land they need. Governments can intervene to acquire the land, directly or through the creation of industrial estates, although the acquisition of land will still be a time-consuming and discouraging process, but the problem created by the lack of land-collateral is not so easily avoided. With tribal or communal land tenure, one of the ways in which small businesses in other areas of the world acquire loan capital and grow big is shut off. Elsewhere, a man who wishes to borrow money to enlarge his business can use his (or a relative's or friend's) land as security for a bank loan; land is often, indeed, the best security. Not being able to do this will continue to handicap industrialists in Africa.

Selected Bibliography

Economic Growth and External Debt. (Report EC-121b, Economic Department of the International Bank for Reconstruction and Development.)

ELKAN, W. "Criteria for Industrial Development in Uganda," *East African Economic Review*, January, 1959, pp. 50–57.

———. *Migrants and Proletarians.* London and New York: Oxford University Press, 1960.

GEIGER, T., and ARMSTRONG, W. *The Development of African Private Enterprise.* (Planning Pamphlet No. 120.) Washington, D.C.: National Planning Association, 1964.

GREAVES, IDA C. *Modern Production Among Backward Peoples.* London: Allen & Unwin, 1935.

HAZLEWOOD, A., and HENDERSON, P. D. "Nyasaland: The Economics of Federation," Oxford University Institute of Statistics *Bulletin*, XXII, No. 1 (February, 1960), 1–91.

LEWIS, W. A. "Development With Unlimited Supplies of Labour," *The Manchester School*, XXII (May, 1954), 139–92.

———. *Industrialization on the Gold Coast.* Accra: Government Printer, 1953.

MAIZELS, A. *Industrial Growth and World Trade.* Cambridge: Cambridge University Press, 1963.

MASON, E. S., *et al. The Economic Development of Uganda.* Baltimore, Md.: The Johns Hopkins Press, for the International Bank for Reconstruction and Development, 1962.

MOUSSA, P. *Les Nations Prolétaires.* Paris: Presses universitaires de France, 1959.

NYHART, J. D. "The Uganda Development Corporation and the Promotion of Entrepreneurship." Paper delivered at a conference of the East African Institute of Social Research, Kampala, Uganda, December, 1959.

STALEY, E., and MORSE, R. *Modern Small Industry for Developing Countries.* New York: McGraw-Hill, 1965.

WALKER, D. "Criteria for Industrial Development in Uganda: A Comment," *East African Economics Review*, July, 1959, pp. 58–66.

VIII

Infrastructure

*The most valuable of all capital is that
invested in human beings.*
ALFRED MARSHALL, Principles of
Economics

The economic infrastructure is, essentially, the basic services, or
public utilities, necessary to the commodity-producing sectors of a
nation. Provision of these basic services is essential to, but not sufficient for, the growth of these sectors, and, in time, particular needs
for basic services not only grow but change in character.

In general, it has come to be regarded in Africa (as elsewhere) as
almost axiomatic that governments are responsible for providing this
infrastructure, but it is a responsibility inherited almost by default.
In the early years of the twentieth century, chartered companies, concessionaires, and other private interests generally provided whatever
modern infrastructure there was: Union Minière's continuing private
ownership of the Bas Congo–Katanga railway and of power plants in
the Katanga (although now the Congolese Government is a large
shareholder in Union Minière), the control of the Benguela railway
by Tanganyika Concessions, and the important role that missionaries
continue to play in education are relics of the earlier arrangements.
But most governments everywhere in the world (with the exception
of the United States in railroads and power) hold themselves re-

166

sponsible, and are held responsible by their citizens, for developing these sectors of the economy.

The introduction of modern transport means into Africa was completely financed from abroad. And, generally speaking, dependence on foreign sources of capital to finance a substantial part of the infrastructure has continued throughout the twentieth century, even though national governments and not foreign interests in time came to provide these services. This heavy dependence on outside sources of finance is a unique characteristic of African development of infrastructure; no other region of the world is in a similar position.

There is no completely satisfactory measure of the development of the economic infrastructure in sub-Saharan Africa. Because the economic infrastructure is there to serve the rest of the economy, physical measures are not of great use to establish a standard of its adequacy. If one compares the number of miles of railway per square mile in two countries, the fact that Country A has a lesser railway density than Country B does not mean that its railway network is less adequate. In fact, if Country A's railways are running at less than capacity, it may be that they have actually been overbuilt. In other words, a proper appraisal of an economic infrastructure's adequacy can only be made in relation to the economic needs of a given country. I will not try to present here such evaluations but will, rather, be content to make a *tour d'horizon* of the subject.

Transport

Until late in the colonial period, the main impediment not only to economic development in Africa, but to her development in most fields of human endeavor, was lack of transport, and consequent impossibly high transport costs. (Wrigley, *passim.*) To raise the African standard of living above a bare subsistence level, it was necessary for Africans to be able to produce a surplus of commodities, and to transport and sell them abroad, so that they could purchase, in exchange, the products of industrial societies and the skilled services of foreign technicians and administrators. Transport had to be cheap enough so that African products could reach world markets and could sell for a price that, after paying for it, would leave an adequate return. And this could not be provided for most of Africa before railways had been built.

The threshold to development represented by transport obstacles, then, that the Africans had to surmount was too high for them to climb over it on their own—help from outside was needed.

The transport of goods was impeded, first, by difficulty of access to the continent, caused by the scarcity of good natural harbors and deep inlets of the sea. On the entire African coast south of the Sahara, the really good natural ports can almost be counted on the fingers of one hand: Dakar, Bathurst, Libreville, Cape Town, Durban, Lourenço Marques, Mombasa. The plateau formation of much of the continent ending near the coast, results in the rivers ending in falls or rapids and prevents their use as routes into the interior. Once a landing was made, therefore, penetration into the interior almost always depended on land transport. Internal trade routes were difficult to establish, however, because of the impossibility in much of Africa of using draft or pack animals—due to trypanosomiasis, carried by the tsetse fly, and to other animal diseases; because of the presence of dense forests, swamps, deserts, or steppes; and in many cases because of the resistance of the local people. And, in any event, reliance had to be placed on the wholly inadequate transport capacity of human carriers.

Modern economic development of Africa, then, had to await the coming of the "iron horse" immune to the tsetse fly and other natural enemies. "The bulk of the African resources lay inland and their development could not begin until the railroads made it possible." (Van Dongen, p. 3.) But the railway is a capital intensive activity *par excellence*, requiring amounts of investment that no primitive economy can hope to muster. It came to tropical Africa, therefore, only when the colonial countries were ready to turn from their own railway building in Europe and North America, and looked abroad to the Argentine, Australia, and Africa. The main railway building effort in Africa was from about 1885 to about 1914.

Aside from South Africa, where mineral development in large part necessitated the building of railways, in Africa they were built for strategic military or imperial reasons. Often, they were pushed ahead well before the area they served had developed enough to make them economic. The railways were built first, then attempts would be made to find ways of making them pay. Only after the Kenya-Uganda railway was built was the idea of finding settlers to farm along its route to provide traffic put forward. Cecil Rhodes's British South Africa Company began in the 1890's to push a railway north from the Cape Colony through Bechuanaland, to avoid the Boer states, and through Southern and Northern Rhodesia. While the railway securities were sold to investors on the basis that the railway would be the means of tapping the mineral wealth of Southern and Northern Rhodesia, Rhodes was probably motivated more by his dream of acquiring central Africa for the British Empire and having a Cape-to-Cairo railway all on British territory. Exploitation of the mineral wealth of Northern Rhodesia did not really begin until the 1930's.

Highways began to take over the function of railways as a means of opening up new areas for development while Africa was still getting its first railways. (Since World War II, the airplane has also taken on some of this task.) The automobile, truck, and highway perform this task much better than railroads, in fact, being more flexible and less capital-hungry. Investment in transport can now proceed in stages, beginning with a dirt or gravel road with a few trucks and building up to a modern highway with an enormous volume of traffic, so that the territory opened up can largely pay for the investment as its needs grow. A highway, moreover, allows development to take place all along its length, whereas a railway concentrates development at its stations.

In industrialized countries, rail networks are tending to shrink as highways and airways absorb large amounts of what was formerly rail traffic.* In Africa, however, there is still a tendency carried over from colonial times to associate railways with development and to underrate highway and air transport. In some cases, of course, building new railways is justified—particularly to carry heavy, low-value, bulk traffic over long distances. Africa continues to be the only region in the world where there is actually a justifiable reason for a large-scale

---

* In air transport, Africa at least started on a par with the rest of the world. In fact, since government subsidy of air lines is general practice, Africa suffers a smaller absolute economic loss from the uneconomic, overly rapid development of air travel than other countries do, since she has less investment in other forms of transport to lose in the process. The *relative* size of this loss is another matter, however, and cannot easily be estimated.

building of railways (though this does not imply that all the railways recently built or projected are really needed): in Nigeria, to make Bornu Province accessible and to stretch rail transport out toward the northeast and Chad; in Sudan, to open up new areas in the south and west; in East Africa, to replace a most costly and complicated land-water transport route to northwestern Uganda and to tie the Tanzania and Kenya-Uganda lines together; in Swaziland, to give a new outlet to the sea and make possible exploitation of iron-ore deposits; in Mauritania, the Congo (Brazzaville), and Liberia, for the exploitation of new ore deposits; and in Angola and Mozambique, to open up new areas.

During the 1950's, the Belgians constructed a Kamina-Kabalo link in the Katanga and brought the rail network of southern Africa (South Africa, Rhodesia, Zambia, Angola, Mozambique, and Congo) into contact with the rail system of East Africa across Lake Tanganyika. At present, the southern African network, with African standard gauge (42 inches) cannot, however, exchange rolling stock with the East African system, with meter gauge, but officials of the latter have been working toward an eventual change-over to standard gauge. In the meantime, the East African railway, which once consisted of two separate systems, has linked the whole together with a line opened in 1963 from Kenya to Tanganyika. It has also been pushing north through Uganda to the Nile River within 70 miles of the Sudanese border thus giving the southern Sudan shorter access to the sea than by way of the Sudanese rail system.

In December, 1965, east and west Cameroon were linked by rail; the railway is now being extended across the entire country, and is planned eventually to reach Chad and the Central African Republic.

Tropical Africa in 1964 had about 28,000 miles of railway—this for an area of more than 6 million square miles. This figure can be contrasted with that for South Africa and South-West Africa, an area one-twelfth this size where there are 18,000 miles of railway, traffic on which is considerably heavier. Thus in 1948, the South African railways carried 11.3 billion ton-miles, while for all the African tropical railway systems, the figure was 7.5 billion; in 1959, 19.3 billion and 11.6 billion ton miles, respectively; by 1959, the traffic in the rest of sub-Saharan Africa had caught up to the position of South Africa eleven years earlier.

RAILWAYS, TROPICAL AFRICA
(1964)

	Length (in track miles)
Kenya, Tanganyika, and Uganda	4,240
Congo (Léopoldville)	3,720
Rhodesia and Zambia	3,430
Sudan	3,320
Nigeria	2,360
Angola	2,100
Mozambique	1,890
Ivory Coast	820
Ghana	760
Senegal	730
Madagascar	620
Congo (Brazzaville)	580
Ethiopia	530
Mauritania	440
Guinea	440
Mali	400
Dahomey	400
Cameroon	380
Malawi	350
Sierra Leone	350
Togo	300
Eritrea	220
Total	28,380

SOURCE: *World Railways*, 1963–64, pp. 110–15.

Railroad development not withstanding, the main expansion in ground transport in Africa, as elsewhere, has come to be in roads; road-building as an important part of the investment plan has become a world-wide phenomenon.

Statistics on road mileage in Africa are unfortunately not very good; a reasonable estimate is that there are about 50,000 miles of road in tropical Africa. A table on the following page gives the number of vehicles by country and provides some insight into the development of road transport. The total is about one half that of South Africa's and about equal to the total that the 10 million citizens of the Netherlands possess.

In relation to this highway development, it should be noted that oil-marketing companies have become major investors in sub-Saharan

MOTOR VEHICLES IN CIRCULATION, 1964
(in thousands)

	Passenger Cars	Commercial Vehicles	Total
Rhodesia	95	23	118
Congo (Léopoldville)	43	33	76
Kenya	62	9	71
Nigeria	46	24	70
Malagasy	30	26	56
Angola	31	16	55
Ivory Coast	28	21	49
Zambia	38	10	48
Senegal	27	19	46
Ghana	27	17	44
Mozambique[a]	37	6	43
Tanzania[b]	33	10	43
Sudan	21	20	41
Uganda	29	6	35
Cameroon	13	20	33
Guinea	8	13	21
Ethiopia	14	7	21
Mauritius	12	5	17
Malawi	8	8	16
Sierra Leone	9	4	13
Somalia	4	6	10
Dahomey	6	4	10
Gabon	3	6	9
Mali	3	4	7
Upper Volta	3	3	6
Chad	2	4	6
Niger	2	4	6
Central African Republic[c]	4	2	6
French Somaliland	3	1	4
Gambia	1	1	2
Togo	1	0.5	1.5
Mauritania	0.5	0.5	1
TOTAL	651	333	984

SOURCE: UNITED NATIONS. *Statistical Yearbook, 1965.* Pp. 428–30.

[a] 1962.
[b] 1963.
[c] 1961.

Africa. In this respect, Africa is like the industrialized countries: the gasoline service stations that are scattered across Africa are duplicates of the stations in the United States and Europe. The ultimate economic and cultural effect of this development will no doubt be staggering.

Most African countries have also had to make large investments in ports, often to make up for the deficiencies of nature in providing shelter and deep anchorages. Ghana's two ocean ports, for example, Takoradi and Tema, are both artificial. (The latter, Africa's largest artificial port, cost £17 million to build.) Since 1939, an enormous effort has been made to build or expand existing ports all around Africa. Port Etienne, in Mauritania; Conakry, in Guinea; Port Harcourt and Lagos, in Nigeria; Matadi, in the Congo (Léopoldville); Lourenço Marques and Beira, in Mozambique; Dar es Salaam, in Tanzania; and Mombasa, in Kenya, have been expanded. And the

INTERNATIONAL PORT TRAFFIC, 1964
(in millions of tons)

Nigeria	11.7
Mozambique	8.4
Liberia	6.0
Ghana	4.8
Kenya	4.1
Angola	3.6
Ivory Coast	3.6
Senegal	3.5
Sierra Leone	3.0
Sudan	2.4
Guinea	2.2
Congo (Brazzaville)	1.9
Gabon	1.9
French Somaliland[a]	1.7
Tanzania[b]	1.7
Mauritius	1.3
Congo (Léopoldville)	1.2
Cameroon	1.1
Malagasy	0.8
Ethiopia[a]	0.7
Somalia	0.4
Dahomey	0.3
Togo	0.2
Gambia	0.1
TOTAL	66.6

SOURCE: UNITED NATIONS. *Statistical Yearbook, 1965.* Pp. 439–42.

[a] 1963.
[b] 1962.

new ports of Abidjan, in the Ivory Coast; Cotonou, in Dahomey; Lome, in Togo; and Monrovia, in Liberia, deserve special mention. Another artificial port in Liberia, Buchanan, was completed in 1964 to handle iron-ore shipments from new mines and in 1966 may move as much as 10 million tons. Somalia, which had no deep water port, is now building one with American aid at Chisimaio. Indeed, tropical Africa has moved ahead more rapidly in the provision and use of ports than in inland transport. In 1963, ports handled more than 57 million tons of shipping—about three times the volume handled in the Republic of South Africa. Since then, with a rapid increase in iron-ore shipments from several countries and in oil from Nigeria, the total tonnage should surpass 85 million tons in 1966, or more than double what it was in 1959.

African nations are likely to put a higher proportion of their total investment into transport than industrialized countries do, for a number of reasons. Investment in roads, bridges, and ports has gone on for 2,000 years in Europe (in Cyprus, for example, recent expansion of the port at Kyrenia changed the contour of a port, established by the Venetians, to one that takes advantage of a breakwater left by the Romans); the African patrimony of infrastructure goes back scarcely sixty years. Secondly, the African populations are usually spread very thinly over enormous areas, which means there is a relatively high investment per head in the increased transport facilities required as internal production gradually changes from subsistence to the market. Also, topography and climate make difficulties, and the investment in providing a given level of transport must consequently be greater; thus, the Kenya-Uganda railway from Mombasa to Kampala has to climb from sea level to 7,600 feet, descend to 6,000 feet in the Rift Valley, rise again to 9,000 feet, and finally reach Kampala at an altitude of 4,000 feet. Transport must also be emphasized because commodities make up a much larger share of Gross National Product than in industrialized areas, where services are more important. And, finally, the commodities to be transported in Africa are mostly primary products, which are bulkier in relation to value than fabricated industrial products.

Of the roughly £360 million capital investment carried out by the government and public agencies in Nigeria in the years 1955–62, transport was allocated about 34 per cent. In the French territories, about half of the commitments made by the French agencies Fonds des Investissements pour le Développement Economique et Sociale (FIDES) and Caisse Centrale de la France d'Outre-Mer (CCFOM) in 1946–54 were for transport and communications. In a second FIDES plan, for 1954–58, transport and communications were allocated 42 per cent of the total, even though a special attempt was made to allocate a higher proportion of funds to commodity-producing sectors. (United Nations, *Transport Problems*, pp. 79–80.) Of World Bank group loans and credits of $1.35 billion in Africa from 1950 to 1965, 45 per cent went to develop transport facilities. (In the rest of the world, World Bank loans for power and for transport were about equal, but in Africa, for every $1 loaned for power, $1.50 went for transport.)

Though adequate transport infrastructure must remain an indispensable part of economic development, the word "infrastructure" has a broader meaning. Africa's earlier needs were essentially for transport facilities; African farmers, or European concessionaires or miners, required little else than the means to get their products to market. Until World War II, Lugard's comment was essentially true: "The material development of Africa may be summed up in one word—transport." But, as the economy of Africa broadened and the first stages of industrialization and urbanization began, the necessary infrastructure also broadened. Electric power became essential, if products were to be processed in Africa itself. Assuring electric power for industry has thus come to be generally accepted as one of the basic services that governments hold to be their responsibility.

Electric Power

Electric-power output has been growing rapidly in Africa. Between 1951 and 1960, it more than doubled; since then, it more than doubled again. This rate of increase is higher than the world average, even though the absolute level reached is still low. The very great unevenness in the production of power shown by different countries in the table on the following page is an indication of the degree of industrialization or mining development reached by them; in the Republic of South Africa, it was almost triple that of the total of the other countries.

ELECTRIC-POWER PRODUCTION IN SUB-SAHARAN AFRICA
(in million kilowatt hours)

	1962	1963	1964
Rhodesia		3,369	
Congo (Léopoldville)	2,610		
Cameroon	1,095		1,062
Nigeria	752		1,023
Zambia		730	
Uganda	452	530	521
Ghana	410	470	
Kenya	220	263	
Liberia	90		260
Mozambique	240		
Tanzania		200	
Senegal	204		197
Mauritius		180	
Ethiopia	130	175	
Guinea	39		168
Angola	160		
Ivory Coast	114	159	
Sudan	153		174
Madagascar	120	125	129
Sierra Leone	56	72	
Malawi		42	
Congo (Brazzaville)	52	34	
Mali	19		26
Gabon	24		
Dahomey	11	17	
Chad			15
French Somaliland		15	
Somalia	12	13	
Central African Republic		12	
Niger	11		
Rwanda		11	
Burundi		10	
Upper Volta	10*		
Togo			9
Gambia		7	

Total of latest estimates for each country 12,418

* 1961.

SOURCES: 1962 figures: U.S. Federal Power Commission, *World Power Data,* 1962; 1963 figures: U.N. Economic Commission for Africa, *Conference on Harmonization of Industrial Development Programmes in East Africa* (E/CN.14/ NR/104), and U.S. Agency for International Development, *Economic Data Book, Africa,* December, 1965; 1964 figures: U.S. AID, *Economic Data Book, Africa,* December, 1965.

Hydroelectric power is peculiarly important to Africa. For it appears likely that tropical Africa is not rich in coal—the basic source of energy for Western countries when they industrialized. (The most important coal deposits are in South Africa. Aside from the Wankie coalfield in Rhodesia, the Tete field in Mozambique, and some inferior coal found in northern and eastern Nigeria, no other coal is being exploited in sub-Saharan Africa. Coalfields in Tanzania and Zambia have not yet been found economically exploitable.) For Nigeria, Gabon, and Angola, oil and possibly gas may become main sources of energy, but for the rest of the continent, for domestic sources of energy, attention must be turned to hydroelectric power at this stage of knowledge. (Nuclear energy may eventually prove to be economic for such relatively small markets as the African countries are likely to be for some time. But, this is not probable for another perhaps twenty or thirty years.) Until then, nuclear power will be economic only in large units and only where it provides a portion of the total power output.

Hydroelectric potential appears to be one of Africa's most important natural assets. Indeed, the geographical formation that kept Africa isolated for millennia—the great central plateau with the rivers plunging off it to the coast—gives Africa the greatest hydroelectric potential of any continent in the world: an estimated 200 million kilowatts, or about two-fifths of the total world potential, more than Europe and the two Americas put together. (The Inga site alone on the Congo River near its mouth has a potential equal to that of North America.) Now, with most of the sites in North America and Europe where cheap hydro-power can be produced already utilized, what was once a handicap for Africa has become an attractive asset for the rest of the world.

The greatest hydroelectric potential in Africa is in Congo (Léopoldville) (500 billion kwh annually), Angola (200 billion kwh), Malagasy Republic (100 billion kwh), and Cameroon (100 billion kwh). Congo (Brazzaville), Central Africa Republic, Gabon, and Liberia also have significant potential, especially in relation to the size of their populations.

The problem, however, is to find uses for this potential electric power. While cheap available electric power is an important aid to industry, it is not an irresistible attraction. Uganda discovered this the hard way when she built a power station at Owen Falls in 1954 with an ultimate capacity of 150,000 kw, which was not sufficiently utilized to pay its way until 1962. The *market* for electric power, as in industry proper, is the key. With a domestic market that is too small, the solution is often to look to export—either of the power itself or of industrial commodities that are highly intensive users of electric power, like aluminum or the products of electro-chemical industries.*

So far, the expectation of export has usually been the rationale for building large-scale hydroelectric power projects in Africa. Owen Falls, the first of these, eventually paid its way by adding to growing domestic consumption the export of power itself to Kenya, and by the use of its electricity to refine exportable copper from the Kilembe mines. The Kariba Dam and power plant on the Zambezi River border between Rhodesia and Zambia—which began operations in 1960 with an initial capacity of 600,000 kw (four times the size of Owen Falls), one of the world's largest stations, with the dam forming the world's largest man-made lake—was based on the need for power in the mines and electrolytic copper refinery of Zambia's copper belt and for power in Rhodesia's factories and mines (including an electrolytic ferrochrome plant that came into existence only because cheaper power from Kariba made it economically possible).

And the Volta Dam Project in Ghana, officially inaugurated in January, 1966, with an ultimate capacity of some 860,000 kw (and creating an enormous lake almost the size of Lake Kariba), depended completely for its construction on the decision to commit a large bloc of its power to a huge aluminum refinery to be built, based on the use of Volta power.

Communications and Public Utilities

The spread of modern governmental administration into Africa brought with it the need for better public communication systems —post office, telephones, and telegraphs. Private arrangements, however, have by no means disappeared. In Uganda, for example, the

---

* The kilowat hours of electricity required to produce a ton of metal are, as follows, for selected metals: titanium, 40,000; aluminum, 17,000; electrolytic manganese, 11,000; ferro-chromium, 7,700; electrolytic copper, 2,500.

volume of mail transported privately may well exceed the volume the post office handles. The growth of Africa's cities has made water supply and sewerage essential public utilities, although over most of Africa individuals and companies still make their own provision for these; they are yet to become fully a part of the economic infrastructure.

Education

Education was not always considered a part of the economic infrastructure: in economic terms, it was regarded more as an expensive consumer good than as a necessary prerequisite of economic growth. It is not possible to make a reasonable estimate of education's *economic* effects; it is difficult to distinguish, that is, what part of the cost of education can reasonably be assessed as the cost paid for increased productive capacity.

Concern with modern education occurred in Africa really only in the twentieth century; at first, education was left to the missionaries to handle. In the 1920's, however, governments in Africa began to take an active interest in the education of Africans, although the missionaries remained dominant. This government activity in education was increasingly emphasized after 1950. But many Africans still had a suspicion and a fear of education. Then suddenly in the early and mid-1950's, their attitude changed; African parents began to express a great desire for education for their children, and the children too seemed enthusiastic. Since 1960, the high *economic* yield of expenditures on education has also been widely recognized, and investment plans are influenced by this fact.

In Africa, there has been a special reason for this. During the first decade after World War II, the general approach of government policy-makers in Africa on the subject of economic development was that the provision of economic infrastructure, strictly defined, was the main essential. It is true that the capacity of the infrastructure in many African countries then was the major bottleneck holding back economic development, since the infrastructure had been neglected during the depression of 1930's and during World War II. With the world market for African products growing after World War II, investment in infrastructure was imperative to get these products to market. And it has continued to be the decisive element in many countries. But in many others, once the infrastructure caught up with or even ran ahead of the needs of the rest of the economy, governments were faced with the central task of stimulating the growth of the commodity-producing sectors directly—that is, with the need to increase agricultural production through the voluntary action of millions of small farmers and to develop entrepreneurial, managerial and skilled worker groups where none had existed. It is understandable that governments began to consider investment in education as a means of achieving this.

The development of the educational infrastructure in Africa was no less uneven, however, than in the other fields we have considered. "If one considers only the investment aspects of education, the typical country in sub-Saharan Africa might set as its first target 50 per cent of each age cohort of children in primary school, 5 per cent in secondary school, and 0.5 per cent in university." (Lewis, p. 77.) There are no comprehensive statistics on education in the African countries on this basis. The best available is in the accompanying table on elementary and secondary education, where the definition of secondary education is considerably broader than that given by Lewis, probably including, in most cases, junior secondary schools, or the seventh and eighth years of schooling (which Lewis would have included in his primary school category). The figures as given cast a dim light on the extent to which educational infrastructure in the various African countries has developed.

During the late 1950's and early 1960's, there was a great expansion in the number of and enrollment in elementary schools and universities. More recently, expansion has begun in secondary schools, and special programs, like the Peace Corps', have provided expatriate teachers for them. By 1970, African education will probably have caught up with Southeast Asian and Latin American schools in numbers graduated or will have surpassed them—with more than 30 per cent of children of school age in elementary school and more than 10 per cent in secondary school.

What this means for a particular African country can be seen from the experience of the Ivory Coast, which can be taken as a median African country in this respect. In 1927, the Ivory Coast had 2,600 pupils in primary school, and a large proportion of these were non-Africans. In 1947, there were 22,000; in 1959, just before inde-

ENROLLED STUDENTS AS PERCENTAGE OF SCHOOL-AGE
POPULATION AROUND 1960

	Elementary	Secondary	Elementary and Secondary
Mauritius	69	36	59
Basutoland	78	5	57
Rhodesia	60	12	46
Congo (Brazzaville)	58	7	43
Swaziland	53	6	39
Cameroon	51	4	37
Gabon	49	6	36
Kenya	49	4	35
Zambia	48	2	34
Spanish Equatorial Africa	46	3	33
Congo (Léopoldville)	43	3	31
Bechuanaland	41	2	30
Ghana	40	3	29
Malawi	41	1	29
Nigeria	35	5	26
Madagascar	34	5	26
Uganda	32	6	24
Ivory Coast	31	4	23
Togo	29	4	21
Zanzibar	26	5	20
Mozambique	26	2	19
Central African Republic	22	3	16
Rwanda and Burundi	22	1	16
Tanganyika	19	2	14
French Somaliland	16	6	13
Senegal	17	4	13
Dahomey	18	2	13
Liberia	16	2	12
Sierra Leone	14	3	11
Spanish Sahara	13	6	11
Guinea	13	3	10
Chad	14	1	10
Sudan	11	6	9
Gambia	10	5	8
Angola	9	3	7
Ifni	4	8	5
Mali	6	1	5
Upper Volta	6	1	5
Mauritania	6	1	5
Somalia	5	1	4
Niger	4	1	3
Ethiopia	5	*	3

* Less than 0.5 per cent.

SOURCE: UNESCO, *Statistical Yearbook*, 1963, pp. 96–99.

pendence, 165,000; in 1964, 330,000. By 1964, 45 per cent of all
children in the Ivory Coast of primary-school age attended school.
At the secondary level, the number of pupils quadrupled from 5,000
in 1958–59 to 20,000 in 1963–64. A further increase has been held up
by the shortage of qualified teachers, most of whom still have to
come from abroad. Of the total of 898 secondary-school teachers on
the job in 1965, the sources were:

Ivory Coast	117
French technical assistance	468
Individual contract, mostly French	269
U.S. Peace Corps	44
	898

In 1964, the University of Abidjan was inaugurated, taking over
from the teaching center established in 1958 by the University of
Paris. The university now has some 2,000 students; 1,200 Ivory Coast
students, in addition, are in universities overseas.

Even with the help provided by foreign aid, the financial burden
on the Ivory Coast for education is very large: the percentage that
education represents of the government budget has gone up from
12½ per cent in 1960 to 22 per cent in 1964, and 40 per cent of all
civil servants are employed in education.

The educational systems of Africa are still far from ready to contribute what is needed to build the new African states and economies.
Discovering and developing physical resources, with all its difficulties, is relatively simple compared to training human resources.
Although the knowledge of how to design the right kind of educational system for economic development is still very limited, it is
possible to indicate in some respects how the educational system that
the Africans inherited on independence was lacking.

The purpose of education can be for earning as well as learning,
and the first had been much neglected in Africa. The content of
African education was until recently geared to people who were un-
interested in practical affairs. "It is only now, with independence,
that it is realized that the basic problems of tropical agriculture, the
social organization of a society still based on the tribe and the extended family, and the cultural traditions of the African nations

themselves have been neglected in favor of producing people who could enter the Sorbonne or Oxford without difficulty." (Vaizey, p. 353.)

What kind of education the Africans devise for themselves will probably determine the future of their continent. Certainly, if the African economy is to develop, it will be necessary to train children in rational modes of thought and in an objective, empirical attitude toward nature and society. Problem-solving abilities must be developed, rather than the knowledge of how to pass examinations. The Japanese example is probably not a bad one to take, for the educational system of Japan is largely responsible for the extraordinary adaptability of its economy. Aside from ensuring a good supply of entrepreneurs and technicians, it has promoted mobility and versatility and encouraged inventiveness. "More generally, it is not unreasonable to ascribe, in part at least, to the character of the education systems some of the intense loyalty to their country and of their eagerness for work, which are notorious among Japanese people." (Hicks, p. 28.)

Agricultural Extension Services

Rapid progress in agriculture, as we have seen, depends on a revolution in farming techniques. And this to an important degree depends on governmental expenditures on agricultural research and extension services, as well as on education. Expenditures on research and extension workers, however, have not thus far been regarded as infrastructure investment, but simply as recurrent expenditures. In consequence, countries have not included them in development plans for which a major national effort is justified, nor have they been regarded as clearly eligible for financing from external sources. Actually, expenditure in creating and maintaining a network of extension agents is as much investment in building up the economy's productive capacity as investment in highways, and this is slowly being acknowledged. In 1960, the World Bank made a loan to the Republic of the Congo (Léopoldville) for agricultural development of which a portion was to pay the salaries of extension workers. Uganda's development plan includes a large item for the development of extension services and agricultural research.

184 The Economics of African Development

Selected Bibliography

HAEFELE, E. T., and STEINBERG, E. B. Government Controls on Transport: An African Case. Washington, D.C.: The Brookings Institution, 1965.

HICKS, U. "The Economics of Educational Expansion in Low-Income Countries," Three Banks Review, No. 65 (March, 1965), pp. 3–29.

HUNTER, G. "Education and Manpower," in The New Societies of Tropical Africa. London and New York: Oxford University Press, 1962.

IVORY COAST, GOVERNMENT OF. Ivory Coast Year V: Education. 1965.

LEWIS, W. A. "Education and Economic Development," Final Report, Conference of African States on Development of Education. (UNESCO/ED/181.) New York, 1961.

SAMPSON, H. (ed.). World Railways. London: 1963–64.

SCHNEYDER, P. "Les Problèmes Africains de l'Energie," Problemes Economiques, Notes Rapides (Institut National des la Statistiques et des Etudes Economiques), No. 855 (May, 1964), pp. 13–17.

Situation, Trends and Prospects of Electric Power Supply in Africa. (U.N., E/CN.14/EP.3/Rev.1.) New York, 1965.

Transport Problems in Relation to Economic Development in West Africa. (U.N. Economic Commission for Africa, E/CN 14/63.) New York, 1960.

VAIZEY, J. "Education in African Economic Growth," in E. A. H. ROBINSON (ed.), Economic Development for Africa South of the Sahara. London: Macmillan, 1964. Pp. 340–55.

VAN DONGEN, I. S. The British East African Transport Complex. (Research Paper No. 38, University of Chicago, Department of Geography.) Chicago, 1954.

WRIGLEY, C. "Economic Problems of Development," Proceedings, Conference on Research in West Africa. Ibadan, March, 1961.

IX

Foreign Investment
and Aid Programs*

> *If you find any Island or maine land populous, and that the people hath need of cloth then you are to devise what commodities they have to purchase the same withall. If they be poore, then you are to consider the soile, and how by any possibilities the same may be made to enrich them, that hereafter they may have something to purchase the cloth withall.*
>
> Instructions given by RICHARD HAKLUYT to merchants of the Moscovie Company, 1850
>
> *Their gain shall be the knowledge of our faith, and ours such riches as the country hath.*
>
> SIR FRANCIS DRAKE, speaking of the American Indians

The time period in which there has been substantial foreign lending and investing in Africa is not long—for most of the continent,

* The help of Badri Rao and Dina Driva in assembling much of the material used in this chapter is gratefully acknowledged.

185

considerably less than the sixty-odd years since a significant economic contact was established with the rest of the world.*

There are two aspects to any provision of capital by foreign private investors: the private investor must expect to get a return adequate to induce him to invest; and the receiving country must expect that the investment will make a net contribution to its Gross National Product.

Let us consider first the financial return to lenders. Formally, this consists of interest and amortization. If we accept this as a working basis, and assuming the bond or the loan is made at par, the amortization is the repayment of the original capital; the interest is the return on the capital. But this assumes that there is no risk involved and that no risk premium is included in the interest. In foreign lending, though, risk is always involved, and the return to the lender must include not only a return on the capital but a differential payment for the particular risk taken. In addition, the lender will usually have administrative costs that have to be covered. Until quite recently, the make-up of the World Bank's interest rate, for example, was explicit on this point: it was made up, grosso modo, of the cost of money to the Bank—the rate the Bank was paying on money it borrowed at a given time—plus ¼ of 1 per cent for administrative expenses and 1 per cent for a Special Reserve against losses; that is, it explicitly combined the return on capital, administrative costs, and the risk premium. (In actual fact, the first element was interpreted liberally in favor of the developing countries: it was raised only after a considerable time lag when interest the Bank paid on its borrowings was going up, and was lowered rapidly when the rate went down; furthermore, the administrative charge of 0.25 per cent did not fully cover the Bank's administrative costs. On the other hand, as the Bank had no losses to charge to the Special Reserve, the risk premium seems to have been too high. The Bank now no longer sets its rate in this mechanical fashion but, taking all these factors and other

* Until about 1860 in West Africa and 1900 in East Africa, the bulk of foreign investment was devoted to the slave trade. Very little is known about the returns on this investment. Presumably, the slave trade was very profitable, else the large losses in men and ships would not have been borne for so many centuries. It was certainly an important part of the commerce in England, western Europe, and the New World. And the Arab slave trade in the Indian Ocean must also have paid handsome returns.

policy considerations together, sets a final rate without attempting to break it down into the various elements.)

The return to foreign *investors*, companies or people making direct investments in a foreign country, is even more complicated, including some similar elements (return on capital, payment for risk premium), and also payments for the services of management, supervision, and technicians (engineers, accountants, salesmen, etc.). It can also consist of something much more: of profits, in the Schumpeterian sense—that is to say, of profits made by a foreign entrepreneur because his knowledge of the business and techniques learned in his own economy are in advance of those available in the host country, enabling him to produce at lower cost than the local producers.

The direct investment made by foreign entrepreneurs takes advantage of their access to know-how, managerial techniques, or capital equipment superior to the local entrepreneurs'. The sector of the economy which they control may expand quite rapidly and, if it has tariff protection or transport-cost protection, it will keep most of the benefit of the high productivity for quite a time, rather than pass it on to local consumers. In essence, such enterprises gain from exploiting a type of quasi-rent—which in some cases lasts for a long while, until the indigenous population adopts similar techniques, methods, or organization, or until other foreign investors come in. The degree of difference in the levels of technique between the foreign firm and that of the indigenous economy helps to determine how long it will take before the catching up occurs and the quasi-rents are wiped out—in the case of Africa, it could be a very long time. The persistence of the gap varies inversely with the openness of the country to imports and the entrance of additional foreign investors. (In Australia, however, the data appear to show that there is now no marked divergence in earning rates between foreign-owned companies in general and domestic companies, probably as a result of both a large amount of competitive foreign investment and improvement in Australian competitiveness.)

A somewhat similar quasi-rent arises from the exploitation of natural resources in any underdeveloped country. At Africa's present stage of development, it is a far more important factor than the quasi-rent discussed above. Investors in developing countries very often stand to gain most by providing the missing cooperating factors—transport, technical knowledge, management, or the command over capital—without which it is impossible to exploit an important natural resource. In Africa, the natural obstacles to mining development are so great, and the exploitation of most mineral resources requires so much capital and so many managerial and technical resources, that the indigenous population cannot possibly do the job unaided. For the investor, then, where it is possible to buy resources at prices corresponding to their value in their present uses and then to turn them over to other more profitable uses, which the rest of the local economy is at present in no position to exploit, large gains can be made—gains that provided and provide one of the main inducements to invest in the first place. And one of the chief benefits of foreign investments in African development is that they make it possible to secure an economic use for natural resources, for which before there was none, and thus to convert objects without economic value into economic resources. (Lachmann, pp. 698–713.)

This discussion so far has assumed that the returns on investments can be measured solely in terms of the money made. But direct investment is often motivated by other, less easily measurable expectations. One important reason for investing in the development of iron-ore and bauxite resources in Africa has been the desire to have a sure source of raw materials. And a good part of the foreign investment in manufacturing plants in South Africa, Rhodesia, East Africa, and Nigeria was made in the hope of gaining a foothold in a market that was likely to be (or was being) otherwise cut off by tariff barriers. Some machinery manufacturers make direct investments as a result of their sales of machinery: as a partial return, they take an equity in the factory. There are other motives, too: for example, the "empire-building" instinct in corporate managers who want to run a far-flung corporation.

The philanthropic motive is not unimportant. The Uganda Company, which has contributed a great deal to the development of Uganda through spreading improved agricultural techniques in Uganda and encouraging new crops, was organized around the turn of the century under the inspiration of the Church Missionary Society as a practical way to help the people of Uganda. (*The Economic Development of Uganda*, p. 16.) Much of the impetus to accelerate the development of what is now Zambia and Rhodesia through intensified search for investment opportunities, backed up with the money to put into them, came from Sir Ernest Oppenheimer, Chairman of Anglo-American, de Beers, British South Africa Company, etc., and his wish to make a personal contribution to the development of southern Africa. (Source: conversations with the author, Johannesburg, 1955, 1956.)

Investing in Africa

It is not possible to make a comprehensive study of the returns on private foreign investment in Africa—much of the information is inaccessible, or impossible to collect. But I have been able to get together enough information, which I believe is fairly representative, to present a fairly consistent story.

In Africa south of the Sahara (except in South Africa, which we shall discuss separately), major investments prior to World War I were made through the chartered companies. Most of these companies tried mainly to exploit existing resources—simply going into a territory and taking out what could be easily taken out, such as ivory or gold—and to invest as little as possible. (See, in particular, Conrad, *Heart of Darkness*, and Gide, *Voyage au Congo*.) There were some exceptions—like the East Africa Company, set up to build a railway to Uganda and abolish the slave trade in East Africa. But, as it happens, there are little in the way of *easily* exploitable riches in Africa. By World War I, one after another, nearly all of the companies went bankrupt or ran into such financial difficulties that the European governments then controlling the African territories had to take them over as bankrupt or buy them out.

In French Equatorial Africa, a few remained in existence into the 1930's. The British South Africa Company (BSA) survived longer. After it lost the last of its privileges (mineral rights in what is now Zambia) on the eve of Zambia's independence in October, 1964, it merged with two other mining companies with interests in other parts of Africa and the world, forming a new company, called Charter Consolidated. The three Belgian charter companies (the most important being the Comité Speciale du Katanga [CSK]), established in 1901, 1902, and 1928, after the Congo ceased to be the personal property of King Leopold, still exist. By agreements made in February, 1965, between Belgium, the Democratic Republic of the Congo, and the companies themselves, the Congolese Government took over the portfolio of the former Belgian Congo, consisting in part of shares in the chartered companies, and the companies lost their remaining concession-granting privileges as well as rights to royalties from the mines. (Kredietbank, *Weekly Bulletin*, Brussels, April 24, 1965.)

The chartered companies that went out of existence before World War II in no case had given positive returns on the invested capital. In some cases, the investors were able to get a short-lived return while the territory was initially exploited, but very soon, most of these companies found themselves unable to pay dividends. The BSA did not pay any substantial dividends until World War II.* And even then, the rate paid by BSA was very small: the dividends of £400,000 paid in 1940 represented 5 per cent of the company's book value at that date. Of the three Belgian chartered companies in the Congo, the Comité Speciale du Katanga, with the rich mineral resources of the Katanga to exploit, appears to have become quite profitable as early as the 1920's, but the other two did not become prosperous until after World War II.

South Africa was an early and important exception to the history of frustrated hopes of foreign investors. Like the investments in the CSK and the BSA which finally began to pay off, the profitable investments in South Africa were in mining, showing fairly good returns mostly in the range of 6–8 per cent, which in fact was nothing particularly spectacular for most investors, especially when one remembers that this was the average return of a *successful* company. (See Statistical Appendix, Table 6.) The contrast between South Africa and the rest of the continent is indicated in Frankel's classic study, which showed that in 1936 the largest share of direct foreign

* The BSA and the three Belgian companies differed from other chartered companies in that they did make substantial investments in permanent productive facilities. BSA built the railway from South Africa through Bechuanaland and the Rhodesias to the Congolese border, as well as the one connecting Southern Rhodesia with Beira, in Mozambique. The Belgian companies opened up and exploited mineral resources in the Katanga, established plantations in Kivu, and built the rail connection between the Congo River at Stanleyville and Lake Tanganyika.

investment in Africa south of the Sahara had taken place in South Africa.

But, in general, outside of South Africa and of mining in particular, returns on direct investment were very low before World War II. The experience of Lever Brothers (now Unilever) in Africa prior to World War II is instructive in this regard. (Wilson, *Unilever*.)

Prior to the war, as it is still today, Unilever was the single largest foreign direct investor (outside of the mining companies) in Africa, the biggest single foreign industrial interest (outside of South Africa), and the biggest trading, farming, and transport complex in Africa. Unilever is still probably the biggest single factor in the world oils and fats market, buying nearly a quarter of the 10 million tons moving in international trade in 1965, for example. (*The Economist*, April 30, 1965, p. 525.)

In 1906, Lever Brothers was Great Britain's leading soap manufacturer. Its growth had been of a fairly simple "vertical" type, encompassing the entire manufacturing process from raw-material production to output of soap. Because imported vegetable oils were required, William Lever was particularly conscious of the importance of foreign supplies—and he feared being "squeezed" by merchants and brokers who, he thought, conspired against the manufacturers; he also feared that other manufacturers might take competitive action to secure their own raw materials.

Because of the British colonial policy of refusing to alienate African land for the establishment of plantations, Lever was unable to get land in West Africa as a secure raw-material source. (He did, however, buy trading companies in Nigeria, Sierra Leone, and Liberia.) In 1911, therefore, he established the Société Anonyme des Huileries du Congo Belge to buy wild-palm oil and grow oil palms in the Congo. The Belgian Government empowered Lever's company to establish communications and other facilities (which were to be made available to others) and required it to provide schools and hospitals and to pay a guaranteed minimum wage to labor in the areas it controlled: the Société, in fact, like the chartered companies of the period, was almost more of a government than a business. The original concession covered 1.8 million acres leasehold, of which about 500,000 eventually became freehold. Lever also acquired some 6 million acres from a French concessionaire, the Compagnie

Propriétaire du Kouilou Niari (CPKN) in the French Congo. But on closer investigation it turned out that only 10,000 acres of this were suitable for planting and this proved a total loss.

A second product of the oil palm is palm kernels, and Lever decided to have them crushed on the spot, for palm kernel oil, to save on transport costs. But he found that shipping the oil alone was more expensive, since the valuable by-product, the cake, had no market in Africa. (This industry has still not shown itself economic in Africa.)

The Huileries du Congo Belge, the single largest enterprise that Lever had undertaken, ran into difficulties almost immediately. The available manpower was not sufficient for the double task of collecting wild-palm oil and constructing new plantations. Costs were high and progress was slow. By 1914, about £1.5 million had been sunk in the African businesses. The CPKN was a dead loss; the Congo operations showed no profit; the oil mills lost more than £50,000 in 1913 alone.

The war years proved prosperous for Lever Brothers in general, but the African investments were evidently a burden on the rest of the business. Ordinary dividends of 10 per cent were declared in 1914, 15 per cent in 1917, and 17.5 per cent in 1918. The years 1919–29 were difficult, and became more so when Lever Brothers took on the Niger Company and merged it with the other Lever companies in Africa into the United Africa Company (UAC). (In 1929, after the merger of Margarine Unie with Lever Brothers into Unilever, UAC also acquired Margarine's West African trading companies.) For years, UAC was in severe financial trouble and did not declare any dividends. Unilever's Congo plantations, now closely associated with the UAC, were producing palm oil at a cost higher than market price—and the latter was a little more than a third of the value of palm oil when the original concession had been secured. But, because of its investments, Unilever felt compelled to continue to use African oils rather than other, possibly cheaper, products. By the autumn of 1931, banks and finance houses were pressing UAC to cut its commitments, but Unilever found the £3 million of liquid capital that UAC required and decided to stay in Africa—a decision reached by looking hopefully at Africa and her resources rather than by looking at balance sheets. Better management and rising commodity prices served to improve UAC's prospects between 1932 and

1936. But commodity prices broke again in 1937, bringing new trouble.

While Unilever's rate of return since World War II is comparable to prewar rates, the return on UAC investment remains smaller than on Unilever's investment as a whole. Unilever's policy over the last seven or eight years appears to have been to reduce UAC's relative share in the total investment, while reorienting its activity in such a way as to withdraw from politically sensitive areas, such as the buying of African agricultural produce, and to expand in manufacturing by setting up factories for textiles, pots and pans, soap, etc., as well as assembling trucks for local markets in Nigeria and Ghana, and for making plywood for export from Nigeria.

RETURN ON CAPITAL OF LEVER BROTHERS, LTD. AND UNILEVER

	Lever Bros. 1922	Lever Bros. 1927	Lever Bros. and Unilever 1938	Unilever Ltd. and Unilever N.V. 1955	Unilever Ltd. and Unilever N.V. 1962
	(in millions of £)				
Capital Employed*	64.4	68.1	100.5	425.0	690.0
of which in Africa	n.a.	n.a.	n.a.	118.0	116.0
Profits	4.6	5.4	9.9	42.3	54.3
of which from Africa	n.a.	n.a.	n.a.	7.6	3.7
	Percentages				
Rate of profit, as % of capital employed	7.1	7.9	9.9	9.8	7.9
of which from Africa	n.a.	n.a.	n.a.	6.5	3.2

* Figures for capital employed in 1922, 1927, and 1938 are based on data shown for aggregate liabilities and may not strictly conform to the definition of "capital employed" used in the later balance sheets.

SOURCE: Data for 1922, 1927 and 1938 are from *Moody's Manual of Investments*, volumes dealing with "Industrials" of 1928 and 1939. Figures for 1955 and 1962 are from *Unilever's Report and Accounts, 1962*.

Since World War II, then, the outlook for returns on direct private investment in African enterprises no longer appears so bleak as it did in the past, and there are indications that the opportunities for good returns on well-chosen investments are as favorable as anywhere else.

A number of comprehensive estimates have been made of private investment in the Belgian Congo before and after World War II, but not of returns. According to these, total private investment in the Congo in 1939 equalled about $800 million; for 1953, the estimate was almost $2 billion. (Banque Centrale du Congo Belge, *Bulletin,* August, 1955.) Of this latter amount, half derived from non-African sources and the other half was ploughed-back profits on the foreign investment. In a 1958 study, the Banque Centrale calculated that the dividends payable abroad by Congolese enterprises averaged between 11.6 per cent and 13.1 per cent during the years 1951–56. If one adds to this the "allocations to reserves," total profits ran at 30–35 per cent during the early 1950's, admittedly years of unusually high primary-product prices. The Banque Centrale's conclusion that firms in the Congo had much greater returns than firms in Belgium during those years, certainly appears justified.

The Banque Centrale also compared the capital/net-domestic-output ratio in Belgium (1950) and the Congo (1953); with a total capital-investment figure of $2.2 billion equivalent in the Congo, it found a ratio of 3 to 1, and, to its surprise, it found the same ratio in Belgium. The implication here is that the productivity of capital in the two countries must have been roughly the same. (Banque Centrale du Congo Belge, *Bulletin,* January, 1958.)

The improved situation for foreign investors in Africa can also be seen from figures on American activity in this field.

Using U.S. Department of Commerce figures on U.S. direct investments abroad, we have made some calculations of the rate of return. Obviously, these are only rough comparisons, including as they do both value of investments and annual earnings. Still, there is no reason to believe that the figures for Africa should not be comparable to those for other areas. (See the Statistical Appendix, Tables 7, 8.)

The first point that emerges is that the average rates of return on American investments in Africa were, for five years out of the seven in the period 1957–63, below average rates shown for world-wide American direct investment (outside the United States). The African rates of return also fluctuated more—from a high of 21 per cent to a low of 2.6 per cent, while the world figures remained within the range of 10.7–13.2 per cent. Comparing the African returns to those in other developing areas, it is clear that the Western Hemisphere and Asia paid better—Asia, in fact, much better.

However, these figures for average return on *total* investments are somewhat misleading. Figures on return by *sector*, which are more helpful, can be calculated only for the years 1958–63; these show that returns on most types of American direct investments in Africa tended to be higher than in other parts of the world—and that it was the petroleum investment that dragged down the over-all average. Return on manufacturing investment in Africa (this is mostly in South Africa) was fairly consistently higher, usually around 16 per cent but going as high as 23 per cent and 24 per cent. Earnings on mining and smelting fluctuated more—from 8.8 per cent to 24.7 per cent—but again tended to be higher than similar earnings elsewhere, though not so consistently as in manufacturing.

Apparently, however, the returns on American direct investments in Africa (excluding the petroleum investments) were higher than those secured by other investors. (This is also true in Australia.) Different tax laws of the United States and other capital-providing countries may be at least in part responsible for this. Using the available data on foreign direct investment in South Africa for the same years, 1956–63, rough calculations show a fairly consistent return of 4.6–6.2 per cent per year.

Loans to Africa

Until World War II, the main sources for loans to Africa were the private and institutional bond buyers in the capital markets of London and Paris, and the main borrowers were the governments of Africa. Today, most lending to African, as to other, developing countries is done by governments or their official agencies or by international development institutions. Of the developing nations selling public issues in the major private capital markets of the world in the first twenty years after the war, only the English-speaking African countries were successful. Since 1960, neither the free, independent African states nor the southern African governments have been able to secure any appreciable amounts in this way. The British Government, like the French, has replaced the private capital market as the main source of external funds.

Because information on the French record is less known, and because France's policy orientation on this issue has led the way for other countries, the French experience is particularly interesting.

THE FRENCH TERRITORIES

Before World War II, most of the funds needed for capital works in the French colonies of Africa was raised on the French market and in almost all cases carried the guarantee of the French Government. (A few loans were made directly by government agencies such as the Caisse des Dépôts et Consignations and the Caisse de Garantie des Assurances Sociales.) Because French Government credit was involved, in order to raise a loan on the market, the borrowing colony first had to get a special act passed by the French parliament, and had to submit its total budget to the parliament for approval.

From 1900 to World War I, the total of these loans amounted to some 315 million francs, the equivalent of a little over $60 million at the time—all but 35 million francs of which went to French West Africa and Madagascar. Most of these loans were paid off after World War I at depreciated franc rates; the investors lost from two-thirds to four-fifths of their original investment.

From 1919 to 1931, only 510 million francs were raised (all by French West Africa and French Equatorial Africa), or about $20–$30 million. During this period, too, interest rates went up. One part of the loans to French Equatorial Africa was issued at a rate of more than 8 per cent; this was a loan a large part of which was devoted to what was then a somewhat dubious project—the construction of the first railroad in French Equatorial Africa from Brazzaville to Pointe Noire, which duplicated the existing Belgian line from Léopoldville to the sea.

In 1931, the French parliament passed laws authorizing new loans for public works in all of France's overseas territories. For the first time, a general program—the Maginot Program—was spelled out for the development of the colonies, but no direct financial aid was granted other than the usual guarantee. By the end of 1939, about 3 billion francs had been issued, at interest rates which rose steadily from 4 per cent to 6.25 per cent. During World War II, new authorizations of more than a billion francs (around $150 million at the exchange rates of the time) were made to those colonies not adhering to free France, these advances being made by the French Treasury in view of the unpropitious market conditions. Again, of this capital, the investors have since lost 80–90 per cent of the capital value.

The total capital lent by French investors to Africa prior to World War II came thus to the equivalent of perhaps $200–$250 million (pre–World War II dollars). According to a calculation made by the French National Institute of Statistics, investment in bonds between 1914 and 1940 gave a negative yield of minus 3 per cent to minus 7 per cent. ("L'Intérêt du capital.") Since World War II, the bulk of the external capital provided to the public sector in the ex-French areas of Africa has been provided by the French Government on a grant basis, with only a small amount extended in the form of loans (and this mostly in soft loans). Since 1957, the governments of other European Economic Community members have also contributed. (For a more detailed discussion of the aid program, see below, pp. 200–207.)

THE BELGIAN TERRITORIES

By 1920, private investors had lent a total of some 170 million (1914) francs (equivalent to about $35 million) to the Belgian Congo Government; another $4 million equivalent was lent by 1939. Again, as in the French case, most of the value of the loans was wiped out by the inflation connected with World War II, and the net return to investors was definitely negative. ("Les Investissements . . . du Congo.")

Between the wars, the Belgian Government had found it necessary to finance the Congo directly. From 1921 to 1925, it advanced 17 million gold francs equivalent. In principle, these were repayable, but repayment was never demanded. Then, beginning during the depression and until 1940 and the German occupation, it provided 104 million gold francs to meet the Congo budget deficits. Altogether, from the beginning of the Congolese Free State until 1951, the Belgian Government had to pay some 209 million gold francs net (around $140 million foreign-exchange equivalent as of 1965) as grants or non-reimbursed advances. (*La Belgique et l'aide éco-nomique*, p. 191.)

THE BRITISH COLONIES

On the conclusion of World War II, the British Government began an expanded program of grants to the colonies under the Colonial Development and Welfare Acts (CD & W), and created the Colonial Development Corporation (CDC) to make direct investments in the colonies and the Overseas Food Corporation for investment in food production. This last ceased to exist after several disastrous investments; the CD & W became irrelevant to most of the African colonies as they gained their independence. But the British Government has gradually been recreating a substitute for it: first, by setting up Commonwealth assistance loans with interest rates geared to the government's own borrowing cost; then, by waiving interest charges on some loans for an initial seven-year period; and, since July, 1965, by making interest-free loans in appropriate cases. (See the Statistical Appendix, Table 11.) The CDC, at first not permitted to operate in independent countries, has since been renamed the Commonwealth Development Corporation and is now allowed to function.

The Flow of Capital Funds

Based on figures provided by S. H. Frankel, I have estimated that the total foreign capital invested in Africa south of the Sahara before World War II was around $6 billion; of this, about half was borrowed by the public sector of the African territories on private capital markets, mostly in London and Paris; about half was private. From 1945 to 1960, probably another $6 billion (at current prices,) came in from private sources and around $10 billion in public funds. At varying dates in much of Africa, and certainly since 1960 for all of Africa south of the Sahara, it has not been possible for the African public sector to secure an appreciable amount of funds from private lenders or investors at a reasonable range of return. Official

sources, that is, governments and the international development institutions, have therefore been the main providers of funds at conces-
sional rates. In the 1960–65 period, the total net inflow of capital has
been under $5 billion, with the net inflow of private capital (including
ploughed-in profits) of around $500 million in southern Africa,
Nigeria, Ivory Coast, and Liberia largely offset by capital flight or
repatriation from other parts of the continent. The indications are
strong that, except in mining, the prewar returns on private direct
investment were poor and not very exciting. Since the war, the situation seems to have improved: manufacturing, at least in South
Africa, and mining appear to give very good returns. On the other
hand, investment, other than in mining, outside of South Africa
does not appear particularly favorable.*

According to estimates compiled by the Organization for Economic Cooperation and Development (OECD), the total net flow
of official long-term financial resources to developing countries in
1964 was $6 billion, of which $1.75 billion (net of amortization)
was loaned. In the same year, the total amount of new bonds sold
by all the developing countries in foreign capital markets was $97
million; in 1965, $112 million. (And these figures are gross, since
refunding or amortization is not deducted.) Of these amounts
raised on the capital markets, only South Africa among African
countries participated, to the amount of $13 million in 1965.

In Africa south of the Sahara, the net flow of official capital
reached just over $1 billion a year in 1964, with net official lending
over $200 million a year.

Of the total financial resources made available to the developing
countries by members of the Development Assistance Committee
(DAC) of OECD on a bilateral basis, more than half are now
grants or grant-like contributions. In 1962, the percentage was 60;
in 1963, 56; and in 1964, 54. For Africa south of the Sahara, grants
represent 70–75 per cent of the total. The loans themselves are
made on quite favorable terms. The weighted average maturity of
official loans has been increasing: it was 23.9 years in 1962, 24.6

---

* In this field, as in most African ones, more research and statistical work are
needed: on the returns to foreign investment, and on the flow of capital and
the returns to capital. The World Bank, in cooperation with OECD and the
IMF, has started a program to improve the various data components on the flow
of capital, but progress is likely to be slow.

years in 1963, and 27.6 years in 1964. The weighted average interest rate was 3.6 per cent in 1962, 3.4 per cent in 1963, and 3.5 per cent in 1964. These terms quite clearly are considerably below the cost of capital to developed countries; they do not cover an economic return on capital, much less any allowance for risk premium or costs of administration.

Aid Programs

Until World War II, economic aid to Africa was sporadic and was never included as a part of the over-all foreign economic policies of the metropolitan or industrialized powers. After the war, both the British and French governments started aid programs to their dependent territories—so did Portugal, on a much smaller scale—and since those territories won their independence, the aid programs have continued, without interruption by the French; after a pause by the British. Indeed, the largest single aid program in Africa is still France's bilateral program to her former colonies (supplemented since 1957 by the Economic Development Fund of the European Common Market). These countries have received foreign aid amounting on the average to around 8 per cent of GNP (with the range between 6 per cent and 12 per cent) and to about 65 per cent of gross investment (which averaged around 12 per cent of GNP in these countries during 1960). Since 1960, the aid they receive has increased by about one-quarter (mostly from the Economic Development Fund), or somewhat faster than the GNP, and is now probably about 9 per cent of total GNP, with gross investment about 13 per cent of total GNP. Their volume of aid per capita is around $9 equivalent. In the rest of sub-Saharan Africa, aid has increased even more rapidly—going up by some 70 per cent between 1960 and 1963—but it still is only about half as important to the economy, averaging over the whole area about $4 per capita in 1965, and about 5 per cent of GNP. Since 1963, however, French policy has been to reduce dependence on bilateral aid, in order, presumably, to encourage self-reliance and independent action on the part of the African aid recipients and to free French resources to be used elsewhere in the world. (*La Politique de Coopération.*)

The United States came on the African aid scene for a brief period during the Marshall Plan and after, mostly because of the use of local-currency counterpart funds generated in the European aid programs. The amounts of the American aid contribution are lost or obscured in the intricate accounting of these counterpart funds—particularly in France, where a strict division was not maintained between the use of funds in France and overseas. Since during this period France and the U.K. were receiving aid from America and simultaneously extending aid and exporting capital to their currency areas, it is admittedly arbitrary to identify one final user as the "recipient" of aid. But in any case, about half a billion dollars of real resources made available to France and the United Kingdom under the Marshall Plan were passed on to Africa. Most of this went to North Africa, but as much as $100 million of the French and British aid to sub-Saharan Africa might at least be ascribed to the Marshall Plan. That is, the $100 million is essentially an accounting estimate of the amount of counterpart funds generated by Marshall Plan aid that were made available to sub-Saharan French and English colonies. In general economic terms, one could just as well argue that the aid given to African countries by Britain and France during this period was a marginal use of resources, and that if the Marshall Plan aid had not been received in the first place, there would have been no aid to Africa. On this basis, one could label all the French, British, and Portuguese aid to Africa during this period as indirect American aid.

It was essentially after the African territories became independent that the United States began to give aid directly to Africa. Although the American program at first extended to virtually every independent country, it is now concentrated on Nigeria, Tunisia, the Congo (Léopoldville), Ethiopia, and Somalia. The Soviet Union and East European countries also began aid programs to Africa at about the same time, starting in 1959; they concentrated from the beginning on particular countries—mainly Ghana, Guinea, Ethiopia, Mali, Somalia, and Tunisia. Communist China came on the scene first in North Africa, with help to the Algerian nationalists, and then in 1964 south of the Sahara, with aid to Guinea, Kenya, Mali, Somalia, and Tanzania. While no detailed reports are available on aid programs from the Soviet Union and East Europe, from the information available on the actual agreements and given the exceptional slowness of disbursements under them, one can conclude that it is unlikely that total disbursements exceeded $100 million for 1960–62, with a maximum of $50 million in 1963. Mainland China through 1964 had made commitments of $160 million in Africa (mainly Algeria); in 1964, it committed $80 million, mainly to Tanzania and Kenya. Total Chinese disbursements through 1965 are not likely to have exceeded $30 million.

A number of other countries have also extended aid to independent Africa—notably West Germany, with capital and technical-assistance programs, and Israel, with technical assistance.

The Net Flow of Financial Resources from Multilateral Agencies and the Flow of Official Bilateral Net Contributions from Individual OECD Member Countries to Sub-Saharan Africa (Excluding South Africa)

(in millions of dollars)

	1960	1961	1962	1963	1964	1965[1]
Multilateral Agencies						
World Bank Group	48.7	51.9	44.0	8.3	24.3	60.5
Other U.N. Agencies[2]	16.0	39.9	29.5	36.0	49.4	(50.0)[1]
EEC	3.3	15.2	51.3	58.9	77.4	97.0
TOTAL Multilateral	68.0	107.0	124.8	103.2	151.1	(207.5)[1]
Bilateral						
France	280.1[3]	275.7[3]	288.1[3]	294.0[3]	281.0[3]	310.9[3]
United Kingdom	123.6	228.0	172.5	163.5	211.3	135.0
United States	39.0	75.0	197.0	159.0	161.0	126.7
Belgium	86.0	70.5	63.4	75.8	76.5	103.9
Germany	5.3	13.4	59.2	54.1	41.4	19.0
Portugal	36.6	32.4	40.7	51.1	61.9	7.8
Italy	16.6	18.5	12.5	22.5	16.4	16.6
Other[4]	20.8	27.5	33.8	35.2	14.9	17.4
TOTAL Bilateral	608.0	741.0	867.2	855.2	864.4	737.3
GRAND TOTAL	676.0	848.0	992.0	958.4	1,015.5	....

[1] Preliminary figure.

[2] Disbursements net of subscriptions payments for UNICEF, UNWRA, U.N. High Commissioner for Refugees, the U.N. Fund for the Congo, the U.N. Special Fund, and the U.N. Technical Assistance Programmes.

[3] Excluding aid to French overseas territories.

[4] Including funds from Australia, Austria, Canada, Denmark, Japan, Netherlands, Norway, Sweden, and Switzerland.

SOURCES: Organization for Economic Cooperation and Development and the World Bank.

International and multilateral assistance programs are also important to Africa. About 10 per cent of the total flow of funds has come from the World Bank Group and the European Common Market's Economic Development Fund. (See the Statistical Appendix, Tables 15–17.)

Of course, not all of the amounts we have mentioned should properly be called "economic aid"—i.e., funds made available on a subsidized basis, below market cost, to help a nation's economic development.* Certainly some of these funds were provided for political or military ends—to influence the political orientation of the recipient country or to secure military bases. Some funds were provided and accepted for cultural reasons: the President of the Central African Republic, David Dacko, stated in a speech to his legislature, "Our countries have been rebuilt in the image of the West, and we have agreed to keep the French language here; it is because we have learned this language that we have adopted French civilization. We are called upon to build in the heart of Africa a nation in the image of France." Also, some part of these funds were supplier or exporter credits designed primarily to sell machinery or equipment—in some cases, machinery that was basically unsuitable or uneconomic to use in the country to which it was sold. Probably only the international and multilateral aid programs can be described without reservation as being wholly devoted to economic development. But capital made available for other ends can be helpful to economic development— even aid to military forces, through the army's construction of roads, the training of soldiers in useful skills, etc.

A substantial part of the aid programs in Africa provides technical assistance; indeed, Africa receives a greater volume of technical assistance in both relative and absolute terms than any other region of the world; almost half of France's contribution is in technical assistance; almost a third of all aid to Africa south of the Sahara consists of expenditures on or is connected with technical assistance.† In

---

* Economic aid might more precisely be defined as the residual left to the borrower after subtracting the present value of the debt service installments (discounted by the rate of yield on the investment made with the funds). A loan at 2 per-cent interest "invested" in a prestige project with no return would have no aid element in it.

† The great importance of technical assistance in Africa is indicated by the following figure: bilateral technical-assistance personnel from the OECD nations

Africa, technical assistance in the form of trained personnel is often even more important than additional capital, and in most African countries, the ability to absorb capital depends on the amount of technical assistance received.

During 1963, there were 31,000 technical-assistance personnel stationed in Africa south of the Sahara—40 per cent of the total provided to developing countries by the OECD (there is another 40 per cent in North Africa)—10,000 teachers and the rest administrative personnel and technicians. Of these 31,000, 14,000 were provided by France, at a cost of $136 million equivalent; 10,000 came from and were largely or partly financed by Great Britain, at an annual cost of around $40 million equivalent; 3,000 (including Peace Corpsmen) from the United States; almost 3,000 from Belgium. In addition to the 31,000 from the OECD countries, the various international agencies supplied 3,000 technical-assistance personnel, and around 500 came from Israel.

The distribution of French personnel among the African countries varies in intensity from country to country. It is seven times higher per million Africans in the Ivory Coast than in the Congo (Brazzaville), for example. In general, the higher the per-capita income, the greater the intensity, so that Senegal and Ivory Coast each receive four times as much assistance as Upper Volta, for example. (Upper Volta's population is greater than either, but its per-capita income is about a quarter or a fifth that of the others.) This certainly is not the criterion on which the assistance is made available—the criterion being rather the ability of a country to use the assistance well and its desire for it—but it is clear that the more resources a nation has and the more developed it is, the more help it can use to accelerate its growth. After a certain point, it will obviously be able to cut back on technical assistance. But this point is not likely to come before the African countries have multiplied their present per-capita income several times and are at least semi-industrialized.

---

form about 1 per cent of the university teaching staffs of all developing nations; in Africa, however, *three-quarters* of the university teachers come from this source. "The total input of foreign personnel probably represents about 2.2 per cent of the high-level manpower of developing countries and about the same fraction of middle-level manpower. . . . [But] in Africa south of the Sahara, the majority of the high-level skills are possessed by foreigners." (Maddison, pp. 18–19.)

Consideration of the French-speaking countries in this regard is particularly revealing, since it represents what amounts to a controlled experiment. Because of the French Government's generosity in paying for technical assistance and because of its willingness to meet almost any reasonable request, we can safely say that French aid before 1963 was close to being the maximum amount that could be usefully employed in the recipient countries. That this assistance appears to have varied directly with the country's level of development is therefore particularly significant. It should be possible for a country, in the course of its development, to reduce its use of technical assistance—and this appears to have happened among the English-speaking nations of Africa—and still maintain a favorable growth rate. But, when technical assistance is available on favorable terms and is politically acceptable, the nation's capacity to substitute its own manpower in activities that were once foreign technical-assistance programs apparently, as in the French-speaking countries, makes it possible to absorb and use still more technical assistance, and to secure an accelerated rate of growth in this way.

In conclusion, then, economic development in Africa clearly does not depend solely on the flow of aid from non-African sources, but, just as clearly, aid is very important. Insofar as it is possible to disentangle them, the main outlines of present policies and actions concerning the principal sources of capital and aid appear as follows:

Aid from bilateral donors is beginning to level off. France and the United States are cutting back, the United Kingdom is increasing its aid but at a slow pace. Belgium, Germany, and other Western countries are together about holding their own. The Communist aid programs, after an initial flurry of commitments, are unimportant in actual disbursements and economic effectiveness and are likely to proceed cautiously.

Aid from multilateral and international sources is still slight but shows possibility of growth. The European Common Market's FED and the European Investment Bank are increasing their activities, but the funds allocated to Africa are only slightly above those available in the past. The World Bank Group in 1964 assigned a representative to Addis Ababa to work with the Economic Commission for Africa and the Ethiopian Government; in 1965, it opened two regional offices (in Nairobi for eastern and southern Africa and in Abidjan for western Africa) to help African governments to prepare projects for finance. (The Abidjan office is also helping in the organization of the African Development Bank.) The World Bank Group has also re-invigorated two Consultative Groups— groups of donor countries organized to aid in the development of particular countries—for Nigeria and the Sudan. While all this activity should result in a considerable increase in the World Bank's role in Africa, the amounts are likely to be limited without a substantial increase in IDA funds made available to the Bank Group. (The IDA, or International Development Association, provides money on concessionary terms to developing countries. The source of these funds is contributions made by the principal developed countries who are members of the Bank.) Few African countries are in a strong enough economic and financial position to take on a substantial volume of foreign debt on conventional terms; consequently, the World Bank Group has to provide a large proportion of the loans to African nations on IDA terms. (In 1966, these were 50 years; 10-year initial period of no principal repayments, 0.75 per cent.)

The African Development Bank has only just begun operations. Unfortunately, in organizing the Bank, the Africans decided to exclude non-African countries; and, as South Africa is not a member for obvious reasons, the African Bank, unlike the Inter-American Development Bank or the Asian Development Bank, has no capital-exporting countries among its members. (The Asian Development Bank, in contrast, not only was lucky enough to have Japan, Australia, and New Zealand as members—all developed enough to be able to help other countries—but shrewdly made provision for non-regional members. It was thus able to secure over a third of its capital of $1 billion from the United States and Western Europe.) The African Bank has had to try to derive all of its much smaller authorized capital of $250 million from the African countries—all of whom need capital themselves—and has no ready source of outside funds. Inevitably it will be more difficult for the African Bank to persuade industrial countries to provide it with funds than for the Asian Bank, which already has these countries as members.

Conclusion

No large-scale increase in private foreign investment is likely to occur in Africa in the foreseeable future, although some of the individual countries may do quite well. No substantial increase in the supply of capital, therefore, is in sight—a most disheartening conclusion. There is so much to be done in Africa that is beyond the capacities of the local economies at their present stage of development, yet at the same time, the Africans' eagerness to move ahead and their receptivity to new ideas and techniques puts their continent in a unique category among developing regions. A major effort in research, education, training, institution-building, and investment— at this point in history, when the Africans are still not weary or disillusioned—could bring about a real break-through in economic development.

But there are no major new initiatives at present, there is no coherent or organized approach to the problems of the continent. The organizations principally concerned with African affairs are too fragmented, scattered, and understaffed to provide the kind of dynamic drive necessary to galvanize support and action to help Africa. An organization coordinating all the principal donor countries and economic agencies, with African participation and a strong Secretariat to focus on African economic and financial problems, is needed to stimulate and coordinate new provision of aid. Only such a stimulus would make it possible to get the African aid programs out of the rut, to assess and correct the deficiencies in the various sectors where action is needed, and to coordinate the programs and approaches in an effective attack on Africa's problems.

Selected Bibliography

BANQUE CENTRALE DU CONGO BELGE ET DU RUANDA-URUNDI. *Bulletin* (Brussels, Léopoldville), IV, No. 8 (August, 1955); VII, No. 1 (January, 1958).

La Belgique et l'aide économique aux pays sous-développés. Brussels and The Hague: Nijhoff, for the Institut Royal des Relations Internationales, 1959.

Colonial Development and Welfare. (U.K., Secretary of State for the Colonies [Acts, Cmd. 672, February, 1959].) London: H.M. Stationery Office, 1959.

CONRAD, J. *Heart of Darkness.* London: J. M. Dent & Sons, 1902.

The Flow of Financial Resources to Less Developed Countries, 1956–1963. Paris: OECD, 1964.

FRANCE, MINISTÈRE D'ETAT CHARGÉ DE LA RÉFORME ADMINISTRATIVE. *La Politique de Coopération avec les pays en voie de Développement.* Report of the Jeanneney Study Group, 1963.

FRANKEL, S. H. *Capital Investment in Africa.* London and New York: Oxford University Press, 1938.

GIDE, A. *Voyage au Congo.* Paris: Gallimard, 1927.

HAILEY, LORD. *An African Survey, Rev. 1956.* London and New York: Oxford University Press, 1957.

"L'Intérêt du capital de 1914 à 1965," *Études et Conjoncture* (Paris, Institut Nationale de la Statistique et des Études Économiques), XX, No. 10 (October, 1965), 47–64.

"Les Investissements Belges et Étrangers au Congo," in Banque National de Belgique, *Bulletin d'information et de documentation,* I, No. 3 (March, 1952), 174–81.

LACHMANN, L. M. "Investment Repercussions," *Quarterly Journal of Economics,* LXII (1948), 698–713.

LITTLE, I. M. D. *Aid to Africa.* Oxford: Pergamon Press; New York: Macmillan, 1964.

MADDISON, A. *Foreign Skills and Technical Assistance in Economic Development.* Paris: Development Center of the OECD, 1965.

MASON, E. S., et al. *The Economic Development of Uganda.* Baltimore, Md.: The Johns Hopkins Press, for the International Bank for Reconstruction and Development, 1962.

Private Overseas Investment in Australia, supplement to the Commonwealth of Australia Treasury *Information Bulletin,* (Canberra), May, 1965.

U.S. DEPARTMENT OF COMMERCE. *Survery of Current Business* (Washington, D.C.), various issues, various years.

WILSON, C. *The History of Unilever.* 2 vols. London: Cassell, 1954.

X

Economic Plans
and Planning in Africa

> *The reality of economic planning in
> the hustle and bustle of a fast de-
> veloping African country bears little
> or no relation to the theoretical work
> on elegant models constructed in
> statistical laboratories of more de-
> veloped countries.*
>
> TANGANYIKA DEVELOPMENT PLAN

Africa is the continent of economic plans. Every country in
Africa (except South Africa) has had at least one since World War
II, and most have had several. The preparation of economic plans
began under the colonial regimes and under the stimulus of the
colonial powers. Both the British and the French decided that aid
to their colonial territories after the war had to be provided within
the context of development plans, worked out for each colony by the
territorial governments themselves with help from London in the
case of the British colonies and by Paris for the French colonies.

Perhaps the one point in colonial history upon which everybody
now agrees is that these development plans were defective: they were
prepared by administrators with little or no economic background;
coordination of the investments in various sectors was largely non-

existent; there was no consistent development strategy. In short, the plans were "no more than lists of projects."

Yet, it must be said (nostalgically) that these plans did have one virtue: they were usually carried out. They did represent something that was actually planned to take place, and the probability was high that it would take place. And when, to the preparation and execution of these plans, an economic intelligence was added to influence government policy (as in the case of the Rhodesias during C. H. Thompson's tenure as Economic Adviser, 1951–58, or in Nigeria after the 1953 World Bank Economic Survey Mission), the results were probably as close to the economic optimum as one could have reasonably expected to attain.

In the era of independent African countries, the highest rate of economic growth may well have been reached in the production of plans—increasingly more "comprehensive" and sophisticated plans. *The Plan* has become a symbol of independence, and a great deal of public attention is devoted to, and incantation of praises made over, the Plan document.

The planning process is in many countries depressingly similar: An expert or team of experts arrives to prepare a plan. They set to work to construct or fill in a model of the economy, build up intersectoral input-output tables, construct a system of equations, and present an internally consistent over-all development plan complete with capital/output ratios; marginal savings coefficients; import, consumption, and production functions; investment; savings; and import gaps. A plan is worked out for the whole economy which lays down a growth rate, sectoral targets and allocations of funds, a balance-of-payments projection showing the need for foreign aid. The plan is turned over to the government; the visiting experts depart. At that point, the government may simply file the plan away on a shelf (as Upper Volta did, in one case); or it may adopt it with great fanfare and a year or so later request someone else to prepare another one (as happened in Sierra Leone and Senegal); or, as in most cases, it may continue to give lip service to the plan but otherwise pay little or no attention to it. "The majority of the plans . . . are only vaguely operational in the sense that decisions with respect to investment and other policy matters are often made by the government without respect to the plans' objectives and priorities." (Forrest, p. 6.)

But when the government tries to carry out the plan, it may find it to be of not much help. In Guinea, for example, the Three-Year Development Plan 1960–63, devised by two foreign advisers, had as objectives: decolonization and economic independence by restructuring the economy; accelerated growth as far as possible within the framework of collective property of the means of production, with the state sector and cooperatives playing a dominant role in all domains; amelioration of the standard of living of the population; etc. The plan was unrealistic, its stated goals completely out of line with the administrative capacity of the government and the existing information on the resources and problems of Guinea. The government tried valiantly to carry out the plan, however; with the help of substantial foreign aid, it got investment to well over 20 per cent of GNP. But the GNP grew more slowly than the population, so that the per-capita standard of living went down; foreign aid and voluntary domestic savings were insufficient to finance the investments, so the central bank had to print money, resulting in a rise in prices and a discouragement to export; export earnings (outside of the foreign-owned mines) went down.

On the other hand, the plans in Kenya and the Sudan (and, in North Africa, Tunisia) have certainly been of help—perhaps, to greater or lesser degree, in other countries as well. But over all, an objective observer must inevitably conclude that for most of Africa the plans have so far made little or no contribution to economic development. The improvement of planning in Africa depends in part on some general factors, and in part on some specifically or especially African characteristics.

I would venture to say that a general consensus on planning has arisen among most economists who have had extensive experience in development planning: A. K. Cairncross, W. Arthur Lewis, E. S. Mason, G. M. Meier, and the World Bank economic advisers give roughly similar advice in this field. What matters most, they all say, is not whether a plan is well coordinated or internally consistent, although this is desirable, but whether it is based on good economic judgment and reasoning. Uncoordinated decisions are bad, but so may be coordinated ones: even if the Tanganyika groundnut (peanut) project of the Overseas Food Corporation had been perfectly coordinated, it would have been no less a disaster, for the original decision to grow peanuts by large-scale mechanization in Tanganyika was wrong. A plan should be a focus, not a substitute, for decision-making.

In fact, an economic plan is nowhere near as important as the process by which a government makes economic and financial decisions. It is much better to have a good planning process in this sense than to have a good plan. As Albert Waterston puts it:

Development planning as a process involves the application of a rational system of choices among feasible courses of investment and other development actions based on a consideration of economic and social costs and benefits. Planning as a process is an indispensable precondition for the formulation of effective development policies and measures. A plan can play an important part in the planning process when it makes explicit the basis and rationale for planning policies and measures. But if a plan is prepared before the process has begun in earnest or if it is unable to generate the process, it is likely to have little significance for development. (Waterston, p. 5.)

The pressure that international aid agencies have exerted on governments to prepare national plans and the priority that the governments have given these plans are, then, misapplied. The priority belongs to building up a proper economic policy-making machinery and using it effectively. What is important is not to set a target in a document called a plan, but establishing the right economic policies and targets and then deciding on the action to carry them out. Once these are secured, an effective and realistic plan can be easily produced. It is really useless, for example, to produce a plan for a nation that has not yet succeeded in preparing and administering a proper government budget—as is true of one African country now launched on its Second Five-Year Plan.

Perhaps one of the biggest wastes in developing countries is in the way economists are used. It is not at all unusual to find the scarce economic talent available segregated in a planning office, working on a sophisticated macro-economic model, while policy decisions that are shaping the economic future of the country are made without the benefit of economic analysis or advice. What makes the whole matter worse is that the model and plan being constructed often bear little relation to reality. This is not a defect peculiar to Africa: "The latest Turkish plan, according to one observer, is a workmanlike job, complete with intersectoral input-output tables.

But it has one defect: the underlying statistics are either unreliable or absent." (Watson and Dirlam, note 4, p. 187.) But if the time and effort spent on such unrealistic exercises were devoted to improving basic statistical and economic information, economic development in Africa would be speeded up.

In other words, an African government would be well advised to use its own and any available foreign economists as advisers in the Prime Minister's or President's office and the principal economic ministries, and in strengthening the statistical services—*before* it turns to the problem of providing personnel to build ultra-refined econometric models.

It is true that the economists and foreign advisers involved may find it easier to play with models and write papers than to engage in the demanding task of finding out the real facts of the nation's economic problems, working out the policy solutions, and trying to persuade a ministry or government to adopt them. The kind of talent required is exactly that described by Keynes:

> The amalgam of logic and intuition and the wide knowledge of facts, most of which are not precise, which is required for economic interpretation in its highest form is, quite truly, overwhelmingly difficult for those whose gift mainly consists in the power to imagine and pursue to their furtherest points the implications and prior conditions of comparatively simple facts which are known with a high degree of precision. (*Essays in Biography*, pp. 191–92.)

That is to say, what is required is an economist who understands how the economy really works in the African context and what broad institutional forces affect it. Unfortunately, in today's scientific environment, governments too often believe that an economist-mathematician, if sufficiently incomprehensible, is the best planner. That this results, in Keynes' phrase, in losing "sight of the complexities and interdependencies of the real world in a maze of pretentious and unhelpful symbols" is considered not a drawback but a virtue. This is because plans are regarded as "magic"—pointed to with pride, expected to result in growth, but not regarded as a guide to action.

Aside from the misuse of economists, the planning process should be realistic in regard to what is administratively feasible in the country concerned. "A due regard for these considerations would limit the size of the public investment sector in a development program to dimensions capable of effective administration; it would counsel against the imposition of controls whose implementation lies outside the competence of existing public services; it would emphasize the importance of training programs and of necessary changes in government procedures." (Mason, p. 72.)

In addition, planners all too often spend their time on the aggregates and never get to the sectors or projects. For development to occur, concrete investment plans for individual projects must have been prepared—investigating technical feasibilities, computing the costs and benefits, and dealing with problems of administration and management. It does no good to be told that investment of x amount is necessary on roads. What roads, going from where to where, what quality, costing how much, saving how much in road-user costs and conferring how much in development benefits?

A major constraint, in other words, is what Hirschman calls the shortage of "the ability to make and carry out development decisions." It is illusory to think in terms of complex plans in countries where the administrative structure is in disarray. This was obvious in countries like the Congo (Léopoldville) after independence. But even in a number of other African countries that did not go through the same disastrous experience, the rapid departure of "expatriate" government officers and their replacement by inexperienced local people meant that even normal administrative tasks were difficult to carry out; much less was it possible to carry out bold new plans. In Tanganyika in 1962, I was told that an AID project for town water supplies was proceeding exceptionally slowly—because it was necessary to dig up the streets to find out where the existing pipes were, the turnover in personnel having been so great that no one was left who knew how to find the files that had the information!

Even without the special disruptions of the independence process, "the ways in which economic policy is formed and institutions are adopted are . . . much messier than is normally . . . acknowledged by economists. Since these changes are part of economic progress *and yet are not fully determined by it*, the process of development is by implication far too complicated to be fitted into the elegant (or should one say naïve) fantasies of the model builders." (Seers, p. 159.)

The colonial governments were governments by bureaucrats, trained to be good administrators, but men with little or no economic training. For such men, the transition was easy from issuing directives to the administration to issuing directives to the economy. Even the public utilities were run as government departments instead of as business enterprises having to meet the economic test of profit and loss.

This tendency to administer the economy by directive has been inherited by the independent African governments, and it is reinforced by an easy perversion of "comprehensive" planning, which is always believed more desirable than something that sounds as incomplete as "partial" planning. In any case, it does make sense to prepare plans for the public sector in terms of and within a framework of comprehensive estimates and forecasts for the structure and evolution of the entire economy; it also makes sense to include the policy plans and instruments the government intends to use to help, persuade, and induce the private sector to develop. But it is easy to go too far, especially among the African governments whose neo-colonialist tendencies to indulge in government by directive are strong, and to attempt also to plan the private sector in detail. This is not an ideological mistake, but simply a matter of ineffective development tactics.

Perhaps the most telling criticism of bureaucratic or centralized economic planning was made by Trotsky, when he foresaw the dead end that Stalinist planning policies would lead to. As we now know, bureaucratic planning can secure growth for a time but with such inefficiency and sacrifice that eventually they are insupportable. As Trotsky put it:

> If there existed the universal mind that projected itself into the scientific fancy of Laplace; a mind that would register simultaneously all the processes of nature and of society, that could measure the dynamics of their motion, that could forecast the results of their interreactions, such a mind, of course, could a priori draw up a faultless and exhaustive economic plan. . . . In truth, the bureaucracy often conceives that just such a mind is at its disposal; that is why it so easily frees itself from the control of the market and of Soviet democracy. . . . The innumerable living participants of the economy, State as well as private, collective as well as individual, must give notice of

their needs and of their relative strength not only through the statistical determination of plan commissions but by direct pressure of supply and demand. The plan is checked, and, to a considerable measure, realised through the market. . . . Economic accounting is unthinkable without market relations. (*The Soviet Economy in Danger,* pp. 29–30, 33. Quoted in Lerner, pp. 62–64.)

For the African countries to achieve a satisfactory rate of growth will not be easy. It is much more difficult than in developed countries, where growth may be stimulated or induced by manipulating the macro-economic variables—increasing the rate of investment by appropriate tax measures, or increasing total gross national expenditure by a budgetary deficit, or shifting the relationship between the domestic cost-price structure and the international one by changing exchange rates, etc. One is able to rely on the law of large numbers and, therefore, on the statistical equations that describe economic behavior and the relationships in the economy. But to use this approach in Africa, and to use it as the main analytical policy guide, leads to meaningless and irrelevant conclusions.

At this stage development planning in Africa does not require elaborate statistical exercises. The main problem is to identify the development potentialities—unexploited minerals, fertile soils, water supplies, commercial crops, technological improvements, and opportunities for import substitution. Mathematical models are needed by countries where the growth of internal demand is the engine of development, since full identification of the possibilities then requires demand projections and input-output analysis of inter-industry transactions. In Africa development planning is primarily an exercise in detecting new opportunities; its tool is not mathematics, but lavish expenditure on surveys and research. (Lewis, "Aspects of Economic Development," p. 9.)

Successful development in Africa will consist in large part of discontinuities—not of even movement along a curve but of kinks in the curve, jumps from one production function to another. It will proceed not so much in the form of small increases in industrial output, for example, but of a whole new industry getting started, or a new mineral resource suddenly becoming economic. Even in agriculture, where progress is more likely to be slow, jumps will occur—when the answer is found to a plant pest or a new hybrid is developed. (In Ghana, cocoa production, after remaining on a plateau for a quarter of a century, shot up by 50–70 per cent in the space of a few years in the 1960's.)

Macro-economic models imported from the developed world also suffer from another defect as far as Africa is concerned: they emphasize investment. "It is one of the weaknesses of development programming generally, and one based on aggregative investment targets specifically, that it may concentrate the attention too much on tangible investment as the only method of raising incomes." ("Problems Concerning . . . African Countries," p. 32.) Obviously, investment is important and necessary, but often a greater contribution to development can be made by governmental economic policies. In Ethiopia, for example, reform of the feudal land-tenure system, which would give farmers the incentives to improve agricultural practices, would increase the national income more rapidly than the various power and road projects, etc., now under way— even though these latter may be economically justifiable. The very important role of the government in African economies notwithstanding, most economic activities take place *outside* the public sector. Economic growth in Africa can to some extent be measured by the shrinkage of the public sector's importance as agricultural, industrial, and mineral production grows. It is, therefore, of prime importance for governments to maintain policies that encourage private investment. It helps greatly, too, if a government provides the environment for growth: honest and efficient housekeeping of its own affairs and finances, political and legal security for private investors and producers, etc.

Macro-economic models often rest on the rather questionable assumption that capital/output ratios (or capital coefficients) or the technical coefficients of an input-output table remain stable in a developing economy. But much of the problem of development is precisely to increase the output per unit of capital per worker. The model will be even more questionable if the parameters are often not even taken from the economy in question but imported from other quite different ones. (Again, this does not mean they are not useful rule-of-thumb checks; but to rely on them is dangerous.) What makes the whole process often somewhat ridiculous is that in an African economy, where the bulk of the output comes from farming, much of the investment carried out by the farmer is not even included in the GNP estimates! A more relevant model for African economies would emphasize not capital/output ratio but a coefficient that measured the effort made to raise the general level of skills and broaden the average African's horizons in relation to output—including recurrent government expenditures on education, extension services, radio, libraries, and some part of the political party expenditures, etc.

Another danger of building economic plans in a developing country mainly on macro-economic models is that is has an anti-economic effect in the real sense of the word "economics." It ignores or does not emphasize to governments that it is most important to make the most efficient possible use of scarce resources. The implication of a macro-economic approach is that *any* investment will produce output, whereas what really matters to a development plan is that some investment will have a much higher yield than others—that some, indeed, may have a negative yield. The main problem is to find and take advantage of high-yield opportunities, not to ensure that all input requirements in the model have been accounted for and that there is an exact matching of domestic resources and requirements and of foreign exchange requirements and capabilities. In the economies of Western Europe and the United States, this problem does not matter, for the government can assume that the private enterprises whose behavior is described in the aggregative model will operate to maximize profits. But in a centralized planned economy, or in a developing country where the government may be taking the initiative in investment, it is a matter of top priority to keep firmly in the foreground what yield can be expected from each investment. "We can allow the investment of capital to remain at the center of the picture; but we must insist, while we do so, that economic growth is not merely a matter of investment as such, but of investment in ways that are sufficiently productive." (Hicks, p. 177.)

Lastly, it should be emphasized that in Africa, non-economic factors are at least as important as purely economic ones in the achievement of economic development. Yet the more "advanced" and rigorous a mathematical model is, the less it is likely to take into account the non-economic factors. We have seen how complex the problem of African development is and how important some of the noneconomic characteristics of the society are in this regard. Planning which excludes such factors or throws them into a simple variable is simply not relevant, for economic development in Africa depends on the transformation of a society, and this must always be kept fully in mind.

In conclusion, then, the first importance is in staffing and organizing the government to improve day-to-day economic management of the government and the economy. Any plan for development should flow out of and be based on this work, with the following points firmly adhered to:

1. The planners—with a thorough understanding of the economy's resources and problems, including the main institutional, sociological, anthropological, and political factors involved—should study the impediments and opportunities for growth, sector by sector, and the international market possibilities.

2. Inventory should be made of the costs and benefits of public-sector investment projects already under way, and as much information as possible should be gathered on private investment under way or planned.

3. A rough forecast of how the economy will grow without further action should be prepared.

4. A policy program should be prepared of recommendations for action required to stimulate a faster rate of growth, sector by sector and over-all. Where possible, the costs and yields of each should be calculated.

5. Based on a rough financial forecast, which should include the fiscal impact of the plan and be governed by an estimate of administrative capacity (and, where applicable, the constraints of construction or contracting capacity) and by a realistic growth assumption, a public-sector program should be prepared. The projects in it would not need to be fully worked out at first, but one should have a rough idea of their costs and benefits. The program should include projects and programs *affecting* the private sector but not the projects *of* the private sector (i.e., provision of capital to industrial or agricultural development financing agencies, industrial estates, etc.). A check should then be made of the private sector, where appropriate, to see how its plans would be modified by the proposed public-sector policies. The program would then be reworked to be made internally consistent.

6. The decision in each sector to accept projects should be made

220 *The Economics of African Development*

on the basis of a partial equilibrium model. That is to say, it should be based on a calculation of the costs, forecasts of demand and prices (in the light of a realistic forecast of GNP growth), and calculation of yield. The latter would be the determining factor. No attempt should be made to screen projects on the basis of capital/output ratio, input-output matrixes, or any other kind of general equilibrium model.

7. The resulting economic plan should be regarded as a working plan, a stage in a process and not a blueprint. It should be reviewed constantly and revised periodically.

Selected Bibliography

CAIRNCROSS, A. K. *Factors in Economic Development.* London: Allen & Unwin, 1962; New York: Frederick A. Praeger, 1963.

CLARK, P. G. "Towards More Comprehensive Planning in East Africa," *The East African Economics Review,* XX, No. 2 (December, 1963), 65–74.

FORREST, O. B. *Financing Development Plans in West Africa.* Cambridge, Mass.: Massachusetts Institute of Technology, Center for International Studies, 1965.

HICKS, J. R. "National Economic Development in the International Setting," *Essays in World Economics.* London: Oxford University Press, 1959. Pp. 161–95.

HIRSCHMAN, A. O. *The Strategy of Economic Development.* New Haven, Conn.: Yale University Press, 1958.

JULIENNE, R. "L'Afrique à l'heure des plans," *La Documentation Africaine* (Paris, Penant), January, 1964, pp. 1–26.

LERNER, A. P. *The Economics of Control.* New York: Macmillan, 1946.

LEWIS, W. A. "Aspect of Economic Development." Background paper for the African Conference on Progress through Cooperation, Makerere University College, Kampala, 1965. Mimeo.

———. "On Assessing A Development Plan," *The Economic Bulletin* (Accra, Economic Society of Ghana), III, No. 6–7 (June–July, 1959).

MASON, E. S. "Economic Planning in Underdeveloped Areas: Government and Business." (The Millar Lectures, No. 2, 1958.) New York: Fordham University Press, 1958.

———. "On the Appropriate Size of a Development Plan." Unpublished paper: Cambridge, Mass., 1964.

MEIER, G. M. "The Development Decade In Perspective." Background paper for the Cambridge Overseas Studies Committee Conference, 1965. Mimeo.

Problems Concerning Techniques of Development Programming in African Countries. (U.N. Economic Commission for Africa, E/CN 14/42/Add 1.) Addis Ababa, December, 1959. Mimeo.

SEERS, D. Review of *Journeys Toward Progress: Studies of Economic Policy-Making in Latin America*, by A. O. Hirschman, in *American Economic Review*, LIV, No. 2 (March, 1964), 157–60.

VINER, J. *International Trade and Economic Development*. (Lectures delivered at National University of Brazil, 1953.) Oxford: The Clarendon Press, 1953.

WATERSTON, A. *Development Planning: Lessons of Experience*. Baltimore, Md.: The Johns Hopkins Press, 1965.

———. "What Do We Know About Planning?," *International Development Review*, VII, No. 4 (December, 1965), 2–9.

WATSON, A. M., and DIRLAM, J. B. "The Impact of Underdevelopment on Economic Planning," *Quarterly Journal of Economics*, LXXIX, No. 2 (May, 1965), 167–94.

WILSON, T. *Planning and Growth*. London: Macmillan, 1964.

XI

Economic Development, Politics, and Diplomacy

> *No country can reasonably be expected to cut its own throat.*
>
> DR. HASTINGS BANDA, President
> of Malawi

The economic forces and economic structure of a country are major factors in its domestic politics and foreign policy. Very simply, to survive you must eat. What an individual or nation must do to get food and other needed commodities is bound to be an important influence; the extent of this influence, however, cannot be so easily explained as some Marxists or other economic determinists would have us believe. It depends on the strength of the economic forces at work, on the awareness in the government leaders and among other leading elements of the economic factor, and on the strength of other forces such as nationalism, cultural objectives, etc.

In some cases, economics may be determinant, as seems to be true in Malawi's refusal to take drastic action against Portuguese Africa. Even though there is no doubt of Dr. Hastings Banda's solidarity with and commitment to the African independence movement, the influence of the economic factor was clear in his decision to continue to utilize Beira as a port and to ship Malawi's exports and imports on the Portuguese railways to and from Beira.

In most cases, however, the economic factor is not so overridingly important or it may not be so well appreciated, or other factors may be given more weight. Economic considerations were clearly deemed of secondary importance, for example, in the Moroccan Government's insistence on the United States removal of its air bases from Moroccan soil, even though these provided a considerable income to Morocco and gave employment to thousands of Moroccans. (In addition, the air bases undoubtedly gave the United States a special interest in giving Morocco priority in economic aid.) On the other hand, these considerations may have influenced the slowness with which the bases were finally "phased out." (Elsewhere in Africa, the financial and economic advantages of foreign military bases were more appreciated. When France reduced her armed forces in Africa from 40,000 to 6,000 between 1963 and 1965, the decision was regretted by almost all countries where troops had been stationed. Senegal estimated that it had enjoyed the equivalent of $40 million a year from the French military establishments at Dakar and Thies, and their loss was a severe economic blow.)

The economic forces affecting politics and foreign policy stem from (a) the structure and nature of the domestic economy, and the nation's external economic and financial relationships; (b) the objectives of the government and people as to the kind of economy and foreign economic relationships they want; and (c) the tension between the first and second, that is, the tension between "what is" and "what ought to be."

THE STRUCTURE OF THE ECONOMY

As we have seen, African economies are heavily dependent on the outside world for capital; external markets are the main propulsive force for their growth, etc. And we have seen that it is their *market* or *money* economy—the economy of the future—which is dependent on the outside world, so that the dynamic parts of the economy and the people most interested in change are the ones who must be oriented to foreign affairs.

Indeed, most of Africa is still at that stage of development where the main engine of economic growth is growth in export earnings. Consequently, the richer a country, the higher the relative per-capita importance of its foreign trade; the richer a country, the more it depends on other nations in the continuation of its existing economy and for further economic growth. (South Africa is becoming an exception to this because it has passed beyond this stage and, at its present industrializing phase of development, depends more on an increased internal market than on an increase in exports.)

African nations also, as we have seen, depend heavily on imported capital and on key trained personnel from non-African sources. African countries receive more finance from abroad, on the average, than countries in other parts of the world—around $4 per capita of capital annually (Algeria and Swaziland received more than $25 per capita of capital imports in 1963), as opposed to rather less than $3 in developing countries elsewhere. In many African countries, almost all of the recorded investment is financed from abroad; in most, the size and pace of inflow in investment funds makes the difference between rapid economic growth—as in the Ivory Coast, for instance, with a 10 per-cent growth or more in the last few years—or very slow growth or near stagnation. (Here again, South Africa is an exception, being now practically independent of inflows of capital from abroad.)

Although the rest of the world is vital economically for the African countries, African trade and investments are of little importance outside of the continent. Even if the African countries were organized in a bloc, which they are not, they could not use their economic power as a bludgeon to serve their political interests in the world arena. They simply do not have that much economic strength. They are, rather, in the position where it makes more economic sense to use their political power—for example, in their votes and influence in the U.N.—to serve economic ends.

Still, it is difficult to argue that any nation has or can have decisive economic influence. Even the United States with its enormous economic power cannot successfully wield its economic power alone to force another country to adopt policies or programs that the latter wants strongly to resist (*vide*, Cuba). Today, nations are bound closer together economically, and, at the same time, any one nation has only a small degree of economic influence over others. Certainly no developing nation or group of developing nations can exercise decisive international economic power.

The New International Economic Environment

In the 1930's, many small countries were forced into separate face-to-face bargains over trade with a larger economic power. And it is not surprising that many of them fell into the economic clutches of a dominant great power. Today, with international economic affairs (except for some remnants of bilateral relations, preserved mostly by the Soviet countries) based on multilateral trade and convertible currencies, a small country has a multiplicity of markets and suppliers to choose from, and it can choose on the basis of the economic advantages in each individual transaction. Developing countries, which usually produce only a few commodities, and primary products at that, do not have the flexibility and alternatives open to developed nations in this regard, but the present situation is still an immense improvement over the prewar world.

The growth of international economic and financial organizations since World War II has resulted in more and more international economic and financial decisions being made through negotiations—in organizations like the World Bank, the International Monetary Fund, the General Agreement on Tariffs and Trade, and the new U.N. Trade and Development Board—than through unilateral imposition by any one nation or group of nations. In these instances, no one country is dominant, and decisions are reached more by consensus than by vote; the African states are able to exercise a legitimate influence and get a hearing for their needs and aspirations.

African Aid Options

The economic ends which African countries strive to achieve in the present international economic and financial context are, usually, the best paying markets, stable remunerative prices for their exports, and the most generous provision of economic aid and technical assistance. An African country, in some cases but not all, may have the option to develop close relations with a particular donor nation or group in order to gain the optimum benefit; or to maneuver among various donor countries, perhaps playing one off against the other; or, thirdly, to play the "multilateral game."

Most of the ex-French colonial countries have chosen the alternative of working closely with France. From the *economic* point of view, it is hard to argue that they have been wrong; essentially, they were offered no comparably generous alternative. The two countries which did not initially follow this pattern, Guinea and Mali, have in recent years re-established relations with France. (Mali, in fact, had remained an associate member of the European Common Market and never destroyed all her links to the franc zone.)

Other newly independent African countries did not receive from other Western powers the kind of treatment the French provided their former colonies, and most of them have been quick to learn that close ties with the Communist countries are not an adequate substitute. And to play the field successfully, that is, to play potential givers of aid off against one another, requires a large cadre of diplomatic and financial negotiators that only two or three countries in Africa possess. In general, African nations, in most cases from choice, have made no attempt to use political maneuvers as a means of securing aid, but have remained politically true to the principles of nonalignment. On this score, Ghana was temporarily successful, but by the end of 1965, aid to Ghana from both east and west was drying up. Tunisia has probably been most successful in securing aid from a whole range of sources, in both the west and the east, while at the same time eliminating the vestiges of its former dependent status and becoming no country's client. (She has been given economic aid by France, the United States, West Germany, the Netherlands, Sweden, Italy, Switzerland; the U.S.S.R., Poland, Czechoslovakia, Bulgaria; Yugoslavia; and the World Bank Group—including the Bank, the International Development Association, and the International Finance Corporation, the U.N. Special Fund, and the U.N. Expanded Program of Technical Assistance.)

AFRICAN TRADE OPTIONS

The eighteen African associate members of the European Economic Community—with free entry for their products into the Common Market—have a direct interest in trying to preserve this rapidly growing market for themselves as against Asian, Latin American, and other African producers of the same products. For they could in this way secure more rapid growth in exports and, therefore, in their economies than if they had to gear production to the slow over-all growth of the total world consumption of primary products. The other African producers have two alternatives in this situation: one is to try to join with Latin American and Asian producers to persuade the Common Market to eliminate or to reduce the preferences given to associate members; the other alternative is to attempt to have the preferences extended to their products too. It is also possible to try to operate on both fronts simultaneously. Nigeria and the nations of East Africa, which are strongly affected, have negotiated with the EEC for an agreement permitting entry of their products into the Common Market on some basis of equality with the African associate members. Tunisia, Morocco, and Algeria have also intermittently tried to work out acceptable relations with the Common Market. (It is not at all surprising that these African countries appoint some of their ablest economic negotiators as their diplomatic representation in Brussels.)

The bulk of African trade is now with Western Europe. North America is a poor second—except in the case of a few countries, notably Liberia and Ethiopia—although coffee exports from Uganda, Angola, etc., to the United States are becoming important. The Soviet bloc is a very poor third, yet the Communist bloc presents the biggest potential unexploited market for Africa's primary producers. These countries' consumption of coffee, cocoa, palm oil, etc., in relation to their per-capita income levels, is only a fraction of the Western figure; if they bought tropical products in the same proportion to per-capita income as the West Europeans or Americans do, the African producers could sell another $2 billion or $3 billion of exports—i.e., African exports and the African standard of living could rise by almost 50 per cent, and the opening up of this large market could provide an important propulsive force for the next decade or two.

This "import gap" of the Sino-Soviet countries has many implications for African-Soviet relations in particular and for African international relations generally, and both the Africans and the Soviet Union know it. The Soviet Union's announcement that it had abolished custom duties on tropical products on January 1, 1965, is one indication of this, but this decision is, at present, meaningless for Africa.

In the Soviet Union's centralized economy, the decision to buy or not to buy African products is not taken by consumers, who might be influenced by the price they must pay—which would be affected by whether a customs duty was levied. The decision to import a particular product is a bureaucratic decision made by the government's foreign-trade monopoly. The fact that a customs duty may be levied when a product is passed on to a government sales organization has little influence on the monopoly's original decision to buy that product (assuming that the demand for the product at a price including the tariff was already greater than the quantity permitted to enter when the duty was imposed; under the Soviet system, in any case, the internal price may or may not be related to the foreign-exchange price paid). It is simply that if the foreign-trade monopoly, under a bilateral agreement, can "sell" Soviet machinery (which is not easily salable for foreign exchange elsewhere) in exchange for African products (which are), it will make good business sense to do so. Or if the price at which Soviet equipment is sold, in terms of the world market value of the African products received in exchange, is higher than the price at which it can be sold elsewhere, it makes sense to trade it for African products and then sell the latter in world markets. Both Egypt and Ghana have discovered that cotton or cocoa sold to the Soviet bloc against purchases of Soviet goods has wound up for sale in Western Europe, in competition with cotton and cocoa coming directly from Africa. If the Soviet Union and other East European nations evolve toward a more decentralized economy (as there are some indications that they are), however, with buying decisions determined more and more by price and by the consumers themselves, the elimination of customs duties will increase the volume of African exports.

On the other hand, at present there is little potential for the growth of Chinese-African trade in the near future. The simple manufactured products that China itself is trying to export are in fact of the type that African countries themselves hope soon to export; and the Chinese standard of living is, and is likely to remain for a long time to come, too low to provide much of a market for present African exports; in addition China is likely to exclude them in order to save foreign exchange for purchase of machinery. China's purchase of raw cotton or tea from time to time can only be momentary phenomena resulting from crop failures or ad hoc political decisions.

AFRICA'S INTERESTS AS A PRIMARY-PRODUCT EXPORTER

As exporters of primary products, African countries have a common cause with developing countries everywhere to try to secure cooperative international action that would control the market in such a way as to assure favorable prices and minimize fluctuations. As the most dynamic and lowest-cost producers in many primary commodities, however, their economic interest is in many cases to try to get a larger share of the market away from producers in Asia or Latin America—and to secure a more rapid economic growth in this way than the general sluggish growth of demand for most of the commodities they produce would otherwise permit. Consequently, in regard to international commodity agreements (except concerning commodities where they already dominate the market, as in cocoa), the intelligent thing for African countries to do may be to remain outside the agreement as long as possible to take advantage of the price umbrella created and maintained by the other producers. Once they are within the agreement, their interest may be to secure flexibility in quotas so that they can get a growing share of the market as time goes on. (In the International Coffee Organization, it is precisely the African producers who have applied the most pressure for increased quotas and who have been the most restless with the quotas they have. The long-range coffee situation can be summed up in a few statistics: the Brazilian share of the world coffee market decreased from 70 per cent before World War I to 37 per cent in the early 1960's; the African share has increased from 1 per cent in 1909–13, 5 per cent in 1934–38, 20 per cent in the 1950's, 27 per cent in the early 1960's, to 31 per cent in 1964.) Finally, it may be in their interest to have the prices set by international commodity agreements at a level low enough so that high-cost producers elsewhere will not be encouraged to stay in production or go into production, and to discourage production of synthetic substitutes.

These interests, of course, may, in specific cases, put Africans into direct conflict with other world producers. But Africans have a long-term interest in allying themselves with other primary producers to get more favorable treatment in the markets of the developed world. In particular, the semi-industrialized or industrializing nations of Latin America and, to some extent, India and Pakistan are endeavoring to find markets for their new manufacturing industries in Europe and North America—through liberalized tariff treatments, preferential markets, etc. To the extent that these semi-industrialized countries can succeed and their economies become more industrialized, it will be easier for them to move over and allow the African countries to take over a larger share of the world markets for the primary products.

INTRA-AFRICAN RELATIONS

While the most important economic relations of African states are with non-African nations, some states have important ties to other African countries. For the land-locked African state that depends on another for access to the sea, for example, this dependence can be a dominant factor in its diplomatic as well as economic relations. Malawi has no choice but to use routes through Mozambique to the sea, so good relations with Mozambique are vital, as Dr. Banda has indicated. Uganda, Rwanda, Burundi, the Central African Republic, Chad, Niger, Mali, and Upper Volta each have two or more feasible routes to the sea and their situation is somewhat more flexible. The degree of flexibility may be severely curtailed, however, because of the costliness of shifting trade from one route to another; and the degree of costliness may be a determining factor in foreign policy. In the case of Zambia, not only does its main rail connection to the sea lead through Rhodesia, but still another important factor links it to Rhodesia and that is power. Most of the electric power consumed in Zambia is produced by the Kariba hydropower project, situated at the dam straddling the Zambezi River between the two countries. (This power is especially vital to the continued operation of the copper mines in northern Zambia, which produce Zambia's main export.) The Kariba power plant is controlled by the Kariba Power Board, administered jointly by the two states. Unfortunately, the first powerhouse to use the Kariba potential was built on the south, or Rhodesian, bank. This fact became one of the central issues in the drama of Rhodesia's unilateral announcement of independence in late 1965 and early 1966. Zambia repeatedly asked that British troops enter Rhodesia to take over custody of the Kariba power project in order to safeguard Zambian power supplies, which it feared Rhodesia's rebel government would curtail or cut off. As of mid-1966, no British troops had taken action and Kariba power was still available to Zambia.

Clearly, this situation, and the fact that the Rhodesian Railways are Zambia's major route to the sea, were severe constraints on Zambia's freedom to pursue the kind of policy she might have wished vis-à-vis Rhodesia's declaration of unilateral independence. The Organization of African Unity Foreign Ministers' meeting in Addis Ababa in December, 1965, recommended that a total economic and communications boycott of Rhodesia be imposed at once, but Zambia would be hard put to cut her ties with Rhodesia. The vital importance of the services they share was clearly acknowledged by President Kenneth Kaunda, when he declared to the Zambian parliament that if Rhodesia interfered with Zambia's railway services or supply of power to Zambia, "it would be a declaration of war, and I would not hesitate to order my country into action." (Lloyd Garrison, "Zambian Warning Given to Britain," *The New York Times*, December 10, 1965, p. C.7.)

Another important economic link among African countries is the international movement of labor. To citizens of Lesotho, Swaziland, Botswana, and Mozambique, employment opportunities in South Africa are important, if not vital. "African leaders in the three High Commission Territories and Malawi have stated that they could not support economic measures (against South Africa) because of their dependence on trade with the Republic and on earnings from migrant labor employed in South Africa." (Hance, p. 102.) In 1964 and 1965, the African voters in the three High Commission territories voted for governments that were pledged to maintain economic ties with South Africa, but "None of this means that Africans like apartheid. It simply means that countries held in South Africa's economic thrall, like Basutoland, cannot afford to declare political war upon it." (*The Economist* [London], May 8, 1965, p. 622.) On the other hand, South Africa's need for this labor is considerably less acute than the need of the labor-supplying countries to have the job opportunities in South Africa.

Their citizens' need to continue to be able to work in another country is also an important economic factor for Malawi vis-à-vis

Rhodesia, Rwanda vis-à-vis Uganda, Niger and Chad vis-à-vis the Sudan, northern Nigeria and Upper Volta vis-à-vis Ghana and the Ivory Coast, and Dahomey vis-à-vis most of the other French-speaking West African countries. Conversely, the nation providing the employment wants to keep the labor coming in, although in most cases the need for jobs is more important to the "proletarian" country than the labor is to the "employer" country. For example, Ian Smith, Prime Minister of Rhodesia after her declaration of independence in November, 1965, injected the issue of the migrant labor force directly into Rhodesian foreign policy: with more than half of the African wage-labor force in Rhodesia made up of migrants from other African countries (200,000 from Malawi, 120,000 from Mozambique and Angola, and 70,000 from Zambia), Smith warned those countries that, if economic sanctions against Rhodesia caused unemployment, the foreign workers would be the first to be dismissed. (Dispatch from Salisbury, "Smith Warns He Will Expel Foreigners if Sanctions Cause Job Shortage," *The Washington Post,* December 9, 1965, p. A 18.)

A third important link among African nations is created by the need to have large markets. Aside from Nigeria, the Congo (Léopoldville), South Africa, and to some extent Algeria, none of the African countries has or is likely to have in the near future a market large enough to permit industrialization to get under way. Only by several countries' joining together in a customs union or free-trade area, pooling their purchasing power in a single market, can this be accomplished. But only if the gains—new industries made possible by the larger size of the common market—are clearly beneficial and the distribution of benefits is skillfully carried out will the common market hold together. Politically, the distribution of benefits and allocation of compensations are easier to handle if they are done within the context of a common government. Consequently, the hopes of maintaining common markets in Africa are usually brighter if they are the result of a federation or union of states than if they are only negotiated agreements among sovereign states.

The problems of locating industries have important political implications in the context of common markets (see above, p. 156), but in other areas as well. There is, for example, the question where slaughterhouses handling cattle from Niger which are destined for

Nigeria should be located—a question whose political implications increase when analysis of the economic costs and benefits involved shows that there is no clear-cut economic advantage to one or the other country. The location of natural resources is another such factor. In areas where a frontier is in dispute or there are irredendist claims, an agreed solution may be much more difficult to come by if there are rich natural resources involved. The belief that there might be oil in Kenya's northeast corner reinforces its reluctance to consider concession of this area to Somalia. The discovery of oil in the Sahara made both Moroccan and Tunisian claims to parts of the area under Algerian control politically more volatile.

Economic aid may also be a factor in the political relationships among African states. The financial contribution of around $6 million a year that the Ivory Coast has been making out of its budget since 1959 to the other states (Upper Volta, Niger, and Dahomey) of the Conseil d'Entente helps the Ivory Coast to be recognized as the leader among them.

THE COLONIAL INHERITANCE

Some African countries inherited what might be called a complete "colonial" economic structure. Unskilled African labor faced big foreign mining or plantation concerns; African farmers producing export crops confronted small groups of foreign-owned exporting and processing firms who monopolized the market (although in most countries the colonial governments themselves, after World War II, had set up marketing boards or *caisses de stabilisation*); and, as consumers, they faced the same group of import-export firms selling or distributing imported commodities. In many countries, finally, a middle stratum has grown up between the big European firms and the local population—made up of Asians in East Africa, of Syrians and "Coast Africans" in West Africa.

Now the political effect of these patterns has been significant. Many African governments either have tried to set up "countervailing power" to the strategic power of the big concerns—through encouraging labor unions and increased government controls—or have nationalized them (e.g., Ghana's nationalization of Levantis, a major "expatriate" trading firm).

The United Africa Company in recent years has been shifting out of trade into manufacturing in the English-speaking countries, which should help to avoid the hostility that grows naturally in the colonial trade pattern when a farmer sells his produce to a foreign company or individual trader at a price he feels is too low, and buys commodities from the same trader at prices he easily can come to believe are too high. In those countries where no major change in this "colonial" structure has taken place, the potential for political difficulties continues. Particularly when domestic action to change the status of Europeans, Indians, Pakistanis, Lebanese, or Syrians (as the case may be) in key positions of the economy is not under control, disputes with the nations whose citizens or companies are involved are bound to occur.

A related problem concerns the relationship of African governments to large international corporations—particularly the mining companies. When an African government negotiates with an international mining group whose worldwide net profits are as large as the national income, it may naturally feel the negotiations are not on an equal basis.

While there are ways of equalizing the bargaining capabilities (see above, chap. VI, p. 138), there may also be a case for international cooperative action. The Economic Commission for Africa is already helping to prepare a uniform investment code applicable to foreign investment; oil-producing nations have organized a protective association (the Organization of Petroleum Exporting Countries); conferences have been held of the copper-producing countries on matters of mutual interest. There is still considerable potential for additional ties of this type among African nations.

CONCLUSION

Finally, we must consider the "revolution of rising expectations." There is a tremendous, largely invisible, but important change going on in Africa—the slow growth throughout the continent of the monetary economy. With it, there is an enormous increase in the demands of the African peoples. This is coming from the impact of education, the effect of experiences of migrant laborers, the impact of the transistor radio, movies, and now television. Everything and everybody is influenced, whether or not this is immediately evident, and this change in people is accelerating. The modern economy— with its amazing power to create wealth, to control disease, to satisfy material desires—is becoming desired by Africans throughout Africa. The traditional outlook, with its more passive attitude toward the ups and downs of life, is suddenly discarded. People realize that they are poor, and that something can be done about it; sickness and early death are seen as avoidable; burdensome tribal discipline and respon- sibilities are no longer tolerable. The new African governments are very much aware of these growing demands and new attitudes, but also of the inability to achieve something quickly.

When European officials enjoyed a high standard of living in colonial Africa, this was resented as part of the whole colonial system. Now, the first generation of independent Africa's governing elite enjoy the benefits formerly held by Europeans. More and more peo- ple feel that they should qualify as members of the elite, and even those who may not feel qualified see no reason why they should not have radios and automobiles. (The contrast between the educated elite already in power and those outside can take several forms; there is also the struggle between the "petite" and "grande" intelligentsia— i.e., between school and university graduates; and the struggle between the first-generation graduates in power and the second university gen- eration, who feel shut out.) But the economic reality is that Africa cannot yet afford to extend the elite's standard of living to the masses. In many cases, it is questionable whether they can afford it for the elite, and still have the necessary savings and investment to grow on. On the one hand, these benefits should act as an incentive to greater efforts, but on the other hand, the high consumption of the elite may restrict the amount of savings. (And the wrong lesson may be drawn: that the rewards are made not for economic effort but for political effort.)

Political problems also arise when a government, cognizant of the desirability of cutting down the cost of special privileges for civil- service and government workers, tries to do so. In January, 1966, when the President of Upper Volta proposed a 20-per-cent salary cut for the civil service, the civil-service union struck, there were riots in the streets. To restore order, the army seized power and rescinded the salary cut.

In brief, Africa's modern governing elites are faced with demands for the benefits of the Western economy, but with an unawareness of the costs that must be paid to produce these benefits. People are converted to new wants and aspirations more rapidly than their earning capacity or the national income can be increased. People begin to desire "the American way of life for themselves," with all the products they see on television and in the movies; they also desire social-security schemes, unemployment insurances, old-age pensions, etc., which their leaders, acquainted with these things from their experience of England and France, have promised them. "It would . . . be a crowning point of irony if some backward countries were to turn towards Communism through an excessive fondness for the American and British ways of life." (Myint, p. 132.)

Another danger hovers in the background—exemplified by the case of Haiti, independent for almost two centuries, but with less economic progress than any of the newly independent African countries —the danger that the modernizing elite will lose its power to govern and control, and that a country will lose all its gains and slip back into a situation far worse than the nineteenth-century tribal society from which it has ostensibly liberated itself. Such a retrogression might come in many ways: the elite displaced by new leaders who pander to the masses and promise them the benefits of modern life, while they remove the pressure to make the changes that are the preconditions for a modern economy; the elite using the state machinery merely to provide themselves with a "good life" while letting the economy and administration slip backwards; or, on the Haitian pattern, some soldier, remarkable only for his command of violence, seizing and maintaining power. (That it is possible for a small band of military men to overthrow a government in Africa has been shown in several instances: in Togo, President Olympio's assassination in January, 1963, by a small group of soldiers; and, notably, the coup executed by "Field Marshal" Okello, an ignorant but ruthless freebooter from Uganda, that overthrew the centuries-old Sultan's government of Zanzibar in December, 1963. But that there is resistance to such schemes seems also to be shown by the way in which the abler political leaders eased Okello out of power and out of Zanzibar, and by the way in which the three East African governments promptly overcame any false scruples of pride when they asked for aid from British troops in bringing military mutinies under control in 1964.)

In brief, economic development in Africa is, almost inevitably, creating a situation of high political and social tension. African leaders are confronted with a con*n*ict between the overwhelming desire for change, and the feeling that the social and individual costs involved are close to unbearable, and the obstacles overpowering and perhaps insurmountable. It is not at all surprising that they should turn to the developed countries for sympathy and help, nor that the pressures on them from their citizens to produce quick results become the dominant factors in their relations with the rest of the world.

Selected Bibliography

HANCE, W. A. "Efforts to Alter the Future: Economic Action," in A. C. LEISS (ed.), *Apartheid and the United Nations.* New York: Carnegie Endowment for International Peace, 1965.

MOUSSA, P. *Les Etats-Unis et les nations prolétaires.* Paris: Editions du Seuil, 1965.

———. *Les Nations Prolétaires.* Paris: Presses universitaires de France, 1959. (3d ed., 1963.)

MYINT, H. "An Interpretation of Economic Backwardness" in A. N. AGARWALA and S. P. SINGH (eds.), *The Economics of Underdevelopment.* London and New York: Oxford University Press, 1963.

PREST, A. R. and STEWART, I. G. *The National Income of Nigeria, 1950–51.* (Colonial Research Studies No. 11.) London: H. M. Stationery Office, 1953.

STOLPER, W. F. "Politics and Economics in Economic Development," *Revista di Politica Economica* (Rome), LIII, third series, No. 6 (June, 1963), 851–76.

XII

The Prospects for Economic Development

> Come il viso mi scese in lor piu basso,
> mirabilmente apparve esser travolto
> ciascun tra il mento e 'l principio del casso:
> Che dal reni era tornato il volto,
> ed indietro venir gli convenia,
> perche il veder dinanzi era lor tolto.
>
> DANTE, Inferno, Canto XX,
> lines 10–15

Dante's belief that forecasters belong in Hell was based not only on the idea that it is sacrilegious to try to predict the future but also on his perception that predictions can change the future and, therefore, interfere with God's plans.

Economic forecasts in particular run this danger. In some cases, economic forecasts may be self-realizing—this is largely true of the successful "indicative plans" in the industrialized market economies. In the late 1950's, the Vanoni Plan forecast a rapid growth in the Italian economy. Industrialists assumed this would happen and invested on that assumption; their belief in the forecast made it come true. In other cases, economic forecasts may be self-frustrating: by calling attention to the disastrous future an economy is heading

238

toward, it may stimulate government or other action to make sure the forecast does *not* come true.

This chapter is primarily an attempt to forecast the future economic development of the African countries on the assumption that present and probable future trends continue. It is, if you will, the working out of a model of the present structure and relationships of African economies.

An Economic Forecast

The economic test I am applying in this chapter is the achievement of a per-capita GNP of $400. This is not to imply that the figure represents happiness, or any other non-economic state. Even on economic grounds, $400 is essentially an arbitrary target, chosen because at that level, with any sort of reasonable management, and without special foreign aid, a country's standard of living can continue to grow, *ceteris paribus*. The figure was realized by Mexico, Lebanon, and Malta a few years ago; by Japan five years ago; by Italy ten years ago. (In some cases, the capacity to grow without special aid can develop at lower income levels, but it is virtually assured at the $400 per-capita level—with, at most, the help of foreign loans at conventional interest rates.)

In the African context, the speed with which this goal is attained is important. Until recently, this did not matter much; for most of Africa, it was fairly simple to keep the economy growing at pace with or even a little faster than the population growth. But nowadays this is no longer enough; as a minimum to maintain stability, people must feel that their standard of living is rising perceptibly. What this implies in terms of a GNP growth rate has not been established; it probably varies from country to country and group to group. (As a working figure, I have finally adopted a 7 per cent GNP growth rate, as will be seen later on in this chapter.) As a first assumption, I have arbitrarily begun with a target of a per-capita GNP of $400 by 1980.

For some African countries, this goal is not overly ambitious. The Republic of South Africa has already considerably exceeded it. By 1980, indeed, at its present rate of growth, it is possible that its per-capita GNP will be at a level with that of Western Europe's in the late 1950's (i.e., around $1,000). If the economic benefits of the South African economy were evenly distributed, all the nation's races would then enjoy a good standard of living; on the present basis, the people of European origin will continue to have one of the highest standards of living in the world, while the Africans do as well as the highest-income African nations.

Of the other African countries, Ghana, Senegal, the Ivory Coast, Gabon, and Rhodesia appear to be within striking distance of this objective. To attain it, they would need a per-capita growth of GNP of about 5 per cent yearly, or, assuming a population increase of 2 per cent yearly, a 7 per cent GNP growth rate. This is a high rate—higher than was sustained by the present industrialized countries in their developing stages. But it has been maintained or surpassed for long periods since World War II by some countries (Japan, Taiwan, Israel, Southern Rhodesia during the 1950's, South Africa and probably Gabon and Liberia in 1960–65).

But for most of the continent, the attainment of a per-capita GNP of $400 by 1980 would require a rate of growth two or three times as high—and such rates extended over so long would be unprecedented and, I believe, practically impossible. But if a 7 per cent rate could be reached and maintained, all Africa would reach the $400 per-capita level by the year 2000. This would be no mean achievement: Africa would have made as much progress in a century as it took Europe more than 1,000 years to accomplish. A 7 per cent growth rate is also desirable politically: it means doubling the GNP in ten years or, with a 2 per cent rate of population growth, doubling per-capita income in less than fifteen years—that is, in less than a generation; this would mean an appreciable gain in income every year and would give parents confidence that their children would be better off than they. (Seers suggests that a 7 per cent growth rate is a necessary condition for political stability in Africa.)

Whether Africa can and will achieve these growth targets depends on a large number of factors: the favorable conditions and the obstacles offered by the natural environment; the cultural readiness and receptiveness of Africans to economic growth; the interplay of politics and economics; and the opportunities and constraints presented by the rest of the world to African economic growth.

ENVIRONMENT

The natural environment is still the dominant factor in African economics. To a large extent, development represents mastery over it or escape from its limitations. The fact that man has still not mastered the tropics is Africa's biggest restraint on economic development. But there is always the exciting possibility that the potentials for progress in Africa are greater than anywhere else in the world. For example, in the temperate areas, the gains from increasing the number of a man's productive years or of increasing his efficiency through reducing disease are, while appreciable, nowhere near so great as they would be in the tropics. (In the United States, the average male life-span has scarcely increased in the last ten years.) The announcement on December 25, 1965, that CIBA, the Swiss drug firm, had succeeded in finding a successful quick cure for bilharzia—a disease which persists in a person for years before it may kill him and which is presently debilitating tens of millions of Africans—may be exactly this kind of breakthrough. (*Le Monde*, December 25, 1965.) Since African agricultural production is set by the amount of labor that can be mustered at peak periods (sowing and harvest), the eradication of bilharzia may result in a 50 per-cent increase in output with no increase in agricultural investment.

Certainly, since World War II the volume and quality of research on the tropics and on Africa in particular has risen, although suffering a severe setback with the political turmoil of the 1960's. But it is reasonable to expect that this factor will make a more and more important contribution to African development. Research, especially in agriculture, takes a long time—first to show results and then to be applied. While it is impossible to quantify the contribution research will make, it is safe to say that it will exert a fairly gentle upward push on economic growth during the next fifteen years, growing in intensity as time goes on.

But all this notwithstanding, some natural handicaps are not likely to be overcome in this century. The lack of rainfall in the deserts, the unevenness of mineral distribution—such factors cannot be offset by research, and they will lead to an uneven development among the African nations. On this basis alone (barring any presently unforeseen discovery of oil, *à la* Libya), the task of economic development appears very difficult indeed in countries like Upper Volta, Niger, Chad, Central African Republic, Somalia, Botswana, and Lesotho.

CULTURAL AND POLITICAL FACTORS

The new African governments have, if anything, accentuated the emphasis on and the desire for material goods. The monetary economy has continued to erode the subsistence culture, economy, and fatalistic philosophy of life. The spread of education, the transistor radio, and now television is resulting in an accelerating rate of social change—a difficult and painful process. With its uneven incidence on individuals and generations, its vast political and social tensions, the surprise is that there has been so little unrest in Africa. But the logic of African economic development, the "anguish of disintegration and adjustment," must continue, and at a pace that is often "too urgent for patient reflection and wise action." (de Kiewiet, p. 86.)

The breakdown of law and order in the Congo demonstrated both the importance of political life for economic development and the fragility of the political structure left behind in some cases by colonialism. Development cannot take place without a certain minimum of security and without the provision and maintenance of basic government administrative services. Slow progress, while these are built up on a Congolese basis, is therefore inevitable for the immediate future. This political and administrative factor will be a determining one in the Congo for the next fifteen years.

But the Congo only dramatized a situation that in less acute form is typical of other African countries. I. R. Sinai, in his analysis of what happened in some Asian countries that preceded Africa to independence by a decade or more (*The Challenge of Modernization*), points out that Western imperialism provided no more than a top-dressing of modernization—a tiny intellectual elite, developed export-import sectors, a few big cities and communications geared to foreign trade, little industry, and no transformation of farming for local consumption. Modernity could become an ambition in such countries, but not a reality. Behind the façade of modernity, there was slow retrogression, as the old ways reasserted themselves. Administration became confused and incompetent; corruption spread;

there was an irresistible tendency to confuse talk with action and to blame the rest of the world for domestic shortcomings.

This is a somber picture, and it reveals real dangers for many countries in Africa. It may not be possible for an African government, no matter how well intentioned nor how able its leaders, to avoid retrogression. The difficulty in some cases is that too little real modernity was left behind by the colonizing power. Many of the ex-French colonies are now trying to cope with this problem by continuing to import vast numbers of French technicians and teachers—in a race to shift the balance to the modern world before it is too late. But such a policy requires on the one hand a considerable modern elite and strong enough political leadership to hold on while the transformation continues, and on the other, large-scale foreign assistance. Even in some of the French-speaking countries, the latter does not obtain; the volume of technical assistance available or absorbed in Upper Volta, Niger, and Chad is less than in the Ivory Coast and Senegal; Guinea and Mali are even worse. In the former colonies of the British Empire, Malawi, Zambia, and Tanzania appear to receive considerably less aid than would be justifiable. Various new programs providing technicians and teachers from the United Kingdom, the United States, and some of the West European countries are helping, but they are not anywhere near large enough to eliminate these dangers.

Another widespread political problem that is already interfering with economic progress in Africa is a more sociological one: the yet unfinished problem of nation-building. In most of the new African nations, there are large sectors, often a majority, of the population who regard themselves first as members of a tribe or ethnic group and as citizens of the new country secondarily, if at all. In some cases, there are large groups who still regard themselves as subject peoples, subject no longer to the British or French but to the dominant tribe who inherited the colonists' position. Whether this is justified or not, the fact is that the tension or fighting between southern Sudanese and the government, between Somalis in northern Kenya and in Ethiopia and their respective governments, drains the resources of these governments and makes development that much more difficult.

Finally, it is necessary to take special note of the spread of corruption in some of the new African states. The position in Nigeria before the January, 1966, military revolt was described as follows: "Corruption was widespread. It was almost axiomatic that all members of the government were rich. It was considered standard practice for a federal or regional minister to get a percentage of any new loan on contract being negotiated. Tips or 'dash' greased the wheels of a cumbersome bureaucracy. It was the system and everyone played along. For the average Nigerian, a politician was expected to take 'dash.' He wasn't hated for it. He was envied." (Donald H. Louchheim, *The Washington Post*, January 23, 1966.)

Aside from any economic ill effects, it could certainly be demonstrated that corruption has an undesirable effect on the whole quality of African life. And corruption can certainly destroy a society's chance for economic development. By causing decisions to be made on the basis of the rake-off to the decision-maker, rather than of what pays best for the enterprise or economy, corruption can result in such a misuse of resources that the economy stagnates or retrogresses. But this is not necessarily inevitable. If limited, corruption will simply make the economy a little less efficient; this is probably true in the United States, where corruption in the form of expense-account entertainment used to influence decisions taken on other than purely economic bases not only is legal but is actually encouraged by the tax laws. Corruption can also make a positive economic contribution: in inefficient slow-moving governments, where the bureaucracy attempts to control the economy in every detail, corruption may make it possible for the economy to move. It may also result in the government making major new policy decisions and thus allowing profitable new opportunities to be exploited more rapidly. Corruption may also serve as an efficient—if inequitable—means of capital accumulation.

In the African context, the prevalent one-party systems of politics and government encourages the spread of corruption, for the checks provided by a vigilant opposition and by the threat of losing power are not present. And, whenever "African Socialism" manifests itself in the attempt to regulate the economy in minute detail, when the government tries to make all the important economic decisions, and this is beyond the effective capabilities of the administration, corruption is inevitable. It becomes one of those compromises that are common to all governments: laws and regulations are passed regulating economic activity to satisfy the mass of the people, while the persons or enterprises regulated are enabled, through the judicious use of bribery, to pursue their interests unhindered. (In more sophisticated societies, these compromises are reached within the law: income-tax rates are made progressively high to satisfy the mass of the electorate, but sufficient loopholes are left to allow the rich to avoid the ruinously high brackets.) Still, in all, it is difficult, if not impossible, for an economist to regard corruption in the African states as unquestionably a *major* threat to economic growth. But it is a hindrance.

Probably the greatest contribution the political sector could make to economic development is in the creation of larger political and, therefore, economic units. For the preservation of bigger markets where they already exist, as in Nigeria, or the creation of them elsewhere is the *sine qua non* for substantial industrial growth in Africa. But there is no indication at present that African politicians and statesmen will be able to make a substantial contribution of this kind in the next fifteen years.

EXTERNAL CONSTRAINTS

There is still a great deal that African countries can do (and are doing) to increase their output and improve their standard of living without regard to the outside world—in the improvement of food production, the creation of industries for the home market, the construction of an infrastructure that is not primarily intended for the use of foreign trade, such as electricity for domestic consumption, etc. But these activities cannot result in a good growth rate if the countries cannot at the same time improve their ability to purchase foreign goods. Practically every one of these activities requires imported equipment, tools, spare parts, books, paper, etc. The need for more foreign exchange, either through increased exports or foreign aid, is still one of the most important constraints on African growth.

In the past, Africa's GNP has grown roughly in line with the growth of her export earnings—over the last fifteen years, at around 4 per cent per year. Seers estimates that these are not likely to grow by more than 3 per cent per year in the future, on the assumption that the growth rate of developed countries will be less than 4 per cent (probably 3 per cent); their consolidated income elasticity of demand for primary products is under 1 per cent; and the proportion of African goods in the imports of developed countries grows as Latin America shifts to industrial goods.

Since Seers' estimates were made, the United States, which had held down the average over-all growth rate of developed countries, has shown growth of 5–5.5 per cent. While this rate may not continue as the pool of unemployed labor is absorbed, the conversion of the United States to growth economics makes a higher average rate likely. Secondly, the East European countries are beginning to increase consumption of tropical products to a rate commensurate with their per-capita incomes. Consequently, a higher estimate for African export-earnings growth, perhaps around 4 per cent, now appears more reasonable. Seers' argument that African terms of trade will improve (i.e., that export prices may increase slightly more than import prices) also appears reasonable.

With proper development policies, then, the African countries may be able to increase GNP somewhat faster than export earnings—conceivably to 4.5–5 per cent per year. These figures, however, are based on the assumption that there will be no change in the flow of aid and technical assistance which, at a cost of around $1 billion a year during the early 1960's, facilitated the growth in export earnings and in the African economies. If the growth rate of GNP is to be lifted from 4.5–5 to 7, an increase in capital and technical assistance seems necessary. A 2 per-cent increase in African GNP (excluding South Africa) is equivalent to $400–$500 million a year. Assuming a capital/output ratio of 3 to 1, which may be a reasonable over-all rule of thumb for Africa, an increase in the growth rate would appear to require an increase in the annual volume of aid of around $1.2–$1.5 billion—that is, more than double the recent rate. If the rate of population growth were to be slowed down to 1 per cent per year (we have been assuming 2 per cent), the required aid increase would be $600–$750 million per year.

Obviously, these are very rough calculations, based on daring assumptions, but they may provide some indication of the order of magnitude of the problem.

In actual fact, of course, the prospects and possibilities differ radically from one African country to the next. In any case, a broad distinction should be drawn between mineral producers and the agricultural exporters. As earlier chapters have tried to make clear, the former tend to have brighter prospects than the latter.

Of the mineral producers, Gabon, Guinea, Liberia, Zambia, Nigeria, Congo (Léopoldville), and Rhodesia already clearly have the potential to reach or surpass a 7 per-cent GNP rate of growth. Congo (Brazzaville), with potash and possibly bauxite and iron-ore deposits; the Sudan, a very large and practically unexplored area; and Ghana, if it handles its opportunities from the Volta power and aluminum project wisely—may also belong in this select group. Most of the other African countries depend mainly on agricultural exports, and here the external constraints apply. But this still does not mean that particular countries cannot be successful—especially if others, by mishandling their affairs, open up the opportunities to get a bigger share of a limited market. Among the more likely candidates for such success are the Ivory Coast, Kenya, Uganda, and the Sudan.

Conclusion

In the course of this discussion, it has been possible to identify several African countries where, even with a continuation of existing trends, the chances are good that a satisfactory rate of growth can be achieved. Some others, with substantial improvement in political and economic policies, also stand a good chance. For the rest, it appears clear that there will have to be drastic changes in existing trends —certainly including the lifting of the whole aid and technical-assistance effort to a considerably higher level and planning and co-ordinating it through some new international effort—if they are to be able to move ahead at a proper pace. New development techniques may also be required. Perhaps it will be possible to work out a generation-long contract between an international aid agency and the recipient country, through which the necessary transformation of the country's economy from top to bottom could be systematically and thoroughly carried out. Greater aid efforts should certainly include more investment in research on African problems. Perhaps, even more important, this research should be organized on a more permanent basis, in the form of an internationally sponsored research institute, and be better coordinated and directed toward a coherent set of targets.

Finally, major political changes creating larger economic units would greatly improve the prospects for the African economies.

The next decades are not likely to be easy ones for Africa. The final solutions are certainly not in sight; we are not even sure that the problems have been fully and accurately ascertained. Most of the agony in the process of development is still ahead. Nevertheless, I am confident that for most of Africa the economic future before the end of the century can be bright. The environmental difficulties that held Africa back for so long have not yet been fully overcome but, with the right help from abroad, they can be. In the last analysis, economics, like politics, largely depends on people. The Africans have the will to learn and the talent to make good use of the opportunities offered them.

Selected Bibliography

DE KIEWET, C. W. *The Anatomy of South African Misery.* (The Whidden Lectures, 1956.) London and New York: Oxford University Press, 1956.

LOUCHHEIM, D. H. "Premier Balewa's Body is Discovered," *Washington Post,* January 23, 1966, pp. 1 and 18.

SEERS, D. "International Trade and Development—The Special Interests of Africa," in I. G. STEWART and H. ORD (eds.), *African Primary Products and International Trade.* Edinburgh: Edinburgh University Press, 1965. Pp. 19–25.

SINAI, I. R. *The Challenge of Modernisation: The West's Impact on the Non-Western World.* London: Chatto & Windus, 1964.

TOYNBEE, A. J. "Africa: Birth of a Continent," *Saturday Review,* December 5, 1964, pp. 27–29, 87–88.

APPENDIXES

Table 1

THE INDEPENDENT AFRICAN COUNTRIES

Country	Date of In-dependence	Area (in million sq. km.)	Estimated population at end 1965[1] (in millions)	Density of population (per sq. km.)
1. Algeria	7/3/62	2.2	11.0	5
2. Botswana	(1966)	.5	.5	1
3. Burundi	7/1/62	.03	3.0	100
4. Cameroon	1/1/60	.5	4.8	9.6
5. Central African Republic	8/13/60	.6	1.3	2
6. Chad	8/11/60	1.3	3.1	2.4
7. Congo (Brazzaville)	8/15/60	.3	.9	3
8. Congo (Leopoldville)	6/30/60	2.3	16	7
9. Dahomey	8/1/60	.13	2.4	18.4
10. Ethiopia	Time immemorial	1.3	22	17
11. Gabon	8/17/60	.3	.5	1.7
12. Ghana	3/6/57	.2	7.9	39.5
13. Guinea	10/2/58	.2	3.6	18
14. Ivory Coast	8/7/60	.3	3.9	13
15. Kenya	12/12/63	.6	9.5	15.8
16. Lesotho	(1966)	.03	.7	23
17. Liberia	1847	.1	1.0	10
18. Libya[14]	12/24/51	1.8	1.4	.8
19. Madagascar	6/25/60	.6	6.3	10.5
20. Malawi	7/6/64	.13	4.0	31
21. Mali	9/22/60	1.2	4.7	4
22. Mauritania	11/28/60	1.0	.9	.9
23. Morocco	3/2/65	.5	13.6	27
24. Niger	8/3/60	1.3	3.3	2.5
25. Nigeria	10/1/60	.9	45[19]	50
26. Rwanda	7/1/62	.03	3.0	100
27. Senegal	4/20/60	.2	3.5	17.5
28. Sierra Leone	4/27/61	.1	2.2	22
29. Somalia	7/1/60	.6	2.4	4
30. South Africa	1910	1.2	13.7	15
31. Sudan	1/1/56	2.5	13.7	5.4
32. Swaziland	(1968)	.015	.3	20
33. Tanzania (excluding Zanzibar)	12/9/61	.9	10.1	11
34. Togo	4/27/60	.06	1.6	26.7
35. Tunisia	3/20/56	.13	4.8	37
36. Uganda	10/9/62	.23	7.7	33
37. Upper Volta	8/5/60	.3	4.7	15.7
38. Zambia	10/24/64	.8	3.8	5

250

Annual Growth Rate of population	GDP/GNP[2] (in millions of US $)	Per-capita GDP/GNP[2] (US $)	Annual Growth Rate of GDP/GNP[2] [3]	Annual Growth Rate of per-capita GDP/GNP[2] [3]
2.5	1,939	180	falling	falling
2.5	-	60	-	-
2.5	150	60	2.5[5]	nil
1.5	445	110	4	2.6
1.3[7]	120	100	6.5	5.1
2	202	65[8]	2	nil
2	134	155	7.5	5.4
2.5	1,218[9]	80[9]	6.8	4.2
2.8	140	65	-	-
1.8	880	40	3.5	1.7
1[10]	81[11]	180	20	18
2.6	1,388	247	3.2	1.9
2.7	240	70	-	negative
2.2	736	196	12	9.6
3.1	778	85	4.2	1.1
1.7	-	60	-	-
1	187	187	3.5	2.5
3.6	350	350[15]	-	-
2.6	596	105	3	.38
3.0	147	37	3.2[17]	.19
2.4	305	66	2	-0.39
1.3	98	110	19	17.5
3	2,436	162	3.8	.78
2.7	209	70	3.5	.77
1.9[7]	4,258	80	4.7	2.7
3	123	40	2[20]	-0.98
2.25	657	200	2.6	-0.34
.5[7]	170-250	77-115	-	-
1.25	98-119	40-50	-	-
2.4	10,388[21]	590	6[22]	3.5
2.8	1,333	102	5[24]	2.1
2.6	-	100[25]	-[26]	positive
1.8	684[27]	68	6.5[28]	4.6
2.6	130	80	6.0	3.3
2.5	844[29]	200	5.9	3.3
2.5	613	81	4.7[30]	2.1
2	170	40	-	-
3	600	164	2.3[31]	-0.68

251

Table 1 (cont.)

| | | | Industrial Origin of GDP (in percentages) | |
| | Agri- | Mining and | | |
Country	culture	Quarrying	Manufacturing	Construction
1. Algeria	26		16[4]	-
2. Botswana	-	-	-	-
3. Burundi	60	-	7	-
4. Cameroon	-[6]	-	-	-
5. Central African Republic	49		12	-
6. Chad	-	-	-	-
7. Congo (Brazzaville)	23.4		17	-
8. Congo (Leopoldville)	28		38	-
9. Dahomey	-	-	-	-
10. Ethiopia	70		2	-
11. Gabon	12		20	-
12. Ghana	49.5	3.8	2.4[12]	-
13. Guinea	50	10	-	-
14. Ivory Coast	45		15	-
15. Kenya	40	-	9	-
16. Lesotho	-	-	-	-
17. Liberia	35	39	12[13]	-
18. Libya[14]	-	-	-	-
19. Madagascar	35	-	10[16]	
20. Malawi	57.5	-		9.5
21. Mali	57	-	7	-
22. Mauritania	45	4[18]		
23. Morocco	28		19	
24. Niger	55	-	-	-
25. Nigeria	62	2	5	-
26. Rwanda	60	3	-	-
27. Senegal	29		13	
28. Sierra Leone	50-40	30-40		
29. Somalia	80	-	-	-
30. South Africa	9.2	12.5	27.8[23]	-
31. Sudan	52	3		8
32. Swaziland				-
33. Tanzania (excluding Zanzibar)	58	2	4	-
34. Togo	56	9		-
35. Tunisia	25	14		7
36. Uganda	56	2.7	3.8	-
37. Upper Volta	58	2	-	-
38. Zambia	11.4	49.9	5.9	-

Notes to Table 1

1. Source: <u>U.N. Demographic Yearbook</u>, 1963, except for Algeria, Ethiopia, Liberia, Nigeria and South Africa.

2. Gross Domestic Product at market prices for Algeria (1963), Cameroon (1959), Central African Republic (1961), Chad (1963), Dahomey (1959), Guinea (1964), Liberia (1963), Madagascar (1962), Mauritania (1962), Niger (1961), Senegal (1962), Somalia (1962), and Togo (1962); GDP at factor cost for Kenya, Morocco, Tanzania, and Uganda (all 1964). Gross National Product at market prices*for Burundi (1964), Congo (Brazzaville) (1959), Congo (Leopoldville) (1959), Ethiopia (1962-63), Gabon (1960), Ghana (1964), Ivory Coast (1964), Libya, Malawi (1964), Mali (1964), Nigeria (1964-65), Rwanda (1964), Sierra Leone (1961), South Africa (1964), Sudan (1963-64), Tunisia (1964), Uganda (1964), and Zambia (1964).

3. Figures for Burundi, Cameroon, Central African Republic, Chad, Congo (Brazzaville), Gabon, Niger, and Tunisia at current prices.

4. Petroleum an additional 13 per cent.

5. Long-term: recent annual rate, 20 per cent at current prices.

6. Primary sector 51 per cent, secondary sector 8 per cent.

7. Old estimate; current International Development Agency brief gives "not available."

8. 1960 estimate.

9. 1959 figures at the then rate of exchange (50 FC=U.S. $1). At present rate (150 FC=U.S. $1), GNP would be $406 million and per-capita GNP $29.

10. "Less than 1 per cent."   11.   GNP: GDP at market prices was $128 million.

12. Other industries, 13.2 per cent.   13.   Industry and commerce.

14. No mission since 1960; earlier data rendered invalid by discovery and exploitation of petroleum.

15. 1965 estimate.   16. All industry.   17. 1954-64, with a slight decline in 1963-64.

18. Before enclave investment came into production.

19. Estimated figure. The 1963 census gave 55.6 million.

20. 12 per cent in 1964 in real terms.

21. Includes South West Africa, Bechuanaland, Lesotho, and Swaziland.

22. The real rate of growth in 1948-64 was 5; in 1962-64, 7.5.

23. Private manufacturing. In addition, commerce: 12.9 per cent; transport: 7.7 per cent; and public authorities: 10.3 per cent.

24. Calculated from 1955-56 to 1962-63 by constant prices; only 7 per cent in 1963-64 owing to bad harvest.

25. "Less than 100."   26.   "Probably greater than the growth rate of population."

27. GDP at factor cost. GNP was $725 million.   28.   1964. The 1954-60 rate was 5.

29. 1964 figures at post-devaluation (late 1964) exchange rate (0.52 dinars=U.S. $1). At the pre-devaluation rate (0.42 dinars=U.S. $1), GNP was $1045.

30. 1954-64. Actual rate in 1964, 5.2.   31.   1955-64. Actual rate in 1964, 9.1.

253

Table 2

EXPORTS, BY COUNTRY, 1938-64
(excludes gold imports except as noted)
(f.o.b. values in millions of U. S. dollars)

Country	1938	1946	1950	1960	1961	1962	1963	1964
Total Africa	862[13]	1,512	3,222	5,930	6,076	6,459	7,031	8,090
Total Africa south of the Sahara[1]	612	1,207	2,575	5,051	5,234	5,054	5,443	6,196
Algeria	162	200	333	394	368	800e	700e	710e
Angola	15	39	75	124	135	148	164	204
Cameroon	7	n.a.	47	97	98	103	118	122
Congo (Leopoldville)[2]	50	121	261	335	117	366	379	368e
Central African Republic[3]	7	n.a.	43	14	14	15	22	29
Chad				13	21	17	23	27
Congo (Brazzaville)				18	20	34	42	49
Gabon				47	56	59	72	94
Dahomey[4]	3	2	13	18	14	11	13	13
Ivory Coast[4]	11	15	79	151	191	193	230	296
Senegal[4] [5]	19	35	71	113	124	124	111	123
Niger[4]	1	1	3	13	15	20	20	21

Country							
Ghana	52	57	192	294	292	290	273	292
Kenya[6]	40	76	57	112	116	126	142	150
Uganda[6]	7	7	81	120	116	115	153	186
Tanganyika[6][16]	15	33	66	155	138	146	179	197
Liberia	2	12	28[8]	83	62	68	81	164e
Malagasy Republic	24[8]	40[8]	69	75	78	94	82	92
Mauritius	14	20	32	39	62	64	90	78
Morocco	43[8]	87[8]	190	354	342	348	384	434
Mozambique	8	33	37	73	89	91	101	106
Nigeria	46	99	253	475	486	472	531	601
Reunion	6	19	19	36	37	33	38	37
Zambia ⎫[9]	49	53	140	576	579	587	624	470
Malawi ⎬	n.a.	n.a.	14					n.a.
Rhodesia ⎭	24	68	117					386
Sierra Leone	11	10	22	83	82	57	81	95
South Africa[15]	157	394	626	1,238	1,329	1,336	1,387	1,458
Tunisia	39	34	114	120	110	116	126	130
Gambia[8]	2	3	6	8	9	10	9	10e
Zanzibar, Pemba[16]	4[8]	9	14	16	12	13	14	12e
Togo	2[10]	2[10]	9[10]	14	19	17	18	30
Upper Volta[4]	3	5	11	4	3	7	9	9e
Guinea[4]	5	n.a.	n.a.	52	61	45	55	46e
Cape Verde Islands	1	n.a.	n.a.	11	11	11	11	11e
Portuguese Guinea	n.a.	n.a.	n.a.	4	7	7	8	8e
Ethiopia[11][12]	n.a.	20	27	73	76	80	90	105
Libya	6	9	10	11	22	141	378	620
Sudan	30	41	95	182	178	226	227	196
Sao Thome and Principe	2	n.a.	n.a.	7	6	6	7	7e
All other[14]	2	n.a.	68	378	581	63	39	104

Notes to Table 2

[1]Excluding Algeria, Morocco, Tunisia, and Libya.

[2]Includes Ruanda-Urundi through July, 1960; July-December, 1960, excludes Katanga and South Kasai; 1961, excludes Katanga, South Kasai, Kivu, and Orientale.

[3]Figures for countries of French Equatorial Africa exclude trade with the other French Equatorial African countries.

[4]Trade with former countries of French West Africa is excluded in figures for Senegal, for Guinea prior to 1959, for Niger and Dahomey prior to 1960, and for Ivory Coast (except for January-June, 1959) and Upper Volta prior to 1961.

[5]Includes Mauritania and Mali through June, 1960; Senegal and Mali, July 1-August 20, 1960.

[6]Excludes trade among Kenya, Uganda, and Tanganyika.

[7]Included with Kenya.

[8]Includes gold (usually negligible).

[9]Figures for all periods adjusted to approximate trade of present customs area, with exclusion of inter-territorial trade.

[10]Included with Ivory Coast.

[11]Prior to September 15, 1952 excludes Eritrea.

[12]Prior to 1960, years ending September 10 of years stated.

[13]Added total thus may not agree with total in sources.

[14]Residual figure.

[15]Semi-processed gold included prior to 1947.

[16]Now Tanganyika and Zanzibar; Pemba constitute Tanzania.

Note: Conversions in each year were made at the current exchange rate in that year.

n.a. - not available
e   - estimate

Source: United Nations, Yearbook of International Trade Statistics, 1963; International Monetary Fund, Direction of Trade, 1960-64 Annual and International Financial Statistics, November, 1965.

256

Table 3

GOLD PRODUCTION, BY COUNTRY

(In millions of U.S. dollars at 35 U.S. dollars per fine ounce)

Country	1938	1946	1950	1960	1961	1962	1963	1964
Congo (Leopoldville)	16.6	11.6	11.9	11.1	8.2	7.2	7.9	7.8
Ghana	23.6	20.5	24.1	30.8	29.2	31.1	32.2	30.3
Rhodesia (S. Rhodesia)	28.5	19.1	17.9	19.7	20.0	19.1	19.8	20.1
South Africa	425.7	417.5	408.2	748.4	802.9	892.2	960.6	1,018.9
Tanzania (Tanganyika)	2.9	1.7	2.3	3.4	n.a.	n.a.	n.a.	n.a.
All other	14.5	8.1	5.9	2.7	6.0	7.0	7.4	6.9
Total	511.8	478.5	470.3	816.1	866.3	956.6	1,027.5	1,084.0

n.a. - not available

Source: International Monetary Fund, International Financial Statistics, November, 1965.

257

Table 4

IMPORTS, BY COUNTRY, 1938-64
(excludes gold imports except as noted)
(c.i.f. values in millions of U. S. dollars)

Country	1938	1946	1950	1960	1961	1962	1963	1964
Total Africa	1,393	2,245	3,757	7,451	7,337	7,252	7,653	8,750
Total Africa south of the Sahara [1]	1,096	1,793	2,829	5,431	5,515	5,607	5,950	7,012
Algeria	143	203	434	1,265	1,024	800e	800e	739e
Angola	10[2]	32	58	128	114	136	146	164
Cameroon[2]	6	n.a.	60	84	96	102	109	116
Congo (Leopoldville)[3]	35[4]	744	188[4]	185	130	264	316	254e
Central African Republic	8[2]	n.a.	77[2]	20	22	25	26	30
Chad				25	25	30	29	35
Congo (Brazzaville)				70	79	65	62	73
Gabon				32	36	41	48	56
Dahomey [2] [6]	3	4	12	31	25	27	33	31
Ivory Coast[6]	9[2]	13[2]	61[2]	120[2]	169	156	170	235
Senegal[6] [7]	29[2]	58[2]	140[2]	172	155	155	156	172
Niger[2] [6]	1	3	4	13	19	27	23	33

	(1)	(2)	(3)	(4)	(5)	(6)	(7)	(8)
Ghana	50	58	135	363	394	333	365	340
Kenya[8]	47	82	89	196	193	194	206	214
Uganda[8]	9	9	43	73	74	73	86	92
Tanganyika[8] [16]	17	33	67	106	111	111	113	123
Liberia	2	5	11	69	91	132	107	181e
Malagasy Republic	17[2]	31[2]	85[2]	111	103	122	127	136
Mauritius	12	20	37	70	68	68	70	80
Morocco	62[2]	147[2]	328	397	440	423	442	459
Mozambique	22	43	58	127	129	136	142	156
Nigeria[2]	42	82	173	604	623	569	581	712
Reunion[2]	8	10	26	52	58	63	70	91
Zambia	25	37	84	} 439	} 434	} 400	} 377e	247
Malawi } [10]	n.a.	n.a.	21					n.a.
Rhodesia	41	93	184					346
Sierra Leone	7	16	19	74	91	85	84	97
South Africa[15]	516	975	936	1,711	1,547	1,552	1,853	2,350
Tunisia	45[2]	92[2]	147[2]	189	209	216	222	248
Gambia[2]	2	4	8	9	13	12	12	9e
Zanzibar, Pemba[16]	5[2]	8	10	15	15	15	15	19e
Togo[2] [11]	2	4	9	26	26	27	29	42
Upper Volta[6]		7	24	8	28	35	37	25e
Guinea[2] [6]	5	n.a.	n.a.	50	73	66	46	38e
Cape Verde Islands	5	n.a.	n.a.	12	7	7	6	6e
Portuguese Guinea	1			11	10	10	10	10e
Ethiopia[12] [14]	n.a.	22	30	84	90	103	111	123
Libya	47	10	19	169	149	206	239	292
Sudan	32	47	78	183	238	256	285	268
Sao Thome and Principe[13]	1	n.a.	n.a.	5	5	6	7	7e
All other[13]	136	32	102	153	224	204	93	101

Notes to Table 4

[1] Excluding Algeria, Morocco, Tunisia, and Libya.

[2] Includes gold (usually negligible).

[3] Includes Ruanda-Urundi prior to July, 1960; July-December, 1960, excludes Katanga and South Kasai; 1961, excludes Katanga, South Kasai, Kivu, and Orientale.

[4] Includes partly worked gold.

[5] Figures for countries of French Equatorial Africa exclude trade with the other former French Equatorial African countries.

[6] Trade with former countries of French West Africa is excluded in figures for Senegal, for Guinea prior to 1959, for Dahomey and Niger prior to 1960, and for Ivory Coast (except for January-June, 1959) and Upper Volta prior to 1961.

[7] Includes Mauritania and Mali through June, 1960; Senegal and Mali, July 1-August 20, 1960.

[8] Excludes trade among Kenya, Tanganyika, and Uganda.

[9] Included with Kenya.

[10] Imports f.o.b. Also, figures for all periods adjusted to approximate trade of present customs area, with exclusion of inter-trade.

[11] Included with Ivory Coast.

[12] Excludes Eritrea prior to September 15, 1952.

[13] Residual figure.

[14] Prior to 1960, years ending September 10 of years stated.

[15] Semi-processed gold included prior to 1947.

[16] Now Tanganyika and Zanzibar, Pemba constitute Tanzania.

Note: Conversions in each year were made at the current exchange rate in that year.

n.a. - not available

e   - estimate

Source: United Nations, International Monetary Fund, Direction of Trade, 1960-64, and Yearbook of International Trade Statistics, 1963; International Financial Statistics, November, 1965.

Table 5

ANNUAL YIELD TO CAPITAL INVESTED IN WITWATERSRAND GOLD MINING COMPANIES, SELECTED YEARS 1888-1932
(in thousands of pounds sterling)

	Total "available" profits	Dividends	Capital invested (excluding appropriations from revenue)	Capital invested (including cash premiums and appropriations from revenue)	Dividends as percentage of capital invested (excluding appropriations from revenue)		Percentage of "available" profits as percentage of capital invested (including cash premiums and appropriations from revenue)
					(A)	(B)	
1888	261	251	2,585	2,596	38.0	9.7	10.0
1895	1,247	751	18,843	20,708	5.2	4.0	6.0
1900	121	115	38,537	43,504	0.2	0.3	0.3
1905	4,147	3,232	56,217	64,586	6.1	5.7	6.4
1910	7,435	6,016	67,882	84,139	9.4	8.9	8.8
1915	7,720	6,180	71,588	96,036	8.7	8.6	8.0
1920	9,071	7,842	78,356	110,969	10.2	10.0	8.2
1925	9,775	8,170	82,874	124,958	8.9	9.9	7.8
1930	10,258	8,930	90,630	138,904	10.0	9.9	7.4
1932	9,976	8,877	92,012	142,740	9.7	9.6	7.0

Source: Selected from S. H. Frankel, Capital Investment in Africa (London, New York: Oxford University Press, 1938), Table 15, pp. 96-97. Percentage figures under Column A are from Frankel; these seem to be in error. Figures in Column B have been computed from the data presented by Frankel.

Table 6

EXPORTS OF GOLD, BY COUNTRY

(F.o.b. values in millions of U.S. $)

Country	1938	1946	1950	1960	1961	1962	1963	1964
Algeria	.3	n	n.a.	.1	1.3	n,e	n.a.	n.a.
Cameroon	.4	n.a.	.3	x	x	.2	x	n.a.
Congo (Leopoldville)[1]	14.4	11.4	11.9	11.7	1.2	5.9	7.6	n.a.
Central African Republic	1.0	4.7	1.8	x	x	x	x	**x**
Congo (Brazzaville)				.1	.2	.1	.1	n[2]
Gabon				.6	.4	.4	1.1	n.a.
Senegal	3.4	.6	.8	n	n	n	n	n.a.
Ghana	23.6	22.4	24.4	31.1	30.1	31.5	31.6	30.0[3]
Kenya	3.3	1.2	1.0	.3	.4	.3	.3	.4[4]
Uganda			x	x	x	x	x	x
Tanzania (Tanganyika)	2.9	1.7	2.3	3.4	3.5	3.6	3.6	3.3e[3][4]
Liberia	0.1	.4	n.a.	n.a.	n.a.	n.a.	n.a.	n.a.
Malagasy Republic	n.a.	n.a.	.1	n	n	n.a.	n	n.a.
Morocco	n.a.	n.a.	.1	.1	n	n	n	n[5]
Mozambique	.5	.9	n	n	13.2[5]	3.2[5]	1.0[5]	n.a.
Nigeria	.9	.1	n	n.a.	n.a.	n.a.	n.a.	n.a.
Rhodesia[6]	28.0	19.3	18.2	19.5	19.9	19.3	19.6	19.8[7]
Sierra Leone	1.0	n	.1	n	n	n	n	n[8]
South Africa	355.2[9]	385.7	319.8	802.8	685.7	684.5	832.6	n.a[10]
Sudan	.5	.2	n	.1	x	.1	x	n[10]
Ethiopia	n.a.	10.0	.5	n	1.0	n	n	n.a.
Total	435.5	458.6	381.3	869.8	743.7	745.9	896.5	n.a.

[1] Includes Ruanda-Urundi through July, 1960; July-December, 1960, excluding Katanga and South Kasai; 1961, excludes Katanga, South Kasai, Kivu, and Orientale; January-September, 1962, excludes South Katanga and South Kasai; beginning October, 1962, South Katanga only.

[2] U.S. Embassy in Brazzaville, Exports and Imports, 1964.

[3] Agency for International Development, Economic Data Book: Africa.

[4] East African Customs and Excise, Annual Trade Report for Kenya, Uganda, and Tanganyika, 1964.

[5] Overseas Geological Surveys, Statistical Summary of the Mineral Industry, 1965.

[6] Data refer to trade of the Federation of the Rhodesias and Nyasaland prior to 1963, but these are most likely composed mostly of South Rhodesian exports.

[7] U.S. Embassy in Salisbury, Mineral Exports, 1964.

[8] Sierre Leone, Quarterly Trade Statistics, 1964.

[9] U.S. Department of Commerce, U.S. Treasury, and South African Reserve Bank Bulletin.

[10] U.S. Department of the Interior, Sudan: Annual Foreign Trade Report, 1964.

Note: Conversions in each year were made at the current exchange rate in that year. For comparison purposes, the following table is shown:

	Congo (Leopoldville)	Ghana	South Africa	Southern Rhodesia
Exports of gold 1946-63	199.5	476.5	10,043.6	338.8
Production of gold 1946-63	205.6	472.2	10,118.8	336.2

Table 7

U.S. DIRECT INVESTMENTS BY AREA, 1929-64
(in millions of dollars)

Year end	Total	Canada	Other Western Hemisphere	Europe	Africa	Asia	Other
1929	7,700	2,000	3,600	1,400	-	-	700[1]
1936	6,690	1,952	2,803	1,258	-	-	651[2]
1940	7,300	2,100	2,600	1,900	-	-	700[1]
1945	8,400	2,500	3,100	2,000	-	-	800[1]
1950	11,788	3,579	4,735	1,720	-	-	1,753[2]
1956	22,177	7,460	7,373	3,520[3]	659	1,106[4]	2,059[5]
1957	25,394	8,769	8,052	4,151	664	2,019	1,739
1958	27,255	9,338	8,447	4,573	746	2,178	1,974
1959	29,735	10,171	8,990	5,300	843	2,236	2,196
1960	32,778	11,198	9,271	6,681	925	2,291	2,412
1961	34,667	11,602	9,190	7,742	1,064	2,477	2,593
1962	37,226	12,133	9,474	8,930	1,271	2,500	2,918
1963	40,686	13,044	9,891	10,340	1,426	2,793	3,193
1964[6]	44,343	13,820	10,318	12,067	1,629	3,062	3,447

[1] Including undistributed.
[2] Including Western European dependencies.
[3] Western Europe only.
[4] Middle East only.
[5] Including the Far East.
[6] Preliminary.

Source: U.S. Department of Commerce, Survey of Current Business, issues of 1929; 1940; 1945; November, 1949; 1936; December, 1952; 1950; and November, 1954. For the years 1956-64, figures were obtained from either the August or September issues.

264

Table 8

U.S. Direct Investments in Africa, by Country,
1929-64

(in millions of U.S. dollars)

Country and Area	1929	1936	1943	1950	1957	1959	1960	1961	1962	1963	1964
East Africa			4	12	30	43	46	56			
Ethiopia	*	*	*	5	1	1					
French Equatorial Africa		*		4	9	8					
French West Africa	1	*	3	11	34	76					
Ghana		*			7	9					
Liberia	5	*	18	16	72	115	139	160	184	197	187
Nigeria		*	5	11	15	16					
Congo (Leopoldville)	+	1	4	8	19	17					
Rhodesias and Nyasaland			18	26	59	72	82	85	83		
South Africa	77	55	50	140	301	323	286	309	357	411	467
Total	83	55	102	233	547	680	553	610	624	608	654
All other	19	38	27	54	117	163	372	454	647	818	975
Grand Total	102	93	129	287	664	843	925	1,064	1,271	1,426	1,629

*Not separately shown.
+Less than $500,000.

Source: Department of Commerce: U.S. Business Investment in Foreign Countries, 1960, p. 92; Survey of Current Business, August issues of 1962, 1963, 1964, and issue of September, 1965.

265

Table 9

U.S. FOREIGN DIRECT INVESTMENT* AND EARNINGS,[+]

BY SECTOR AND PERCENTAGE OF EARNINGS ON TOTAL INVESTMENT, 1958-64

(in millions of U.S. dollars)

Year	Total			Mining and Smelting		
	Investment	Earnings	% of earnings to investment	Investment	Earnings	% of earnings to investment
1958	27,075	2,954	10.9	2,856	219	7.7
1959	29,735	3,255	11.0	2,858	315	11.0
1960 ·	32,744	3,546	10.8	3,013	394	13.1
1961	34,684	3,700	10.7	3,061	359	11.7
1962	37,145	4,245	11.4	3,183	367	11.5
1963	40,686	4,572	11.2	3,369	359	10.7
1964	44,343	5,118	11.5	3,564	505	14.2
1958	789	69	8.8	234	37	15.8
1959	843	56	6.6	255	38	14.9
1960	925	33	3.6	247	61	24.7
1961	1,017	28	2.8	285	44	15.4
1962	1,246	80	6.4	307	34	11.1
1963	1,426	170	11.9	349	31	8.9
1964	1,629	343	21.1	356	38	10.7

*Position at the end of period.

[+]Per year. Earnings is the sum of the U.S. share in the net earnings of
subsidiaries and branch profits.

Note: Detail may not add to total because of rounding.

Source: U.S. Department of Commerce, Survey of Current Business, various issues,
Earnings percentage calculated from U.S. Department of Commerce data.

	Petroleum			Manufacturing			Other	
Invest-ment	Earnings	% of earn-ings to investment	Invest-ment	Earnings	% of earn-ings to investment	Invest-ment	Earnings	% of earn-ings to investment
All Countries								
9,681	1,307	13.5	8,485	873	10.3	6,053	555	9.2
10,423	1,185	11.4	9,692	1,129	11.6	6,762	626	9.3
10,944	1,282	11.7	11,152	1,176	10.6	7,635	693	9.1
12,151	1,449	11.9	11,936	1,180	9.9	7,536	711	9.4
12,661	1,716	13.6	13,212	1,310	9.9	8,089	852	10.5
13,652	1,828	13.4	14,937	1,529	10.2	8,727	856	9.8
14,350	1,860	13.0	16,861	1,816	10.8	9,567	936	9.8
African Countries								
276	- 19	- 6.9	139	23	16.6	140	28	20.0
338	- 27	- 8.0	120	17	14.2	130	28	21.5
407	- 77	-18.9	118	19	16.1	152	30	19.7
491	- 84	-17.1	113	19	16.8	180	50	27.8
627	- 6	- 1.0	141	32	22.7	171	20	11.7
702	65	9.3	177	43	24.3	198	31	15.6
830	227	27.4	225	43	19.1	217	35	16.1

Table 10

FOREIGN DIRECT INVESTMENT IN SOUTH AFRICA, BY SECTOR OF INVESTMENT

(in millions of South African pounds)

	Grand Total		Official Sector		Private Sector		Mining	Manufacturing	Trade	Insurance	Other Financial Organizations	All Others
	1963	1956	1963	1956	1963	1956	1956	1956	1956	1956	1956	1956
Great Britain	670.5	556.1	40.0	32.3	630.5	523.8	164.0	186.6	74.9	17.0	47.5	33.8
United States	120.5	126.3	2.0	1.1	118.5	125.2	54.0	36.2	28.7	0.6	1.2	4.4
France	40.5	24.2	2.5	2.4	38.0	21.8	12.2	1.4	5.0	0.6	1.5	1.1
Switzerland	28.5	17.0	0.5	0.2	28.0	16.8	4.3	8.4	1.0	0.6	1.7	0.9
Rhodesia and Nyasaland	23.0	13.0	3.0	3.1	20.0	9.9	2.0	1.7	1.0	3.2	1.3	0.7
Netherlands	n.a.	9.9	n.a.	2.3	n.a.	7.6	0.3	5.6	0.5	0.5	0.3	0.4
Canada	n.a.	9.8	n.a.	0.1	n.a.	9.7	0.4	6.0	2.6	0.5	0.3	0.5
Grand Total (including countries other than those above)	985.0	809.0	56.0	46.9	929.5	762.1	242.5	265.7	119.1	28.4	61.2	45.0

Source: Data for 1956 are from the Final Results of the 1956 Census of the Foreign Liabilities and Assets of the Union of South Africa, published as a supplement to the December, 1958, issue of the South African Reserve Bank's Quarterly Bulletin of Statistics. Figures for 1963 are from the December, 1964, issue of the same bulletin.

n.a. - not available.

Table 11a

The French Colonial Loan of 1931
(in millions of French francs)

	Original Authorization	Issued up to 1939	Subsequent Authorization	Total Authorization	Total issued or advanced by 1946
French West Africa	1,690	734	1,430	3,120	2,630
Togo	73	73	none	73	73
Cameroons	57	46	none	57	55
French Equatorial Africa	1,513	1,104	none	1,513	1,513
Madagascar	735	709	100	835	764
Somaliland	44	41	none	44	37
Reunion	63	45	13	136	68
Total	4,175	2,752	1,543	5,778	5,140

Note: Figures given are amounts realized, not nominal value of issue.

Table 11b

The French Colonial Loan of 1931: Expenditure, 1931-38
(in millions of French francs)

	French West Africa	French Equatorial Africa	Madagascar	Total
Railroads	179	719	272	1,170
Roads and bridges	33		57	90
Ports and rivers	171	179	176	526
Irrigation	207			207
Production	57	51		108
Social services	75	65	78	218
Miscellaneous	29	32	108	169
Total	751	1,046	691	2,488

Note: Expenses given cover only actual projects; loan issue expenses, etc., are excluded. The categories are quite possibly not comparable in some instances. The three colonies tabulated account for some 80 per cent of the expenditure during the period (Indochina excluded).

Sources: Compiled by B. B. King from Ministere de la France Outre-Mer, Annuaire statistique des possessions francaises, annees anterieure a la guerre, 1944; Ministere des Finances, Inventaire de la situation financiere (1913-46), 1946; Royal Institute of International Affairs, The Colonial Problem, 1937.

Table 12

FOREIGN BONDS[a] PUBLICLY ISSUED IN VARIOUS MARKETS BY AFRICAN COUNTRIES, 1946-64
(Nominal amounts in millions of U.S. dollars)

Country	Capital Markets				
	Switzerland	United Kingdom	United States	Other	Total
Belgian Congo					
1950	14.0				14.0
1952	13.7				13.7
1953	14.0				14.0
1956	14.0				14.0
1958			15.0		15.0
Total	55.7		15.0		70.7
Federation of Rhodesia and Nyasaland[b]					
1947		129.0			129.0
1948		20.2			20.2
1950		16.8			16.8
1951		14.0			14.0
1952		21.0			21.0
1953		28.0			28.0
1954		28.0			28.0
1955		28.0			28.0
1958		28.0	6.0		34.0
1959		28.0			28.0
Total		341.0	6.0		347.0
South Africa					
1949		28.0			28.0
1950		16.8			16.8
1952	13.7	2.8			16.5
1953		8.4			8.4
1954	14.0	2.2			16.2
1955			25.0	13.2[c]	38.2
1958		4.5	40.0		44.5
1959	11.6	14.0			25.6
Total	39.3	76.7	65.0	13.2	194.2

270

Federation of Rhodesia and Nyasaland				
1955			7.0[c]	7.0
1958			0.1[d]	0.1
Total			7.1	7.1
South Africa				
1950	11.6	5.6		17.2
1952	5.7			5.7
1954	5.8			5.8
1955	8.2			8.2
1957		8.4		8.4
1958			11.9[e]	11.9
1962	11.6			11.6
Total	42.9	14.0	11.9	68.8

Note: Where country names have changed, the issues are shown under the name of the country at the time of issue (except in the case of Southern Rhodesia, which is shown under the Federation).

[a]Of, or guaranteed by, governments and political subdivisions.

[b]Bonds issued from 1947 to 1953 were issued by Southern Rhodesia; subsequent issues by the Federation.

[c]Issued in the Netherlands.

[d]Issued in Belgium.

[e]Issued in Germany.

Table 13

British Financial Aid to Africa, South of the Sahara, Bilateral Disbursements (Gross), By Country

	1945-60			1960-65		
	Grants	Loans	Total	Grants	Loans	Total
Basutoland	2,140		2,140	8,072	410	8,482
Bechuanaland	4,560	2,351	6,911	9,520	1,256	10,776
Cameroon	1,730		1,730	1,753	1,350	3,103
Congo (Leopoldville)				538		538
East African Common Services Organization	7,086		7,086	7,997	15,297	23,294
Federation of Rhodesia and Nyasaland	1,660	4,700	6,360	1,880	15,026	16,906
Gambia	1,884	1,851	3,735	3,949	98	4,047
Ghana	5,355	325	5,680	374	3,335	3,709
Kenya	38,174	16,510	54,684	28,765	34,315	63,080
Malawi	6,330	4,319	10,649	18,539	7,030	25,569
Mauritania				25		25
Mauritius	2,945	772	3,717	4,000	2,529	6,529
Niger				9		9
Nigeria	36,147	3,958	40,105	6,807	23,076	29,883
Rhodesia		1,000	1,000	2,250	3,855	6,106

	1	2	3	4	5	6
Seychelles	960	250	1,210	1,418		1,418
Sierra Leone	5,376	1,500	6,876	5,507	5,805	11,312
Somalia*	9,065	102	9,167	5,073		5,073
St. Helena and Tristan da Cunha	1,169		1,169	938	2	940
Sudan	3,680	2,440	6,120	165	3,260	3,425
Swaziland	2,782	6,067	8,849	6,001	9,043	15,044
Tanzania Tanganyika Zanzibar	12,169 1,477	3,119	15,288 1,477	19,255	14,936	34,191
Uganda	6,869	5,144	12,013	11,409	14,650	26,059
Zambia	4,006	1,118	5,124	5,565	4,752	10,317
Other and unallocated						
Southern Africa	10+		10			
East Africa	1,837		1,837			
West Africa	380		380	635		635
Central Africa	47		47			
Total	157,838	55,526	213,364	150,445	160,025	310,470

*Disbursements up to July 1960 were made to British Somaliland.
+Includes grants to Basutoland, Bechuanaland, and Swasiland not indentifiable by individual recipient.

Sources: United Kingdom, Treasury, Aid to Developing Countries, 1963; Ministry of Overseas Development, Overseas Development: The Work of the New Ministry, 1965.

273

Table 14

OFFICIAL U.S. ASSISTANCE TO AFRICAN COUNTRIES SOUTH OF THE SAHARA, 1946-65
(in millions of U.S. dollars)

Country	Total, Fiscal Years 1946-60					Total, Fiscal Years 1961-65					
	Net Obligations, Grants		Loan Authorizations	Total	Disbursements under Foreign Assistance Programs	Net Obligations, Grants		Loan Authorizations		Total	Disbursements under Foreign Assistance Programs
	PL 480	Other				PL 480	Other	PL 480	Other		
Burundi						6.5	0.6			7.1	0.1
Cameroon	0.1			0.1		0.2	12.1	9.2	3.2	24.7	9.1
Central African Republic							2.7			2.7	1.0
Chad						1.2	3.1			4.3	1.3
Congo (Brazzaville)						0.2	2.0	0.2		2.4	1.6
Congo (Leopoldville)					*	80.1	125.4	12.6	82.3	300.4	183.7
Dahomey	0.1			0.1		3.8	4.5	0.1	0.1	8.5	3.2
Ethiopia	5.8	38.6	13.0	57.4	29.3	6.8	40.7	2.1	43.9	93.5	58.5
Gabon							4.8			4.8	1.5
Gambia							0.1			0.1	
Ghana	1.3	2.7		4.0		5.3	9.3		147.0	161.6	15.5
Guinea	1.7	2.1		3.8	2.0	4.6	34.7	20.8	5.5	65.6	22.9
Ivory Coast						0.1	8.0	6.5	11.3	25.9	3.7
Kenya	0.5	4.6		5.1	4.1	10.0	13.9	3.8	2.8	30.5	8.1
Liberia	0.6	20.7	43.8	65.1	14.7	1.3	42.4	8.6	113.5	165.8	36.3
Malagasy Republic						1.9	3.3		2.7	7.9	2.3
Malawi						0.1	3.1			3.2	1.2
Mali						0.9	9.4		3.2	13.5	6.9
Mauritania	0.1		1.4	1.5	1.4	1.0	0.3			1.3	0.1
Niger						0.2	6.1		2.3	8.6	3.5
Nigeria	0.2	5.0	1.0	6.2	2.0	2.0	88.0		63.5	153.5	52.3
Rhodesia and Nyasaland	*	0.2	32.4	32.6	10.0		8.4			8.4	3.0
Rwanda						0.1	1.6			1.7	0.3
Senegal						2.8	9.5	2.6	1.6	16.5	6.7
Sierra Leone	0.2	0.3		0.5		2.6	12.2	1.8	10.2	26.8	4.0

Somalia	0.3	6.8	2.0	9.1	4.4	6.9	27.3	11.9	4.2	38.4	22.2
Sudan	*	34.1	10.0	44.1	20.2	5.8	21.0		5.8	44.5	39.4
Tanzania	0.1	0.1		0.2		17.9	13.4		12.9	44.2	9.9
Togo	0.5			0.5		3.9	5.5			9.4	3.1
Uganda	0.2	0.8		1.0	0.3	1.2	10.4		4.8	16.4	8.0
Upper Volta						1.3	4.0			5.3	4.3
Zambia						0.1	0.8			0.9	1.0
Africa Regional	0.5	7.3	23.2	31.0	7.0	1.8	42.6		-9.2	35.2	24.3
Total	12.2	123.3	126.8	262.3	95.4	170.6	571.2	80.2	511.6	1333.6	539.0

Note: A minus figure under "authorizations" indicates cancellations or cancellations exceeding new authorizations.

* Less than $50,000.

Sources: Figures in the first four columns for each time period are from the special report prepared by the U.S. Agency for International Development for the U.S. Congress, House of Representatives, Committee on Foreign Affairs, "U.S. Overseas Loans and Grants and Assistance from International Organizations; Obligations and Loan Authorizations," March 3, 1965, and March 18, 1966 (carrying data through June 30, 1964, and June 30, 1965, respectively).

These data relate only to U.S. bilateral assistance under Foreign Assistance Programs administered by the Agency for International Development, plus assistance under the Food for Peace and the Peace Corps programs, and Export-Import Bank loans.

Authorizations data for Export-Import Bank loans are for loans of five years' or more maturity, and include loans by private financial institutions if guaranteed by the Export-Import Bank.

Disbursements data are from a report of the Agency for International Development entitled "U.S. Economic Assistance Programs Administered by the A.I.D. and Predecessor Agencies," March 5, 1965, and February 24, 1966 (carrying data through June 30, 1964, and June 30, 1965, respectively).

Table 15

World Bank Group Operations in Africa, through December 31, 1965
(in millions of U.S. dollars)

	Bank Loans Net Amounts*	Amount I.D.A. Credits*	I.F.C. Commitments
Bechuanaland	-	3.6	-
Burundi	4.8	-	-
Congo (Leopoldville)	91.6	-	-
Ethiopia	56.7	13.5	4.4
Gabon	47.0	-	-
Ghana	47.0	-	-
Ivory Coast[a]	7.1	-	0.2
Kenya[b]	52.0	10.3	-
Liberia	4.3	-	0.3
Mali[a]	-	-	-
Mauritania	66.0	6.7	-
Mauritius	7.0	-	-
Niger	-	1.5	-
Nigeria	185.5	35.5	2.2
Rhodesia[c]	87.0	-	-
Senegal[a]	-	-	-
Sierra Leone	3.8	-	-
Somalia	-	6.2	-
South Africa	221.8	-	-
Sudan	105.0	13.0	0.7
Swaziland	4.2	2.8	-
Tanzania[b]	24.0	18.6	4.7
Uganda[b]	8.4	-	3.5
Upper Volta[a]	-	-	-
Zambia	67.4	-	-
Total	1,090.6	111.7	16.0

*Net of cancellations, refundings, and termination.

[a]Loans shared with other countries marked [a].
b "   "   "   "   "   " b.
c "   "   "   "   "   " c.

Table 16

WORLD BANK GROUP LOANS AND CREDITS,

CLASSIFIED BY PURPOSE AS OF DECEMBER 31, 1965

(in millions of U.S. dollars,
initial commitments net of cancellations and refundings)

	World Bank	I.D.A.
Electric power	405.6	-
Transportation (total)	545.2	71.3
Railroads	338.0	-
Roads	119.6	71.3
Ports and waterways	37.6	-
Pipelines	50.0	-
Telecommunications	9.2	-
Agriculture, forestry, and fishing (total)	79.9	15.8
Farm mechanization	4.1	-
Irrigation and flood control	47.5	13.0
Land clearance, farm improvement, etc.	26.4	2.8
Crop processing and storage	1.1	-
Livestock improvement	0.9	-
Industry (total)	140.5	-
Iron and steel	-	-
Paper and pulp	-	-
Fertilizer and other chemicals	-	-
General industries	20.5	-
Mining	101.0	-
Development finance companies	19.0	-
Educational projects	-	40.6
General development	40.0	-
Total	1,220.4	127.7

Note: Multipurpose loans are distributed according to each purpose
and not assigned to the major purpose. Detail may not add to
totals because of rounding.

277

Table 17

COMMON MARKET AID TO AFRICAN COUNTRIES
(FONDS EUROPEEN DE DEVELOPPEMENT)

	First FED, as of October 31, 1965				Second FED, as of June 30, 1965				Total, 1st and 2nd FEDs	
	Commitments under contract	Balance of Commitments	Total Commitments	Disbursements	Commitments under contract	Balance of Commitments	Total Commitments	Disbursements	Commitments	Disbursements
Algeria	6,136	19,183	25,319	6,014					25,319	6,014
Burundi	2,951	1,980	4,931	2,722		1,601	1,601	54	6,532	2,776
Cameroon	36,393	16,404	52,797	23,825	1,135	11,452	12,587	747	65,384	24,572
Central African Republic	10,182	8,035	18,217	6,458	386	4,503	4,889	1,529	23,106	6,458
Chad	24,736	3,188	27,924	20,114	1,481	5,251	6,732	87	34,656	21,643
Comoros	2,861	216	3,077	2,367	153	224	377		3,454	2,454
Congo (Brazzaville)	18,531	6,091	24,622	15,565		3,832	3,832		28,454	15,565
Congo (Leopoldville)	13,329	3,823	17,152	7,065	6	4,896	4,902	3	22,054	7,068
Dahomey	11,830	8,947	20,777	8,502		1,011	1,011		21,788	8,502
Gabon	12,505	5,275	17,780	10,439	10	2,107	2,117	5	19,897	10,444
Ivory Coast	27,181	12,481	39,662	23,919	22	32,819	32,841	14	72,503	23,933
Malagasy	50,677	5,590	56,267	36,237		1,643	1,643		57,910	36,237
Mali	35,169	6,784	41,953	24,423	422	3,324	3,746	210	45,699	24,633
Mauritania	10,996	4,382	15,378	10,055		9,836	9,836		25,214	10,055
Niger	23,512	7,779	31,291	13,022	82	3,374	3,456	31	34,747	13,053
Reunion	2,738	6,124	8,862	1,943					8,862	1,943
Rwanda	3,955	1,026	4,981	2,919		3,003	3,003		7,984	2,919
Senegal	29,831	14,003	43,834	24,887	5	10,568	10,573	5	54,407	24,892
Somalia	7,772	2,438	10,210	209	194	7,858	8,052	109	18,262	318
French Somaliland	1,025	174	1,199	826					1,199	826
Togo	10,830	5,105	15,935	8,190		15	15		15,950	8,190
Upper Volta	22,392	5,841	28,233	15,249	207	783	990	66	29,223	15,315
Total	365,532	144,869	510,401	264,950	4,103	108,100	112,203	2,860	622,604	267,810

Table 18

COMMITMENTS BY SINO-SOVIET COUNTRIES FOR ECONOMIC ASSISTANCE
TO AFRICA SOUTH OF SAHARA, 1958-65
(in millions of U.S. dollars)

Country	1958	1959	1960	1961	1962	1963	1964	1965	1958-65 Total
Central African Republic	-	-	-	-	-	-	4	-	4
Congo (Brazzaville)	-	-	-	-	-	-	33	29	62
Ethiopia	2	112	-	-	-	-	-	-	114
Ghana	-	-	40	82	-	-	22	20	164
Guinea	-	35	59	12	13	-	-	-	119
Kenya	-	-	-	-	-	-	55	-	55
Mali	-	-	-	75	10	-	27	-	112
Nigeria	-	-	-	-	-	-	-	14	14
Senegal	-	-	-	-	-	-	7	-	7
Somalia	-	-	-	74	-	22	-	-	96
Sudan	-	-	-	22	-	-	-	-	22
Tanzania	-	-	-	-	-	-	51	-	51
Uganda	-	-	-	-	-	-	15	15	30
Total	2	147	99	265	35	22	214	78	850

Note: These figures are for commitments. Actual disbursements usually take place
over a four- or five-year period following, or the commitment may not be
utilized at all. Total commitments to other countries through 1965 were:
U.A.R., $1,408 million; Algeria, $299 million; Morocco, $17 million; Tunisia,
$48 million.

Source: United Nations, World Economic Survey, 1965: Part I, Chapter IV;
International Flow of Long-Term Capital and Official Donations
1961-65, 1966.

Table 19

FLOW OF EXTERNAL RESOURCES FROM

INDUSTRIAL MARKET ECONOMIES AND MULTILATERAL AGENCIES[a]

(in millions of U.S. dollars)

	Bilateral[b]					
	Grants[e]			Loans		
	1961	1962	1963	1961	1962	1963
Algeria	401	353	286	37	43	12
Libya	36	30	26	1	1	
Morocco[f]	88	53	69	29	31	36
Tunisia[f]	84	60	65	2	4	27
Sub-total: North Africa	609	496	446	69	79	75
Congo (Leopoldville)	60	63	87		3	
Ethiopia	21	25	21	-1	1	1
French franc area[g]	282	313	310	38	26	39
Ghana	3	3	4		3	14
Guinea	1	6	15	1	3	8
Kenya[h]	34	35	32	29	13	22
Liberia	5	7	10	22	72	24
Malawi	...	...	...	...	...	...
Nigeria	7	14	18	24	16	
Portuguese Overseas Provinces[g]	3	3	10	30	38	42
Sierra Leone	10	5	5	4	3	5
Somalia	21	23	22			6
Sudan	13	10	10	2	-3	1
Tanzania[h]	22	37	20	17	10	10
Uganda[h]	10	16	14	11	13	6
United Kingdom Colonies	18	19	21	11	5	7
Zambia	...	...	...	...	...	...
Sub-total: Sub-Saharan Africa[g]	534	613	613	215	206	208
Total[g]	1 143	1,109	1,059	284	285	283

[a] As reported by the source.

[b] From Austria, Belgium, Canada, Denmark, Federal Republic of Germany, France, Italy, Japan, Netherlands, Norway, Portugal, Sweden, United Kingdom and United States.

[c] International Bank for Reconstruction and Development, International Finance Corporation, International Development Association, Inter-American Development Bank, and the European Development Fund (all net of subscriptions and of repayments), and United Nations agencies (other than the World Food Program) for relief and technical assistance (net of contributions).

[d] Preliminary.

[e] Including loans repayable in recipient's currency and net transfer of resources through sales for recipient's currency.

Source: United Nations: International Flow of Long-Term Capital and Official Donations 1961-65, 1966.

Multilateral[c]			Total			
1961	1962	1963	1961	1962	1963	1964[d]
-5	-4	-3	433	392	276	252
	1	1	36	32	26	16
	1	3	117	85	117	107
1		3	87	65	95	71
<u>-4</u>	<u>-2</u>	<u>4</u>	<u>673</u>	<u>574</u>	<u>514</u>	<u>446</u>
26	2		87	67	87	115
6	6	4	26	20	26	...
45	92	74	367	444	448	447
	-1	10	2	6	27	40
	1		2	10	23	...
2	2	2	65	51	56	53
			27	79	34	17
...	...	...	8	12	17	32
2	1	-3	33	30	16	54
			33	41	52	64
			14	8	10	...
3	1	3	24	24	31	...
10	14	8	25	21	19	...
2	-1		41	47	32	44
4	2	1	25	30	21	20
	2	3	29	26	31	...
...	...	...	...	...	...	...
<u>108</u>	<u>125</u>	<u>103</u>	<u>857</u>	<u>944</u>	<u>933</u>	<u>1,038</u>
<u>104</u>	<u>123</u>	<u>107</u>	<u>1,530</u>	<u>1,518</u>	<u>1,447</u>	<u>1,484</u>

[f]French grants to Morocco and Tunisia ($28 million in 1961-62 and $31 million in 1963) have been allocated two-thirds to Morocco, one-third to Tunisia.

[g]Regional totals include figures for countries for which the data have not been separately provided as well as for funds that could not be distributed by country. The following territories have been included in Africa: French Polynesia, New Caledonia, St. Pierre and Miquelon and Wallis and Futuna (all parts of the French franc area), and Macao and Timor (listed with the Portuguese Overseas Provinces).

[h]Grants by the Federal Republic of Germany to Kenya and Uganda have been allocated to Kenya. Net flows to the East African Common Services Organization have been allocated 48 per cent to Kenya, 30 per cent to Tanzania, and 22 per cent to Uganda.

Index

Accounts, national; see National accounts
Activities, sector distribution of, 32–33
ADB; see African Development Bank
Adu, A. L.: quoted, 60
Africa: area of, total, 23; coastline of, 5, 10, 168; compared to United States, 23; exploration of, 4; geography of, 5, 10, 168; geology of, 134, 136–37; isolation of, 3–6; hydroelectric potential of, 179; see also specific countries and subjects
African Associated States (of the EEC): Committee of Association, 81; Convention of Association, 76–77; Council of Association, 40, 81; EEC aid to, 79–82; list of members, 76–77 n.; relations with members of UDEAC, 42; technical aid to, 80; and trade options, 226–27
African Development Bank (ADB), 40, 206
Agence Transéquatoriale des Communications (ATEC), 43
Agriculture: agricultural production, 73; climate and soil, 4; conditions for success of, 90; cooperatives, 111, 117, 118; credit systems, 117–18; during colonial period, 12, 14; government extension services, 114–17, 183; and GNP, 32–33; importance of, 89–91; introduction of maize and manioc, 7; marketing boards and, 125–28; research in, 41, 241; restrictions in South Africa, 58 n.; see also Farms and farming, specific products

Agricultural work patterns: cooperative farming in Kenya, 111; division of labor, 103–4; and industrialization, 162; and leisure, 101; permanent individual farms, 110–12; "progressive" farmers, 104, 106; and security of return, 102; see also Cultivation

Aid programs: to African Associated States of the EEC, 79; to African Development Bank, 206; by Communist China, 201, 202; to education, 80, 182; from European Common Market Economic Development Fund, 203; by foreign grant, 200–6; by France, 200; by International Development Association, 206; by Israel, 202; by Soviet-bloc nations, 201–2; table of, 202; technical assistance, 80, 203–4; by United States, 201; by Upper Volta, 233; by West Germany, 202
Air transportation, 169

Gold: discovery of, 4, 10, 133; export of, 139; production of, 73–74
Gold Coast, 8, 9, 12
Government: agricultural systems and services, 114–17, 117–18, 118–21, 121–22, 164–65; basic services and, 63–64, 166 ff.; bureaucracy of, 63; civil service in colonial period, 59–60; corruption of, 243–44; and economic planning, 209 ff.; and education, 179–83; as employer, 35–36, 39; Europeans in, 19; expenditures of, 35, 63–64; 166 ff.; and head tax by, 57; and industrial development, 154 ff.; and investment in transportation, 169 ff.; in "micro-states," 65; one-party systems of, 244–45; and taxes, 38–39, 57; *see also* specific countries, specific functions
Great Britain: and colonies, 11, 12, 191, 198; and development of minerals, 132; farm policy, 123; formation of chartered companies, 12–13; investments before World War I, 14–15; irrigation projects in Sudan, 121–22; military aid, 136–37; monetary links, 82 ff.; prohibition of slave trade, 8; relations with Rhodesia, 230–31; technical assistance by, 204; and trade with Africa, 72–73
Greaves, I.: cited, 163
Gross Domestic Product, 31
Gross Geographical Product, 31
Gross national expenditures: average, 154; percentage of government expenditures, 35
Gross National Product (GNP): agriculture in, 35; compared to United States, 26; and capital/output ratio, 246; exports and, 35, 72–73; forecast of growth rate, 239–40, 245–46; growth of, 17–18, 25; and industry, 148; and manufacturing, 148; methods of computing, 31; per-capita, 28; percentage of from domestic and external investments, 71, 186; population growth and, 25 n.; public sector of, 35; role of foreigners in, 31; of South Africa, 27; taxes and, 38–39; total, 27; transportation systems and, 174

Groundnuts; *see* Peanuts
Guggisberg, Sir Gordon, 12
Guinea: aid from Communist bloc, 85; central bank in, 85; inflation in, 85; migrant workers of, 23; Three-Year Development Plan, 211

Hance, W. A.: quoted, 91, 231
Harbors; *see* Ports
Helleiner, G. K.: quoted, 127–28
Herding, 32; *see also* Cattle
Hicks, U.: quoted, 183, 218
Highways; *see* Roads
Hirschman, A. O.: quoted, 52, 214
Hoselitz, B. F.: cited, 53
Houphouet-Boigny, Félix, 55
Housing, 26
Huileries du Congo Belge, 123
"Hungry season," 34
Hunter, G.: quoted, 34, 54–55
Hydroelectric power; *see* Electric power

IDA; *see* International Development Association
Imports: in national economy, 32; and money income, 27–28; and quotas, 78; of raw materials and unfinished manufactures, 159
Income: elasticity of, 150, 151, 152; *see also* Per-capita income
Industrialization: automotive industry, 149; and competition from developed countries, 155–56; goal of, 150; and hydroelectric power, 177–78; and imports of raw materials, 159; and labor, 162–64; problems of, 154–65; and technological progress, 152; in South Africa, 148
Infrastructure, 166–83
International Coffee Organization, 229
International commodity agreements, 229
International Development Association (IDA), 200
Intra-African relations: and common markets, 232; and economic aid, 233; and geographical factors, 230; effect of independence on, 41; lack of, 40; links between former French colonies, 40; and location of indus-

War II, 17; iron-ore development in, 141; shortage of labor in, 24 n., 57–58; U.S. investment in, 15
"Lineage system"; *see* Extended-family system.
Literacy, 29
Loans: to Belgian territories, 197–98; to British colonies, 198; capital funds obtained by, 198–200; to French territories, 196; by governments, 195–98; by international development institutions, 199–200; by private capital, 195; theory of, 186; *see also* specific grants, specific countries
Locusts, 113
Louchheim, D. H.: quoted, 244
Lugard, Lord: quoted, 9, 175

Macro-economic variables, 216, 217
Maize, 7, 12
Maizels, A.: cited, 150
Malagasy Republic: non-African population in, 36–37
Malaria, 5
Malawi: breakup of economic union with Rhodesia, 41; density of population, 24; migrant workers of, 23; money economy in, 34; trade with Great Britain, 76; trade with Rhodesia and South Africa, 22 n.
Mali: aid from Communist bloc, 85; central bank of, 85; and federation with Senegal, 41; inflation in, 63, 85; member of UDEAO, 42; migrant workers of, 22; Office du Niger, 120
Manganese, 133, 139
Manioc, 7, 12
Market agriculture, 99, 100
Marketing boards: established by colonial governments, 233; functions of, 125–26; in Ghana, Nigeria, and Uganda, 38
Marshall Plan, 201
Martin, C. J.: quoted, 23
Masai, migrant herdsmen, 22
Mason, E. S.: quoted, 213–14
Mauretania: expenditures, 35; member of UDEAO, 42; percentage of current government expenditures, 35

Mauritius, 23
McKelvey, J. J., Jr.: cited, 96; quoted, 103
Mellor, J. W.: quoted, 128
Merat, Christian, 32
Mhina, J. E. F.: cited, 56
"Micro-states": as barriers to economic development, 65; coined by Léopold Senghor, 65; cost of government, 65; difficulty of establishing new industries in, 65
Migrant labor: as economic link, 231–32; and "extended-family" system, 52; extent of, 105–6; relationship with agricultural work patterns, 105–6; *see also* Labor force
Migration: of Europeans from Africa, 37; of Europeans to Africa, 37; *see also* Expatriates
Minerals: exploitation of, 134–39; importance of in development, 74, 131 ff.; potentials of, 69; production of, 73
Mines: bauxite and iron-ore deposits, 93–94; effects of on economy, 132; in Katanga, 23, 145; mining companies, 144–46
Missions (European) in Africa, 12
Mombasa, 11
Money: currency areas, 82–83; *see also* Banking
Money economy: importance of, 34–35, 234–35; and desire for imports, 87; and development, 34; and foreign investment, 223; effect of increase in, 27–28; influence of on average African, 33–34; and land-tenure system, 108–9; and migrant labor system, 106
Monrovia, 11
Morocco: economic growth of after World War II, 17; removal of U.S. air bases, 223
Mozambique: non-African population in, 36
Myint, H.: quoted, 236

National accounts: British system, 29; French system, 29; importance of expatriates in, 31; interpreting data about, 32; methods for preparing,